THE FAMILY IN GREEK HISTORY

THE FAMILY IN GREEK HISTORY

Cynthia B. Patterson

HARVARD UNIVERSITY PRESS

Cambridge, Massachusetts, and London, England, 1998

Library of Congress Cataloging-in-Publication Data

Patterson, Cynthia.
    The family in Greek history / Cynthia Patterson.
       p.   cm.
    Includes bibliographical references and index.
    ISBN 0-674-29270-7 (alk. paper)
    1. Family—Greece—History. 2. Domestic relations—Greece—
    History. 3. Family in literature. 4. Domestic relations in
    literature. I. Title.
HQ662.5.A25   1998
 306.85'09498—dc21   98-9295

For Richard, Nathan, and Elly

ACKNOWLEDGMENTS

This book has been a long time in the making and has over the years benefited from the support and advice of many people and several institutions. I began work on the project in 1988–89 while a fellow at the Center for Hellenic Studies, where I first presented my thoughts on the problem of the heiress in Greek law. I thank my fellow fellows and Zeph Stewart, then director, for their interest and encouragement. Emory University has provided needed time for concentrated research and writing in two crucial semester leaves, and my colleagues, particularly Tom Burns, have patiently read numerous drafts. Only my husband, Richard, has read more—and his advice has been more appreciated than he may realize. Margot Finn, Mary Odem, Michael Bellesiles, and Stephen White (of the Legal History Reading Group) spent an evening discussing my discussion of Greek adultery law. Audiences at various APA, CAMWS, and AAH meetings and at Stanford University and the University of Georgia offered helpful criticism and further convinced me of the subject's interest and importance. Elizabeth Cottrell and Brent Hardy took time from their graduate studies to help with proofreading and the index. Many thanks to all.

Finally, I owe my longest-term debt to two extraordinary teachers and friends, Antony Raubitschek and Michael Jameson, whose influence may or may not be evident in this book, but without whom it would not have been written.

CONTENTS

ILLUSTRATIONS

THE FAMILY IN GREEK HISTORY

INTRODUCTION

The modern uses of the English word "family" are many and varied;[1] although the "nuclear family" (husband, wife, and children) has a certain ideological and political priority in contemporary society, other kinds of family are readily recognizable. Not only can a single-parent or grandparent household be a family, but someone's "family" might have come to America on the *Mayflower,* while another's "family" might be arriving next week for a "family reunion." The term is clearly flexible and denotes not so much a certain group of people as a family of relationships that binds people together as "one's own."

The use of the term "family" in Greek history, however, has enjoyed neither this practical flexibility nor any clear and precise definition. The central problem is that although "family" has generally been taken by Greek historians to refer to "blood" relationships and lineage, as distinct from the practical relationships of the household, it has also been used as one standard translation of *oikos,* which specifically denotes that household and its relationships.[2] So *oikos/polis* usually translates the "family/state" opposition into a Greek idiom, even though it tends to be "blood kin," rather than household relationships, that are seen as opposing those of the state or polis. The problem is further compounded when the term *genos* is added to the discussion. This word is related to the verb "to become" and has a large range of meanings, from "birth, origin, or natural type" to a composite sense of "kin," to a specific descriptive name for a fictive kin group organized around the management of a

1

particular religious cult.[3] Yet the one meaning that is most generally assumed for *genos,* that is, a corporate and autonomous clan, has no place in the historical record. In sum, it is often unclear in discussions of the "Greek family" just what is intended by the term, especially since "family" has been implicitly used as the equivalent of two specific and quite different Greek words.

Instead of insisting on either *oikos* or *genos* as the proper and only Greek equivalent of "family," I suggest a return to the broadly practical and flexible use of the English word and acknowledge that both *genos* and *oikos* fall under the semantic umbrella of "family." We will still need to look carefully at the meanings of these terms as they occur in different contexts; but an appreciation of the flexibility of "family" language should help make clear the extent to which in Greek society, as in our own, some sorts of family could be more emotionally or politically charged, and some "family" matters more closely regulated in law than others. It will also emerge that the *oikos* or household, though not the only significant form of family, was the most enduring, and stood at the moral center of both family and state in ancient Greece.

This book focuses on the participatory role of the family—family structures, family interests, family ideals—in the historical development of the Greek polis. I am not interested in family history as "prehistory" or primarily as "women's history," but as an important component of polis history. The assignment of family history to the realm of prehistory is a central feature of the paradigm of family history developed in the nineteenth century. Somewhat ironically, the recent energetic and productive focus on the lives and representations of women in ancient Greece has tended to emphasize their separation from the public and political (and historical) world—and for all of its successes has not brought family history out of its "seclusion" in the "women's quarters."[4]

By emphasizing or claiming that the family, especially in the form of the household or oikos, was an active player in the history of the Greek polis, I am not disputing the important point made by contemporary historians that historical development or change in family organization or relationships does not necessarily follow the patterns or periods of political and economic change.[5] Rather I am proposing that the political changes which are so dramatic in the Greek world from the eighth to the third centuries B.C.E. are changes in which the family and family interests often played a key part. The dichotomous equations public/private = state/family = male/female = history/ nonhistory are frequently applied, explicitly and implicitly, to ancient Greek society. A discussion of the part played by the family in Greek history confounds those equations.

The *oikos,* as composite household of persons and property, was the focus of family identity and interest in the historical Greek world as it first emerges in the poetry of Homer and Hesiod. Despite typically vague modern notions of a primitive clan-based society as the predecessor to the historical society of the polis, early Greek society seems securely rooted in individual households—and in the relationships focused on and extending from those households. These were the relationships that determined a man and woman's place and status in the larger community, and formed the basis of his or her participation in that community.

Beginning in the later seventh century, the appointment of polis lawgivers and the publication of public law codes reveal an increasingly self-conscious public state. Yet this development does not represent a simple shift of power and authority from the oikos to the polis. A close look at the character of early family law reveals a more complex and varied story, for the protection and stability of oikos relationships were often, especially in Athens, important elements of early public law.

By the later fifth century one can see developing in Athens a conception of the polis as the highest form of family. Athenian marriage laws assumed the social institution and social process of marriage as the basis for particular rules on legitimacy and on household relationships with non-Athenians. The importance of marriage as the formative political relationship of the household thus underlies Athenian law but is not defined by it. Somewhat analogously, Athenian law on the violation of marriage focused on the specific figure of the *moichos,* a particular sort of unmanly and dishonorable sexual thief, rather than on the larger household connections and connotations of adultery. That violation of marriage was seen as a public danger is apparent in its representation in the two most celebrated and democratic institutions of classical Athens: the theater and the popular courts. In the work of the Athenian playwrights, we can witness the tragic paradigm of adultery represented as a complex crime of betrayal which corrupts the entire household and its relations of person to person and of person to property. As the corruption of the relationship through which citizen households reproduced the legitimate citizen body, adultery endangered the stability of the polis as a whole.

The female members of the adultery triangle are much less prominent in court than on the stage, an illustration of the protective attitude toward citizen women typical of fourth-century oratory. The character of the *moichos,* however, is developed in oratory in ways which illuminate his unsuitability for citizen rights and responsibilities. The rhetorical and ethical possibilities suggested by such a figure result in his frequent appearance in Aristotle's writings on those topics.

The Hellenistic age brings the final turn of this discussion. In the historical context of Macedonian suppression of political independence, Menander's plays present an interesting solution to the public/private divide: a community of households; considering the comedies from the perspective of family history brings them out of the historical backwater and into the main currents of social history.

The issues addressed in the following chapters—early Greek kinship and inheritance, classical Athenian marriage, and the early Hellenistic retreat into private life—are for the most part quite traditional elements of Greek social history as it has developed since the mid-nineteenth century. As a result, my discussion will repeatedly come up against the evolutionary paradigm of family history which was developed in the nineteenth century and which remains influential, if often unacknowledged. This paradigm must be openly confronted, and its principles exposed, before we can make real progress in interpreting the historical evidence.

THE NINETEENTH-CENTURY
PARADIGM OF GREEK
FAMILY HISTORY

Until the beginning of the sixties there was no such thing as a history of the family.
>
> Friedrich Engels, *The Origin of the Family,*
> *Private Property, and the State* (1891)

Family history in the later nineteenth century was a markedly different enterprise from what goes by that name in the later twentieth century—roughly since "the beginning of the sixties." Dominated by an interest in the progressive evolution of human society from "primitive" to "civilized" and in the pivotal role family structure played in that evolution, the family historians of the nineteenth century were looking for "the eternal footprint" which would explain the modern bourgeois family and its relation to the state.[1] Just how that footprint should be read was fiercely debated—was, for example, private property an "original" or "late" historical development; was early human society "matriarchal" or "patriarchal"?—but there was little disagreement about either the importance of the issues or the principle of social evolution. There was also little question about the centrality of the ancient Greek and Roman family in this discussion, both because the classical world was a common historical reference point for educated Europeans and Americans of the nineteenth century and because classical law and literature provided a rich source of evidence. The classical world, taken as the common heritage of European civilization, had the advantage of both cultural authority and temporal distance. Just as the history of Athens and the virtues and vices of its democracy invigorated the political debates of the later eighteenth and nineteenth centuries,[2] so also ancient family history, read primarily through literature and law, was mined for its larger historical relevance. Family history in the later nineteenth century, however, drew also on the rapidly increasing fund of ethnographic data about non-European and non-"civilized" peoples of the world. Thus there emerged a spirited discussion of early family history, in which Athens and Rome retained their pride of place while essential "primitive" and comparative data were supplied from non-European societies. This was a discussion that crossed both national boundaries and professional disciplines; and although the theories it produced were generally disowned by anthropologists by the early twentieth century, the effects of the evolutionary habit of thought have been considerably longer lived outside the bounds of academic anthropology.

The European and American fascination with the idea of social evolution is an important and well-recognized piece of the complex intellectual history of the later nineteenth century. But the continuing presence of the evolutionary paradigm in ancient history, in the field which provided, so to speak, its home base, is less well recognized. In discussing the social evolution of both family and state, nineteenth-century theorists, whether experts in Roman law, Greek myth, or Iroquois kinship, had much to say about the ancient Greek and Roman family and so produced, as something of a by-product of the larger debate, an influential paradigm for the historical evolution of the ancient family, its gender and property relations, and its relation to the ancient state. The creation of the paradigm in the nineteenth century was enlivened both by the general engagement of the intellectual community in the project, and by its clear significance for contemporary concerns about property, family, and in general the relation of the public and private spheres. But with the increasing isolation in the early twentieth century of classics and ancient history from the social sciences and from social politics,[3] and with the waning of classical education as a common intellectual heritage, the paradigm became something of a fossil. To modern historians, the evolutionary history of the ancient family ("from matriarchy to patriarchy" or "from clan to state") is merely a relic of past intellectual debates, and whether or not it is *true* or historically plausible seems generally outside both interest or expertise. Nor, on the other hand, have classicists been interested in excavating the fossil and subjecting it to serious scrutiny. Although individual elements have been challenged or corrected, the categories in which historians and classicists alike think about the ancient family, and even some of the basic assumptions about family history, such as the competition of family and state or the peculiarly repressed condition of women in democratic Athens, are still essentially those of the nineteenth-century paradigm and have not been subjected to the test of the evidence. They remain fixtures of Greek political and social history. One hears clear nineteenth-century echoes, for example, in the 1975 description of the *Oresteia* as the story of "our emergence from darkness to the light, from the tribe to the aristocracy to the democratic state" and "from the blood vendetta of the tribe to the social justice of our hopes," as well as in the more recent judgments of feminist historians that the archaic age was a "crucial period in the history of the subordination of women"—especially in Athens, where "the development of democracy . . . may have been a parallel phenomenon to the subordination of women," or, put more bluntly, "women were the chief victims of the invention of democracy."[4]

What is missing from this late twentieth-century narrative of female and family subordination is historiographic awareness. Apart from a few independent but isolated voices,[5] there seems to be little appreciation of the extent to which the trans-century unison declaring an essential connection between the emergence of the political order and the suppression of the family and women may be the result of a common historical paradigm inherited from past intellectual debate. One of the key ideas, for example, of the earlier discussion is that ancient Greek (and Roman) society in its most evolved form was essentially "patriarchal" in family structure, a word unknown in classical Greek but prominent in debates over the legitimacy of "paternal authority" in family and state in the eighteenth and nineteenth centuries.[6] "Patriarchy" is also a term central to the twentieth-century feminist critique of classical Athens, referring generally to "male-dominated institutions" and often implicitly to a broadly based misogyny seen as pervading Athenian literature and culture.[7] Indeed, extreme patriarchal "male-dominated institutions" are generally taken as given—inheritance is patrilinear; women were secluded indoors without any public role; theater audience was exclusively male; and so on. Instead of examining these assumptions, commentators remark upon the consequences or reflections of such patriarchal institutions and attitudes in Athenian art and literature. This portrait of Athens is a part of the nineteenth-century intellectual paradigm which still informs discussions of ancient Greek society; its historical validity cannot be evaluated apart from that paradigm.[8]

Therefore, I propose first to call to life the nineteenth-century paradigm of Greek family history by direct recourse to the arguments of five of its most distinctive creators, Johann Jakob Bachofen, Denis-Numa Fustel de Coulanges, Henry Maine, Louis Henry Morgan, and Friedrich Engels. Focusing on these five writers—and on the ways in which despite different perspectives and purposes they articulated together a highly influential paradigm for the evolution of political society—brings us face to face with the roots and character of traditional "wisdom" on the history of the family.

The Evolutionary Paradigm

In announcing the inauguration of family history in *The Origin of the Family, Private Property, and the State,* Engels recognized the temporal priority of Bachofen's *Das Mutterrecht (Mother Right)* but found the arguments for primitive matriarchy and matrilinearity in Morgan's *Ancient Society* politically more congenial. To these "matriarchal" theorists, I join Fustel de Coulanges and Maine, whose *La cité antique (Ancient City)* and *Ancient Law,* respectively, argued a contrasting "patriarchal" view of early family history.[9] Numerous others joined in the discussion, but these five vividly illustrate both the disagreements and the underlying common concerns and principles of the debate.[10] Even in the face of disagreement over such issues as the "original" form of the family, their common interest in and ideas about the nature of kinship and the meaning of "family," the interaction or competition of "family" and "state," and the institution of monogamy and the status of women combine to produce a paradigm with distinct structural, historical, and moral components: the ancient family was primarily a lineage or descent group; the territorial state arose at the expense of the family; and as the family was "privatized" women were excluded from public life and secluded in the home.

Despite Bachofen's own claim to be engaged in the scientific mode of historical analysis and not in the least in "philosophical speculation," it is his philosophical embracing of myth as authentic historical tradition in which the "origin, progression, and end" of human social institutions (and most particularly marriage) can be read which most distinguishes his writing and his methods in modern eyes.[11] Further, despite his repeated appeals to a scientific historical objectivity, Bachofen's own inherently romantic attitude toward marriage, women, and religion is evident in the theory of social evolution he constructs. *Mother Right* is thus a vivid exemplar of the seemingly contradictory tendencies that mark nineteenth-century family history: the avowed goal of "scientific" history was particularly difficult to attain when discussing the intimate and subjective realm of private life and marital morality, as well as the topical issue of the nature and social role of women.[12]

To Bachofen, the mythological and historical record of antiquity revealed a clear, primordial, and universally valid history of the family in all its stages. Myth presents an authentic historical record in which can be seen the vestiges of earlier social and sexual orders; the historian's role is to interpret those scattered vestiges with regard to the "origin, progression, and end" of human family organization—in short, to provide the family with a scientific evolutionary history. The very strangeness of the stories myth tells—for example, of Amazon queens, of daughters favored over sons, and of wives killing husbands—were for Bachofen positive proof of their historical validity and of the social revolutions they record; it was impossible that the "patriarchal mind" of the classical Greeks, let alone of modern society, could ever have imagined or invented such things. Likewise, for Bachofen the possibility that the stories of myth are parochial and limited in significance was excluded not only by the discovery of related and similar stories among diverse peoples, but also and more significantly by his faith in the universality of human experience and

in the primacy of the Greek experience.[13] The ancient Greeks represented the childhood of Western civilization, in whose original experience, however, the full course of Western social history could be
traced. Bachofen and others repeatedly present classical Greek society as standing on the threshold of civilization—thus revealing with
simplicity and clarity the crucial evolutionary steps necessary for cultural adulthood.

On Bachofen's view, the evidence of myth suggested a three-stage
course of human progress: first there is the "swamp" of indiscriminate sexuality (which he labels "hetairism") with uncontrolled vege-
tation and growth; second is the Demetrian "tilled field" of matriarchal monogamy, instituted by women themselves in resistance to the
sexual degradation of the previous era; and finally comes the "heav-
enly light" of spiritual paternity and patriarchy. As evidence of the
first phase, Bachofen appealed to the practices of unspecified "peoples of lower cultural levels" known in his own day. The cultural images of his own day—and his own society—are also evident in
Bachofen's depiction of the second or matriarchal phase of development, which rests upon the foundation of settled agriculture
and "tellurian" religious rites and celebrates the earthy and material
basis of feminine power.[14] Although this second phase was not des-
tined to be the final or highest form of human society, Bachofen allowed himself an enthusiastic description of the character of matriarchy and its quintessential feminine affinity for religious piety and
peace:

> the weaker sex can take up the struggle with the stronger and
> emerge triumphant. To man's superior physical strength woman
> opposes the mighty influence of her religious consecration; she
> counters violence with peace, enmity with conciliation, hate with
> love, and thus she guides the wild, lawless existence of the earliest
> period toward a milder, friendlier culture, in whose center she sits
> enthroned as the embodiment of the higher principle, as the mani-
> festation of the divine commandment.[15]

Bachofen's matriarchal woman evokes the contemporary nineteenth-century figure of the angel of the hearth, and his conception
of matriarchy is preeminently one of feminine piety rooted in physi-

cal maternity and conjugal monogamy, reflecting the contemporary ideal of "public man/private woman."[16]

The cultural role Bachofen assigned woman—on the basis, he asserted, of Greek myth—relies on what he regarded as her essential character: her desire for monogamous sexuality, her maternal love, and her innate inclination toward the supernatural and divine, the irrational and the miraculous. Herein Bachofen saw both the strength and the limits of female nature, and the reason for woman's inability to move human society on to the next and highest stage. Man, it appears, has a "higher calling," and his triumph, or the triumph of his paternity, "brings with it the liberation of the spirit from the manifestation of nature, a sublimation of human existence over the law of material life."[17]

At this crucial moment,

> A new ethos is in preparation diametrically opposed to the old one. The divinity of the mother gives way to that of the father, the night cedes its primacy to the day, the left side to the right, and it is only in their contrast that the character of the two stages stands out sharply. The Pelasgian [i.e., primitive] culture derives its stamp from its emphasis on maternity, Hellenism [i.e., civilization] is inseparable from the patriarchal view. The Pelasgians present a picture of material confinement, the Hellenes of spiritual development; the life of the Pelasgians is marked by the operation of unconscious law, that of the Hellenes by individualism; on the one hand we find acceptance of nature, on the other, a transcending of nature.[18]

And so it goes.

Bachofen spoke more prosaically of the legal and political ramifications of this spiritual revolution, asserting that recognition of paternity led to patrilineal succession in a direct (male) line and that it was the city of Athens that "carried paternity to its highest development; and in one-sided exaggeration . . . condemned woman to a status of inferiority."[19] Both of these points, though less developed by Bachofen than the image of matriarchal piety, are central elements of the completed paradigm, which insists that inheritance in Athens was exclusively male and patrilinear and that women in Athens were singularly oppressed. The linearity and teleology of evolutionary movement are conspicuous in Bachofen's account. On this view, Homeric society, in which the importance of both patrilineal and matrilineal kin is indeed quite evident, becomes a society in transition, on its way from one stage to another, while Athens, understood as strictly patrilinear in structure, is a society already evolved. Bachofen's representation of Athens as an "exaggerated" patriarchal society, however, is based not on any objective comparison of Athens with other Greek cities or on an analysis of Athenian law, but on the implicit assumption of a connection between the public and private fate of women: the more developed the public character and achievement of the patriarchal society, the more extreme or exaggerated its private consequences. In the developed Athenian polis, then, where male political participation was most advanced, the differential between men's and women's participation in the public sphere corresponded to a heightened inequality in the private sphere. Politics and patriarchy worked together to deprive Athenian women of status in both polis and oikos. Or so the theory has it. This view of the history of political and gender relationships has a deceptive simplicity as well as an ideological appeal, features which have made it one of the most often repeated elements of the nineteenth-century paradigm of the history of the Greek family.

While Bachofen was at work in Basel finding in Greek mythology the keys to Greek family history, some 120 kilometers farther along the Rhine in Strasbourg, Fustel de Coulanges was independently constructing an alternative theory of ancient society based upon vestiges of primitive patriarchy and (male) ancestor worship in Roman family law and religion. Despite the obvious difference in historical perspective (perhaps largely as a result of the difference in primary material—law as opposed to myth), Fustel shared with Bachofen a strong belief in the importance of religion as the "mighty lever" (Bachofen's term) of ancient society and also the strong aversion to contemporary Germanic historical methods, which he viewed as dry and antiquarian.[20] The two also shared a view of antiquity which embraced Greek and Roman society as "two branches of the same race" (Fustel) sharing one history, but they also insisted on the "radical and essential differences" (Fustel) and "strangeness" (Bachofen) that distinguished that society from their own. In Fustel's call to study the Greeks and Romans "without thinking of ourselves, as if they were entirely foreign to us; with the same disinterestedness, and with the mind as free, as if we were studying ancient India or Arabia,"[21] we can find some explanation of the apparent inconsistency in both authors as they insist on "disinterestedness" yet clearly reflect contemporary concerns in their construction of ancient family history. What both were objecting to was the ahistorical reverence toward antiquity that excluded the possibility of historical difference and historical evolution (moral, religious, and familial as well as political) and encouraged the simple equation of past with present. Neither Bachofen nor Fustel seems concerned that contemporary interests might affect how and with what emphases they read that historical record. Indeed, the contemporary relevance of their work was something that they took for granted. There was a moral to this story.

Although the perspective is different, Fustel's evolutionary scheme might be said to begin where Bachofen's left off—with the emergence of the strictly patrilinear and patriarchal family, which in both its Roman and Greek forms has here the status of a historical "given." What interested Fustel was the way in which primitive religious patriarchy determined, first, the structure and rules of the ancient family, and second, the character of the ancient state and its relation to the family. For Fustel, the central religious experience of primitive society had to do with neither reproduction nor sexuality but with death. "Death was the first mystery."[22] Primitive man—and the emphasis is clearly on the masculine, not the feminine, experience—believed that the dead continue a form of existence under the ground and so require both sustenance and honor from the living. The first important step in the argument is the connection of the care and cult of the dead with domestic religion: the vital link is the "sacred fire" burning at the hearth of each and every Greek and Roman house. From the idea that the dead require food and care comes very naturally the idea that the dead were in fact gods—demons and heroes to the Greeks, *lares, manes,* or *genii* to the Romans. Indeed, "it was perhaps while looking upon the dead that man first conceived the idea of the supernatural." Death, Fustel posited, "raised [man's] thoughts from the visible to the invisible, from the transitory to the eternal, form the human to the divine."[23] Then, the close relation—indeed the identification—of these divine dead with the eternal family fire results in a domestic religion centered on the worship of the ancestors. This step is crucial to the entire argument, since according to Fustel it was the worship of the dead ancestors that determined the nature of marriage, kinship, private property, and inheritance in ancient society. Yet, as Fustel admitted, the connection was "mere conjecture"; it was in fact a supposition based on a comment of a late grammarian connecting burial of the dead within the house and the worship of lares and penates in the house. Nonetheless, he concludes "that the domestic fire was in the beginning only the symbol of the worship of the dead; that under the stone of the hearth an ancestor reposed; that the fire was lighted there to honor him, and that his fire seemed to preserve life in him or represented his soul as always vigilant."[24]

With one more premise slipped in ("we must notice this peculiarity—that the domestic religion was transmitted only from male to male"), the ancient family fell into paradigmatic form around the central cult of the male ancestors.[25] Despite well-recognized deficiencies in argument and evidence, the following elements of Fustel's model remain embedded in many discussions of the ancient family.

Marriage, "the first institution that the domestic religion established," brought a woman from the worship of her father's hearth to that of her husband. For although the family cult was transmitted from male to male, and although the husband/father was its priest, women were celebrants and priestesses, as daughters to fathers and wives to husbands. The two identities were practically separate but structurally identical: "Marriage has been for her a second birth; she is henceforth the daughter of her husband, *filiae loco,* say the jurists. One could not belong to two families, or to two domestic religions; the wife belongs entirely to her husband's family, and to his religion."[26] This is the "original" form of marriage, which despite later modifications, supplements, and adjustments can still be read in the legal record. The aim of marriage, says Fustel, "was not pleasure," but the perpetuation of the family through male heirs. The cult of the ancestors must continue, so "every family must perpetuate itself forever."[27] It is generally recognized both that the form of marriage described by Fustel is a highly idealized description of Roman *manus* marriage, which put the wife formally in the legal position of a daughter, and also that such a formal status does not necessarily reflect the realities of Roman family life. Nevertheless, the idea of lineage "continuity" as the exclusive motivation for marriage remains a common operating assumption in current discussions of ancient family interests in both Greece and Rome.[28]

Kinship, then, could originally exist only through relationship to males. "One could not be related through females," argued Fustel, because "one could not belong to two families, or invoke two fires; the son, therefore, had no other religion or other family than that of the father." Because the wife became part of the family of her husband, primitive religion and law recognized no maternal family. Kinship was based (originally) on "agnatic" relationship—relationship through males—and only "by degrees as the old religion lost its hold" did the "cognatic" relationship gain recognition in the law.[29]

A full commentary on Fustel's ideas on kinship is neither necessary nor possible here, but the method and argument by which he concluded that Roman agnation was the central principle of the ancient family and proof of his own theory deserves some comment. First, it is again notable that agnation and cognation are understood as evolutionary extremes, similar in significance to Bachofen's patrilinearity and matrilinearity, and the legal recognition of cognate kin as kin in both Athens and Rome is taken to indicate a movement away from an "original" and "pure" agnatic structure. Strict rules of agnation, however, are no longer taken as a reflection of the realities of family life in ancient Rome,[30] and they certainly cannot be assumed as the original system in ancient Greece. With his insistence on the discrete and linear character of his ancient "family" ("a man can have only one domestic religion"), Fustel could not recognize the Roman *familia* or the Greek oikos as in any real sense "family" at all. Nor indeed did he allow that there could be a "maternal family." The mother's family was that of her husband, the daughter's that of her father. The "continuation" of each family, therefore, could only be achieved, on this reading, with the production of sons and sons of sons, who would continue to care for and worship the ancestors at their tombs. Despite the obvious problems and historical distortion resulting from the equation of "family" with "lineage," and the assumption of historical priority for a strictly agnatic lineage, Fustel's emphasis on linear male "continuation" of the "family" is still com-

mon among contemporary historians. Lineage and family are taken
to be one and the same.

Inheritance was accordingly reserved for legitimate sons, that is,
those born of a wife who had joined the domestic religion of her husband. A married daughter could not inherit from her father in Rome,
said Fustel; and the daughter in Athens, married or not, was completely excluded.[31] A daughter without brothers could never be an
heiress in the strict sense, but through what Fustel calls a "very natural softening of the rigor" of this principle, she could produce an
heir by marrying her father's nearest kin and fictively bearing her father a son. The real heir was "neither his daughter nor his son-in-
law; it was the daughter's son." The daughter can be only the intermediary in the continuation of the family and its religion, not the
continuation itself; "she did not inherit; but the worship and the inheritance were transmitted through her."[32] The patriline cannot
allow the diverging of property through women, who therefore cannot be true property owners. But what kind of a community or state
can such discrete patriarchal "families," each with its own religion
and family gods, create; and how will it be produced? For Fustel, the
"incorporation" of the primitive family as the Roman *gens* and
Greek *genos*—corporate groups of related family members with their
own institutions of government and judicial and deliberative assemblies—began the process; then "revolutions," through which the
gens (and *genos*) was "dismembered," and the clients freed and
eventually enfranchised, completed it.[33]

The *genos* and the patriarchal/patrilinear "family" of which it is constituted are thus key but hardly uncontroversial concepts in Fustel's
analysis of ancient society. His analysis of the corporate and familial
nature of the *genos* vigorously challenged competing interpretations
of his day, which saw the kinship relationship of *genos* members to
one another (outside of immediate or primary kin) as fictional.[34] But
according to Fustel, it was impossible that the *genos* was simply an
association of families who recognized a mythical, and fictitious,
common ancestor from whom they took their name. The *gens* (or
genos) was, he insisted, "the family itself." And although "it might
either comprise only a single line, or produce several branches, it was
always but one family."[35] Fustel also called upon the evidence of lan-

guage, noting that of the various "family" terms used by both Greeks and Romans, *genos* and *gens* were clearly related to verbs of procreation (*gignere* and *gennan*) and nouns conveying "the same idea of filiation" (*genitor* and *goneus*). Thus the idea that several families would organize themselves into an artificial group, calling it a *genos,* and agree to "pretend" to have a common ancestor was to Fustel simply "absurd." One cannot suppose—"historical science cannot admit"—that human society "commenced by a convention and an artifice."[36]

Fustel's strongly articulated view of the *genos* thus sets up the rise of the state (polis) as the dramatic struggle of the religion of family (that is, lineage) against secular claims of economic class and individual political rights. The state emerges only through the "dismemberment" of the *genos* and the original familial form of human society.[37] Although modern authors avoid such colorful language, the assumption remains prevalent that for the state to rise, the family (on this account, *genē* or lineage groups) must have fallen. The *genos* remains a problematic fixture of early Greek history, partaking of the character of its many different descriptions and seldom carefully analyzed. Translated into modern discussions as "clan" it continues to obscure the social and political history of the Greek family.[38]

Across the English Channel in 1861 (the same year that Bachofen published *Mother Right*), Henry Maine published another major evolutionary analysis of ancient law and ancient society, which was enthusiastically received in both academic and political circles. Maine's *Ancient Law: Its Connection with the Early History of Society, and Its Relation to Modern Ideas* is probably the best-known British contribution to the nineteenth-century debate on the evolution of human society. Like its continental counterparts, it emphasized the historical antithesis of family and state. Maine was a classicist, a professor of Roman law, a political journalist, and an imperial administrator in British India; and his career—with its complex interlocking of academic, political, and imperial interests—exemplified the Victorian ideal of the educated man of "general accomplishment."

Though working independently of Bachofen and Fustel, and writing with an explicitly political agenda rooted in contemporary British politics, Maine's theory of a progressive movement in the po-

sition of the individual "from status to contract," and in social organization from kinship to territorial contiguity, is fully part of the
larger European and American dialogue and remains a dominant line
of analysis. He shared with Fustel and Bachofen a confidence in the
new scientific comparative method of legal and historical analysis,
and as a well-schooled classicist he shared their belief in the centrality of ancient Greek and Roman society for the interpretation of the
history of human society in general and of its British form in particular. Maine's persuasive paradigm of ancient social and family history—read, studied, and discussed on both sides of the Atlantic, in
college classrooms, political reviews, and judicial chambers—has
strongly influenced English-speaking discussions of Greek history.[39]

Maine's theory operates on both the societal and individual level,
with the patriarchal family tying the two together. "The effect of the
evidence derived from comparative jurisprudence," he claimed (distinguishing such legal evidence from the more dubious evidence of
literature), "is to establish that view of the primeval condition of the
human race which is known as the Patriarchal theory." In ancient
Indo-European societies—Greek, Roman, Hindu, and Germanic—as
well as in Semitic Hebrew society, the father ruled; his word was
law. The "corporation" over which he presided, like his father before him and his son after him, was a deathless and inextinguishable
family unit—the "elementary social group." Primitive society was
not a "collection of individuals" but "an aggregation of families"
forming first the Gens, then the Tribe, and finally the Common-
wealth.[40]

Thus kinship was the basis of primitive social organization, and
"the history of political ideas begins, in fact, with the assumption
that kinship in blood is the sole possible ground of community in political functions." But he also allowed that such kinship could be the
result of legal fictions, such as that of adoption and "factitious extensions of consanguinity."[41] Primitive legal fictions thus serve to
preserve the character of primitive society as an aggregation of kin
and families.

When adoption, either familial or communal, ceased to be a
means of incorporating new members into a society, and society
therefore became increasingly split between exclusively "familial"
aristocracies and an inferior resident local population, a powerful

new principle of social organization emerged. This was the principle of "local contiguity"—of community based on residence rather than on family. Eventually the new principle "vanquished and dethroned" the old, so giving, says Maine, "ourselves, our contemporaries, and in great measure . . . our ancestors" a distinctly different "condition of community."[42]

Among those ancestors are both the Greeks and the Romans, for here again classical antiquity provides for Maine a synoptic evolutionary model, and within its historical record the transition from community as family to community as territory is clearly evidenced.[43] This transition is mirrored on the individual level by Maine's best-known evolutionary idea—that "the legal development of progressive societies involves a movement of the position of the individual in private law 'from status to contract.'"[44] For Maine, primitive society was based on the irreducible unit of the patriarchal family, and the position of persons within that family was determined by relation to its head, the paterfamilias. The Roman concept of *patria potestas* thus determined status in primitive society, and the individual had no status or identity apart from the familial "corporate" groups making up society. When, however, the power of the patriarchal family is challenged ("the Patria Potestas, in its normal shape, has not been, and . . . could not have been, a generally durable institution") by the growth of civil law and its persistent emancipation of the individual from paternal authority, and when the familial authority of the aristocratic *gens* gives way to the truly political community based on residence and contiguity—*then* it is possible to enter the higher phase of social and political organization characterized by the individual right of property ownership and contract. Roman law preserves "a nearly complete history of the crumbling away of an archaic system," but the process is a universal one, Maine asserts, at least for "progressive societies" such as Rome, Greece, and modern Europe.[45]

As Maine himself recognized, the theory has interesting implications for evaluating the position of women in both antiquity and the modern world, implications which Maine discusses in *Ancient Law* and in a series of lectures on the history of the legal status of women given in 1872 to law students at Oxford. Like Fustel, Maine emphasized the agnatic principle of descent through males underlying the primitive patriarchal family which, on his view, prevented any person related through a woman from being considered "kin." For Fustel, the explanation lay in the rules of religion; for Maine, it was simply a matter of power. The primitive family was defined by patria potestas—and "all persons are agnatically connected together who are under the same Paternal Power." A woman was the agnate kin of her brothers and father (and his male ascendants), but she could never continue an agnatic line. She was, in the words of the jurists, the "end of her own family."[46]

Together with power over her person went power over property, which was, according to Maine, the most vigorously exercised feature of patria potestas. In the primitive patriarchal family, therefore, the woman did not have, and could never hope to have, the right of property. Indeed, in one of his Oxford lectures Maine asserted that "no class of similar importance and extent was, in the infancy of society, placed in a position of such absolute dependence as the other sex."[47]

Women's increasing property rights in his day were to Maine a sign of "the degree of advance in civilisation," politically and also morally. It was entirely rational to extend to women the same individual right of contract as was extended to men in progressive societies; if men make contracts as individuals, then women must be recognized as individuals as well. It was also a moral step forward: "the assertion . . . that there is a relation between civilisation and the proprietary capacities of women is only a form of the truth that every one of those conquests, the sum of which we call civilisation, is the result of curbing some one of the strongest, because the primary, impulses of human nature."[48] Granting women their property rights is not only the progressive but also the gentlemanly thing to do, and on this score it is clear that Maine judged ancient society, and particularly Athens, deficient. In this way Maine creates an image of Athens as a flawed progenitor of modern European society—politically progressive but morally flawed in respect to its treatment of women. This is an idea which clearly had strong resonance in contemporary society and has found its way, along with "from status to contract," into the mainstream interpretation of ancient Greek social and family history. A particular point of criticism of classical Athens has traditionally been that they did not give women voting or property rights (in the modern sense). Certainly the point only has force when Athens is (anachronistically to be sure) taken as a prototype of modern liberal democracy.

The contemporary theorist, ethnographer, and anthropologist whose work particularly engaged Maine's, and eventually Engels', attention was the idiosyncratic American Lewis Henry Morgan. Morgan's work on the kinship structures of the Iroquois Indians of his native New York intrigued Europeans and Americans alike with its introduction into the debate of evidence about a culture previously unknown or at least unstudied. While Maine examined, from the vantage point of his law office, the society of British India for evidence of primitive law and social relations, Morgan was engaged in direct ethnographic investigation among a verifiably "primitive" and "tribal" people, the Iroquois. (Indeed, his vantage point was that of an adopted warrior, the result of his efforts on the tribe's behalf in Washington.)[49] The American evidence for primitive kinship and family organization, presented by Morgan first in *Systems of Consanguinity and Affinity of the Human Family* (1870) and then in the grand evolutionary thesis of *Ancient Society, or Researches in the Lines of Human Progress from Savagery through Barbarism to Civilization* (1877), both challenged and reinforced conclusions drawn by others from the traditional classical sources.

The second book was, as the subtitle indicates, a full-blown analysis of the evolution of human society through the three major phases of savagery, barbarism, and civilization, based primarily on the conflation of evidence from native American tribes and the ancient Greeks, Romans, and Hebrews. Morgan's argument for an early matriarchal phase of human history on the basis of "primitive" kinship terminology was eagerly embraced by European "matriarchists" and became a key weapon with which they attacked Maine's "patriarchal theory."[50] Morgan shared with Maine, however, the conviction that human society has moved from a family-based (or "gentile" in Morgan's language) organization to a political one, in which "the government dealt with persons through their relations to territory."[51] This step from barbarism to civilization was first taken by the ancient Greeks, who for Morgan and many of his contemporaries stood heroically on the threshold of civilization. Given the importance of gentile institutions for Morgan's theory, it is no surprise that the *gens* (or *genos*) plays a key role in his analysis as the primary social institution of the "barbarian," including both the American Indian and the prehistoric Greek. Taking the name from classical antiquity but the specific data from extensive survey of native American peoples, Morgan created a model of a gentile society originally matrilineal and "democratical," in which members of the same *gens* had mutual rights of inheritance, reciprocal obligations of defense or protection, and common burial plots, and were *not* allowed to intermarry. Ancient evidence was adapted to suit this construction of gentile society—and, on the point of required exogamy, simply assumed.[52] In later stages of barbarism, particularly in Homeric Greece, the matrilineal rule gave way to patrilinearity; and eventually, once again, the *gens* itself yielded to the territorial state and the patriarchal family. "In some respects," said Morgan, this was "the most interesting portion of the history of this remarkable organization, which had brought human society out of savagery, and carried it through barbarism into the early stages of civilization."[53]

The *gens* is thus fixed as the universal basis of prepolitical human society, and the assumed universality of the gentile form becomes an argument against those who view the *gens* (and *genos*) as a group of "fictive kin" secondary to the basic family unit. Like Fustel, to whom he refers approvingly on this point, Morgan insists that, as in America, the *gens* is the original and true "family" organization of ancient Greece. He also displayed notable nostalgia for what he saw as the "liberty, equality and fraternity" of the ancient *gentes,* which in Greece as well as in America were beset by "the elements of an incipient civilization."[54]

One of Morgan's most enthusiastic readers and supporters (against the scholarly critics, who are dismissed as "pedantic bookworms") was Friedrich Engels, whose *Origin of the Family, Private Property, and the State* is to a considerable degree a restatement of Morgan's larger treatise.[55] The feature of Morgan's "materialist" history which most interested Engels was that same insight for which he praised Bachofen: the modern monogamous family, with its age and gender hierarchy, is a product of historical evolution. No matter that Morgan himself viewed monogamy as an achievement of moral progress; Engels was content to note Morgan's demonstration that, in his words, monogamy resulted from "the victory of private prop-

erty over original, naturally developed, common ownership,"[56] and
to press home his own point about the historical consequences for
women and the family of the rise of the bourgeois state. Since Engels' version of Morgan's theories is now much better known and
most likely more influential than its model, particularly among feminist critics and social historians, it merits special attention.

In Engels' paraphrase of Morgan's theory, the history of human
marriage has three main stages: promiscuous intercourse or group
marriage; "pairing marriage" (without exclusive cohabitation) and
organization into matrilinear and exogamous *gentes;*[57] and "world
historic defeat of women" producing monogamy, the patriarchal
family, private property, and the bourgeois state. The first stage
serves primarily to enunciate Engels' point that the monogamous
family is not natural and primordial. The second stage involves some
complex and at times contradictory conclusions ostensibly explicat-
ing the ancient evidence. Following Morgan, Engels saw the early
stages of barbarism as best represented by the native American tribes
and the last stages as represented by the archaic or "heroic" Greeks
and Romans. The institution that linked the barbarian era—identical
in both the Iroquois and the Greeks and Romans—was the matriarchal and matrilineal *gens.* Morgan's discovery of this common barbarian social institution, said Engels, "cleared up at one stroke the
most difficult questions in the most ancient periods of Greek and
Roman history." The "secret" thus revealed, according to Engels,
was the "social constitution of primitive times, before the introduction of the state."[58] Looking at the structures of kinship within the
Iroquois tribe allows us, he declared, to see the "original" and archaic form of the Greek *genos* and Roman *gens,* and so also to understand the historical transformation of that *gens (genos)* into the
historical state in the late barbaric and early civilized era.

The key "fact" for Engels was one he shared also with Fustel and
Maine: the *gentes* were not at all "groups of families" believing in
some mythical common ancestor. Rather, the members of the original *gens* were in reality related to one another through a matrilinear
line and constituted the primary social group of primitive society.
The *gens,* rooted in "blood" relation, was the true family of early society. Bachofen's *Mother Right* conveniently supported this view;
but once the equation of the two systems, American and ancient, had

been made, Morgan's ethnographic evidence for matrilinearity and matriarchy swept away any need for further argument. Then Engels allowed himself to rhapsodize (with Morgan) on the character of these archaic gentile societies: "and a wonderful constitution it is, this gentile constitution, in all its childlike simplicity! No soldiers, no gendarmes or police, no nobles, kings, regents, prefects, or judges, no prison, or lawsuits . . . There cannot be any poor or needy—the communal household and the gens know their responsibilities toward the old, the sick, and those disabled in war. All are equal and free—the women included."[59]

In sum, on the Morgan/Engels view, "once upon a time" all property was communal, and mankind (women included) lived in extended families or *gentes,* which held as their unarticulated first principles "liberty, equality, and fraternity." But with the institution of monogamy, father right, and eventually (patrilinear) private property all of that was swept away; and, as could be seen clearly in the classical record, a state emerged as the defender of the "possessing class" over the "nonpossessing" both within the family and within the society as a whole. The household stood now as a model of class oppression; concomitantly with the defeat of the "family" by the state occurred the "world historic defeat" of women.

For Engels, as for many others, that defeat was most vividly and completely enacted in the history of classical Athens. The crucial transitional moments in Athenian family/state history were compressed into the roughly one hundred historically accessible years between Solon and Cleisthenes (594–500 B.C.E.), and the results of that transition were also more extreme and more complete than in any other Greek polis. For Engels, classical Athens was a thoroughly bourgeois state, which exploited a proletariat composed of both free and slave and in which the exploitative patriarchal family was the rule.

The attractions of taking classical Athens as the quintessential Greek polis and of reading in its history the political and social issues of modern society were readily apparent in Engels' day, as they are in our own. Just as the political lessons of classical Athenian democracy are a recognized staple of modern political science and a highly visible point of debate, so also classical Athens provided the key experience for evaluating the social lessons on marriage, women, and the family to be learned from the ancient world.[60] On the social side of things, however, there has been little debate. Whatever the overall view of the shape of family history envisioned by Bachofen, Fustel, Maine, Morgan, and Engels, there was and still is general agreement that woman's low status and position within the monogamous family represents a morally complicating factor in the history of human society, and one most clearly illustrated in classical Athens. Athens is a distant mirror in which Europeans and Americans read both the achievements and the iniquities of contemporary political society. For such a mirror, complicating historical details—the fact that inheritance was bilateral and the family was not the same as lineage, that women did have public religious authority, that most of the laws regulating women's behavior are archaic not classical in origin—are unwanted and unneeded.

These five distinctive social theorists or family historians of the later nineteenth century together contributed to the creation of a remarkably consistent and broadly popular paradigm for the history of the ancient Greek family. Other paradigms and other aspects of our intellectual heritage are of course important as well in the modern writing of ancient history.[61] But amid the growing self-consciousness among historians about models and methods, this nineteenth-century evolutionary paradigm has enjoyed a distinctly "unexamined" life and influence. Before surveying that influence, it may be useful to briefly review the main components—structural, historical, and moral—of the model.

First, the essential and primary "family" structures in antiquity are generally understood to be lineages and the extended kin relationships such lineages produce. Further, as seen in all five authors, the matrilinear and patrilinear lineages are historically separate and competing structures. So, we imagine (with Bachofen, Morgan, and Engels) a revolutionary move from matrilinearity to patrilinearity, with coexisting features of the two systems explained on the principle of cultural "fossils" or incomplete development. Or we see (with Fustel and Maine) a system of strict agnatic patrilinearity, gradually softened with the admission of the claims of nonpatrilinear cognate relations. Although the term "family" itself derives from an inclusive Latin word for "household," the essential "family" organization of antiquity for these theorists was the *gens* or *genos,* not the household. Membership in the *gens*—either a matrilinearly or patrilinearly defined group of extended kin—determined one's identity in ancient (or "primitive") society, and "continuation" of the *gens* as a "deathless corporation" of common property holders (Maine) or as the priesthood of the cult of the ancestors (Fustel) was of prime importance. It is striking that each of the evolutionary theorists discussed insists on the *actual* kinship of the members of the *genos* and the reality of extended family organization, despite existing arguments from contemporary historians such as George Grote that the relationship was purely fictive. On this point Morgan, who adhered to a matriarchal theory of primitive society, referred approvingly to the "recent work" of Fustel de Coulanges—who, however, argued that the *genos* was a patrilinear clan. Differences over matrilinear versus patrilinear were subordinate to the common belief in the essential "gentile" structure of the primitive ancient family (that is, based on and ruled by the clan or *gens*). Today considerable confusion persists about just what is meant when the term *genos* is employed in discussions of Greek family history, where "fictive kin" sometimes slides into the category of actual kin.

The second component of the paradigm is the historical defeat of the "gentile" family by either patriarchy or the territorial state or individualism—or some combination of the three. The exact historical moment of this defeat differs in different authors; in Greece as a whole it seems to happen in the archaic era, roughly from the time of Homer to the late sixth century B.C.E. In Athens the crucial moment apparently comes with the reforms of Cleisthenes in the late sixth century, although important changes had already accompanied or been precipitated by Solon's law code earlier in the century. The historical argument is essentially that the "state" arose in Greece at the expense of original "family" groups—that is, the *genos* (understood as a corporate "extended family") and the larger composite groups, the phratry and the tribe, into which the *genē* were organized. Whether the emphasis is on family religion, family property, or a general family "rule," the paradigm envisions the authority of "the family" giving way to that of the state. With the emergence of the state, the family became domestic or private; and its institutions, wrote Engels, "sank to the position of private associations and religious societies."[62] Likewise, the administration of the household became "private service"—and since this change went hand in hand with the victory of the patriarchal family, the wife became the first domestic servant. Although Engels' view was a politically radical one, he shares the basic paradigm of historical defeat, and resulting separation of public and private spheres, with even his most conservative contemporaries.

The third and last component of the paradigm centers on the moral status of marriage and of women. The most important point was that Greek, and again especially Athenian, women were denied full moral personhood by the institutions of marriage and the family. We hear outrage over the violations or perversions of monogamy (Morgan) and protestations about the vices of prostitution and pederasty (Engels) against a clear background of the nineteenth-century debate on women's place. Painting the by-now-familiar picture of the secluded and despised Athenian woman, whose husband preferred prostitutes and boys for his pleasure, Engels clearly reveals his indignation over not just her proletarian position within the household in which both her reproductive and productive labor was exploited, but also her personal degradation in the face of an asymmetrical standard of moral behavior. The economic bases of that asymmetry were clear: only the wife's monogamy was necessary to the bequeathal of property "indisputably his own." But the moral consequences for both husband and wife of what Engels bitterly called "civilized" marriage—"monogamy supplemented by adultery and prostitution"—were even clearer. At a time of intense discussion and rising economic and social expectations for women in European (and American) society, the "classically harsh form" of marriage in Athens served, it seems, both to reassure Europeans of their own moral progress and to illuminate the economic inequities, exploitation, and moral faults of marriage still apparent in their own society.[63] Classical Athens was an ideal instructive example of the dangers of excessive domination of the public over the private sphere, the state over the family, and man over woman. In recent years the energetic challenging or overturning of cultural icons has reinvigorated the charges of "misogyny" and "class oppression" that were brought against Athens more than a century ago. The mainstream feminist critique of the culture and society of classical Athens, however, seems to have adopted without examination the dominant paradigm of family and women's history from the nineteenth cen-

tury. Challenges have been made—and, more important, feminist research itself has greatly expanded the boundaries of our knowledge
of women's lives—but apparently the paradigm is too well entrenched, and at times perhaps too useful, to be easily abandoned.

Greek History and Family History: Nineteenth-Century Perspectives

In addition to the rise of modern theories of social evolution, the
nineteenth century saw the emergence of the modern craft of "scientific" history as an academic discipline and of the reading of history
as a popular pastime.[64] The field of ancient history was well represented, and ancient history enjoyed a wide reading public. Two of
the most able and distinctive practitioners of the craft, whose work
also reflects in interesting ways on the relation of family to state and
of family history to history "proper," were George Grote and James
Pentland Mahaffy. Grote's *History of Greece* (1846–1856) is a political history—or, as his friend John Stuart Mill wrote, "an epic, of
which Athens, as a collective personality, may be called the hero."[65]
Mahaffy's *Social Life in Greece from Homer to Menander* (1874),
on the other hand, is avowedly about the "subjective side" of Greek
history—or, as we see in his table of contents, everything "nonpolitical": trade, commerce, religion, eating and drinking, and the status
of women. A look at how the family and family history fit into such
a division of method and topic will illustrate the way in which Grote
and Mahaffy, though by no means entirely sharing the historical
view of the evolutionists (as, for example, on the character of the
gens or *genos*), both contributed to the formation of a model of
Greek history that sharply separated public "politics" from private
"family" and allowed the evolutionary paradigm free rein in the latter. Neither Grote nor Mahaffy refers directly to evolutionary arguments or theories—Grote's *History* was finished five years before
Bachofen published *Mother Right*. In their separation of "private"
from "public," however, as well as in their specific approach to
"family matters," they underline the already quite evident suitability
of the evolutionary paradigm to its historical age. A consideration of
the fate of family history in the work of these two quite different

founders of the modern field of ancient history may help explain the
continuing strength of the paradigm in the twentieth century.

George Grote was a prosperous banker, radical member of Parlia-
ment, and, in his leisure moments, the author of a twelve-volume
History of Greece which appeared (usually in two-volume pairs)
from 1846 to 1856.[66] Responding vigorously to William Mitford's
conservative history of Greece (1784–ca. 1790), which extolled the
virtues of Macedonian monarchy and warned of the excesses of
rabble-run democracy,[67] Grote's history was openly celebratory of
democracy, particularly in its best-known Athenian form. But his political views did not preclude a firm commitment to the new historical standards of his day or a careful and critical use of contemporary
sources. His *History* was clearly superior to any Greek history written previously; and despite some conservative complaints, the
twelve-volume work, with its "genuine fervour in behalf of what is
free and generous and just,"[68] was both a popular and academic success in England and abroad. Grote's *History of Greece* was already
the standard work on the subject at the time Bachofen's *Mother
Right* inaugurated (as Engels saw it) the "history of the family" in
1861, and the authority of his opinions is evident in the energy and
respect with which Morgan and Engels discuss and at times dispute
them. But questions which were central to the construction of the
idea of "primitive" society were only marginal to Grote's view of
Greek history as essentially the documented story (or "epic") of
states and statesmen. Grote's view of history as properly political
history allows and indeed encourages a complementary prehistory in
which the tragic hero was the once dominant but ultimately privatized, and "dismembered," family. What were for Grote "margina-
lia"—for example, suggestions of the power and importance of clan
and kin in the "legendary" world of Homer, or a few details of the
"private life" of Pericles and his love for the cultivated Aspasia—
were central features of the new family history based on the evolutionary paradigm.

By titling the first two volumes of his *History* "Legendary Greece"
and making quite clear here and elsewhere his view of the nonhistorical character of Greek myth, including the poems of Homer, Grote
aligned himself with the skeptical German school of history and its
most famous representative, Barthold Niebuhr.[69] Myth is not even a

distorted image of reality; it is at most a plausible fiction and has no historical value. The Trojan War can by no stretch of the imagination be considered a historical event on a level with the Peloponnesian War. But while Grote could then hardly be sympathetic to Bachofen's claim that myth is "a manifestation of primordial thinking, an immediate historical revelation, and consequently a highly reliable historical source," and shared Niebuhr's belief that absolute beginnings, as opposed to progress or historical change, are beyond the historical faculty, he nonetheless allowed that the "legendary age" was the starting point of historical analysis and that the poems of Homer "are full of instruction as pictures of life and manners."[70] Further, in describing that picture Grote emphasizes the importance of kinship: "not only brother," he wrote, "but also cousins, and the more distant blood-relations and clansmen, appear connected together by a strong feeling of attachment, sharing among them universally the obligation of mutual self-defence and revenge, in the event of injury of any individual of the race." Such feeling, he remarks further, is one of the "bright spots in a dark age" visible also among such "rude and barbarous" peoples as the ancient Germans, the Arabian tribes, and "even the North American Indians."[71] The "private ties" of family in fact, according to Grote, provide all of what moral authority exists in this society. Overall, after weighing in the balance the political and the social habits of Homeric Greece, the latter including the treatment of women, Grote concluded that the poems reveal a society midway between the primitive Thracians, who according to Herodotus tattooed their bodies and sold their children into slavery, and so had no family values at all, and the classical contemporaries, the "civilized countrymen" for whom Herodotus wrote. Thus although Grote refused to speculate about the antecedents of Homeric society, he was not at all averse to emphasizing its primitive elements, evaluating its state of moral progress, and linking both to the strength of "family" relationships.

Grote's clearly articulated view of the *genos* as a fictional kin group did not exclude the possibility of other genuine extended kin groups. Nor was that articulated view always adhered to or distinguished from other kinds of family groups in his narrative, which contained, for example, reference to both the "family" and the *gens* of the Alcmeonidae, who in reality seem to have been a particularly active and self-conscious group of Athenians claiming some common descent, through either paternal or maternal lines, from a certain historical Alcmeon who was active in the seventh century. There is no evidence of their being either a prepolitical corporate group or a *genos* based on a fictional claim of kinship to a mythical ancestor.[72] Similarly misleading is Grote's statement, in his list of the features of the historical *genos* (quoted at length by Morgan), that one of the responsibilities of *genos* members was "the mutual right and obligation to intermarry in certain determinate cases, especially where there was an orphan daughter or heiress."[73] In Athens, however, this was the responsibility not of a corporate descent group called the *genos,* but of a group of kindred called the *anchisteia tou genous,* the "nearest in family" extending bilaterally to the degree of sons of cousins and uniquely focused on each individual male Athenian. Other cities' inheritance systems are less well known than Athens', but in no known case did a corporate clan or *genos* hold this responsibility. I reserve further comment on the *anchisteia* and its significance for later chapters, but emphasize here the prevalent lack of clarity about "family" structures and identity, as well as the open attribution of family authority and power to the "primitive" realm.

According to the paradigm described in the previous pages, the historical evolution of the family culminated in the emergence of the state and of a public realm separate from private and domestic life. Grote's *History* is primarily the story of that public realm, of the public careers of ancient Greek states and statesmen. The "family" connections of such men were significant and notable; being one of the Alcmeonidae clearly made a political difference in Athens. But without such political connections, family affairs belonged in the private realm, where for the most part they could be ignored, like the women of Athens, who "lived in strict and almost Oriental reclusiveness . . . destitute of all mental culture and accomplishments."[74]

Thus it is no surprise to find few women in the primarily political world of Grote's history, or to discover that the most celebrated woman to enter that public world is Aspasia, one of the class of cultivated courtesans who "appear to have been the only women in Greece, excepting the Spartan, who either inspired strong passion or exercised mental ascendancy." Pericles, according to Grote, lived with Aspasia "on terms of greatest intimacy and affection."[75] The elevation of Aspasia and the "cultivated courtesan" along with the corresponding denial of status to Athenian women and wives in general is for Grote a fixed social backdrop for his *History,* requiring no historical argument or footnote. Implicitly agreeing with Engels that "one had first to become an *hetaera* in order to become a woman," Grote excludes Athenian women from the status of historical personhood. History is not about wives or families, but about individuals—primarily individual men; occasionally, however, an extraordinary independent "woman" (that is, a hetaira) such as Aspasia joins the ranks of historical actors.[76] This strong insistence on individual juridical and legal identity and rights as the criterion for historical personhood has helped foster the view, also central to the evolutionary paradigm, that Athens was the locus classicus of both democracy and patriarchy. Of no historical interest in themselves, the lives of citizen women could not be subjected to Grote's historical analysis, and specific legal, literary, and visual evidence which might have led him to question the "oriental" status of Athenian women was left unexplored. The recent boom in the field of "women in antiquity" has provided abundant material for reappraising or adding historical subtlety to the traditional view, but in general the conclusion has remained the same—excluded, secluded, and "other"—even when the evidence presented suggests a more nuanced or complicated picture.

In sum, by implicitly denying that family history *was* history through his placement of family history outside the bounds of the world he calls "historical Greece," Grote cedes family history to the evolutionary paradigm. In that paradigm can be found the explanation of how the public emerged from the private, the state from the family, and history from prehistory.

One of the many eager readers of Grote's *History of Greece* as it appeared over the decade 1846–1856 was James Mahaffy, who at roughly age thirteen happened upon the first ten volumes in the Royal Dublin Society library.[77] Mahaffy went on to become the first professor of ancient history, and eventually provost, at Trinity College Dublin. Like Grote, Mahaffy valued Greek history for its relevance to modern politics, for its modern "perplexities"—although as a conservative Anglo-Irishman he saw the world through a different lens. Along with his politics, Mahaffy's choice of subject matter, well illustrated in his highly successful *Social Life in Greece from Homer to Menander* (1874), distinguished him from Grote. Mahaffy wanted to illuminate the "subjective side" of Greek life, "the feelings of the Greeks in their temples and their assemblies, in their homes and their wanderings."[78] The result is a kind of social history which itself wanders from topic to topic (including, for its day, an unusually forthright discussion of the "romantic affection for boys"), but never engages Grote's political narrative. But while his politics were not radical and his style certainly not "epic," Mahaffy's focus is even more exclusively on Athens than is Grote's. "The Athenians" were the only Greeks whom a modern reader could even begin to "get to know" in the way Mahaffy imagines.

When Mahaffy does get to know them, he is alternately charmed and appalled—as if indeed he were watching the behavior of a precocious child. Though pagan, the Athenians in both their art and their literature were capable of moments of moral grandeur which rivaled that of the civilized Christian world. Family and marital morality, however, was a particularly weak spot in the Athenian character.

The Athenian attitude toward old age and the aged comes in for some strong criticism as Mahaffy maintains that even the "most enlightened Greeks . . . stood near the savage of the present day who regards without affection or respect any human being who has become useless." Mahaffy continues by referring to Athenian laws allowing children to deprive their parents of property, and returns to the theme later, calling upon "the strange account" of the "old people of Ceos . . . who when they came to the age of sixty or upwards, and felt themselves growing useless, drank hemlock, and left the world in which they were becoming a mere incumbrance."[79]

But the most significant "test point" of moral progress in both the ancient and the modern world remains for Mahaffy the "social position of women." His colorful comments on this topic take as a now-familiar given the extreme inferiority of classical and particularly "Periclean" Athenian women in the basic rights of education and liberty—"how far removed from the English gentleman" was Alcibiades in his violent treatment of Hipparete. A contemporary perspective is also evident in Mahaffy's notion that Euripides' plays reveal an incipient "women's rights" movement, in contrast to Sophocles, who as a member of the Periclean circle which elevated political life and "despised the age and the sex that were excluded from its privileges" created heroines who were "coarse, unsympathetic and unfeminine."[80]

But once again, there is one exception to this rule of unrelieved female oppression: the courtesan Aspasia, "the most prominent woman of the day." Mahaffy's discussion is particularly interesting in that, in contrast to Grote, he shows great interest in the details and controversies surrounding her life with Pericles (gleaned primarily from ironic or parodic references in comedy and Socratic dialogues). But to the comic charge that she ran a brothel, the "vilest of professions," Mahaffy indignantly replied that Aspasia may have been a "free-thinker," but "there is no absolute proof of her want of dignity and morality."[81]

The stories Mahaffy tells of female trials and tribulations in classical Athens are egregiously romantic and moralistic; but whatever historical plausibility they have stems largely from the strength of a paradigm of Greek history on which classical Athens represented the magnificent, yet costly, victory of politics and the state over the family and domestic life. That Mahaffy (and many others) could imagine with such certainty, to the neglect of considerable direct complicating evidence to the contrary, a classical Athens in which wives, mothers, and daughters were shut indoors, denied even "the reasonable liberty" granted to women elsewhere, and considered essentially as "property," while courtesans roamed the streets and discoursed on politics and "public" matters with Athenian husbands, fathers, and sons—and that such an image seemed, and still seems to many, historically plausible is an indication of both the past and present authority of this paradigm.[82]

Mahaffy's *Social Life in Greece* and Grote's *History of Greece* stand as models for the radical separation of ancient history into "history proper" and "life and manners" analogous to an assumed separation of public/private spheres. They also represent clearly its strong Athenian focus, in both praise and blame. This historical tradition, and the historical paradigm it has both supported and assumed, has continued in force to the present day.

Twentieth-Century Echoes

Throughout antiquity the female members of the human race shared the fate of the oikos . . . Prior to the emergence of the polis and after its decline, when the household was strong and the political community relatively weak, custom and law accorded women a modicum of personal freedom and independence. But in the classical period, when the polis was in full vigor, they occupied an unenviable status. Women were everywhere denied political rights. In some cities they could neither bring suit in the courts nor own property in their own names. While the men of the town spent their leisure hours loitering about grand public spaces within sight of marble or stone buildings possessed of a magnificence still striking today, their wives and daughters were virtual prisoners, kept in seclusion—all but the wealthiest locked within the squalid, dark, and damp confines of relatively primitive mud-brick houses.

This passage occurs in an article published in *American History Review* in 1984.[83] Indeed, such echoes of earlier discussions are typical of recent discussions of ancient Greek, and particularly classical Athenian, social history. They are also typically unacknowledged echoes. W. K. Lacey begins his scholarly and sober *The Family in Classical Greece* (1968) with the statement that "the family in Greek history is a subject which has hitherto not found favour among historians," and then goes on to incorporate in his analysis the primary elements of the evolutionary paradigm. Likewise, although recent work in "women's studies" has deepened and broadened our understanding of both the representations and the realities of women's lives in ancient Greece, it has rarely challenged the paradigm positing an essential connection between political democracy and female oppression. That connection is also taken as "given" by traditional historians of politics and political discourse, who assume the relevance of nineteenth-century categories of public and private spheres for the ancient Greek world.[84]

In contrast, earlier twentieth-century discussions of Greek social history often acknowledged their debt to and, to some extent, dialogue with the nineteenth century. Gustave Glotz's *La solidarité de la famille* (1904), for example, assigned to *genos* the role of extended kin or "family" increasingly pressured by the rise of the territorial state and was on this central point openly indebted to Fustel's *Ancient City*.[85] Somewhat later, in *Aeschylus and Athens* (1946), an openly evolutionary interpretation of the *Oresteia*, George Thomson appealed first and foremost to the work of Morgan and Engels.[86] The extent to which this way of thinking has left its mark on Greek historical studies is illustrated in the frequently encountered reading of the *Oresteia* as a document of "family history" recounting the triumph of the polis over the primitive family or clan.[87]

Still, not everyone succumbed to the power of the paradigm. In *The World of Odysseus* (1954), M. I. Finley commented wisely that despite what "the anthropologists have taught us" about the preeminence of kin and family in primitive societies, "this is no description of the world of Odysseus, in which the family tie, though strong, was narrowly defined, and in which other strong and often more binding relationships were established outside the blood group." Finley's next comment, however, was that "in evolutionary terms, in so far as they may legitimately be employed, the world of the Homeric poems had advanced beyond the primitive," a view which might seem essentially compatible with Morgan's placing of Homeric society in the stage of "Upper Barbarism."[88] Indeed, the historical component of the evolutionary paradigm is perceptible in Finley's influential discussion of "Household, Kin, and Community." For example, early in that chapter he says:

> Historically there is an inverse relationship between the extension of the notion of crime as an act of public malfeasance and the authority of the kinship group. Primitive societies are known in which it is not possible to find any "public" responsibility to punish an offender. Either the victim and his relations take vengeance or there is none whatsoever. The growth of the idea of crime, and of criminal law, could almost be written as the history of the chipping away of that early state of family omnipotence.[89]

The success of this analysis is undermined by the fact that "family" and "kin" (and elsewhere "lineage") are left undefined and undifferentiated.

In the years since Glotz's *Solidarité de la famille,* Thomson's *Oresteia,* and Finley's *World of Odysseus,* the evolutionary paradigm has

seemed so comfortably entrenched as not even to require acknowledgment of its ancestry. Its comfort derives both from the pervasive
acceptance of its terms and also from the way it validates or reinforces the traditional separation of political history "proper" from
family, social, or "private" history. The paradigm sits comfortably
both for those who decry the seclusion and oppression of Athenian
women and for those who use the assumption of a "men-only" public world to justify the exclusion of women and family from the historical analysis.

As in the nineteenth-century discussions, the society of the Homeric
poems is typically taken today as representing a turning point, at
which the "public" begins to become distinct from the "private"—and
political history from family history. After Homer, family history
(marriage, kinship, and related topics) assumes a separate status from
political history—that is, from history proper. This separation may in
fact be what W. K. Lacey had in mind when he commented that "the
family in Greek history is a subject which has hitherto not found
favor." The designation of his topic as "the family in Greek history"
was promising and significant, for it seemed to challenge the separation of "private customs" from "public history" and to insist that the
family does play a role in the history of Greek society. Nor did Lacey
accept the paradigmatic idea that while the family was important in
the "prepolitical" world of the Homeric poems (Grote's "legendary"
Greece), it retreated or was pushed into the private realm with the
emergence of the post-Homeric polis. Rather, as the "most central and
enduring institution of Greek society," the family, he says, "remained
stubbornly entrenched" in Greek history as well.[90]

So Lacey issued in his preface a strong call for a new social history
of the Greek family. His book, however, was essentially a retelling of
the old story for a new audience. *The Family in Classical Greece* illustrates in a profound way the isolation of the mid-twentieth-
century classical historian, who worked carefully with primary
classical texts and, in sharp contrast with his nineteenth-century predecessors, refused to make direct contemporary moral or political
judgments, but who yet in fact carried along the substantial "bag-
gage" of the older tradition. First, the evolutionary element in
Lacey's discussion is clear in his brief introductory chapter, "The
Family in the City-State," where he announced the theme of a pro-

gressive "emancipation" from "family" control concomitant with the rise of the polis. The oikos (or household) emerged first from under control of the *genos* (clan), and then the individual from under the oikos.[91] And the societies placed at the extremes of this development are the Homeric, taken as a "primitive society" in the Greek "age of settlement" (apparently somewhere between the tenth and seventh centuries B.C.E.),[92] and the classical Athenian, to which the central four chapters of the book are dedicated. Interestingly, the Spartan polis, which does not seem to fit neatly the evolutionary mold, is relegated with Crete to an essentially nonhistorical final chapter. The "historical" component of the paradigm appears fully in control, and it is quite possible that the best way to understand what Lacey intended by the "liberation" or "emancipation" of individual from family is to read Maine on "from status to contract."

Second, the structural question of the nature of the *genos* and its relation to the oikos is a persistent problem throughout Lacey's historical analysis, as it was in the nineteenth-century discussions. Lacey understood *oikos* as the equivalent of "family" but uses it in reference both to the household unit (composed of husband, wife, children, and property) *and* to a patrilineal lineage, which "looked backwards to its supposed first founder" and "forward to its own continuance, and to the preservation for as many future generations as possible of the cult of the family which the living members practised in the interest of the dead." That Lacey imagined this as a male lineage seems quite clear in his paraphrase of Athenian inheritance law requiring that the heiress be married to her "nearest agnatic relative (a father's brother . . . if possible) in order to re-establish the family in the next generation."[93] The way in which an Athenian heiress was actually entrusted to the male members of her father's bilateral and nonagnatic *anchisteia* ("closest" kin) will be discussed in Chapter 3; for now I note that Lacey's emphasis on agnatic "lineage" recalls the more extended discussion of Fustel and Maine. It is striking that although Lacey is well aware of the fictional character of the kinship of the members of the Athenian corporate *genos,* he continues to call the *genos* a "clan" and to emphasize its "family" functions—for example, the common ownership of land by a *genos* or the common taking of revenge for a *genos* member's murder.

Finally, on the issue of the status of women, Lacey's approach, though not overtly political, shares the tendency of his predecessors to read Athens in the light of his own social context and values. Although "middle-class standards demanded by the democracy" may have limited aristocratic freedom, "within this middle class . . . women were probably as well protected by the law as in any century before our own, and, granted a reasonable husband or father, enjoyed a life not much narrower nor much less interesting than women in comparable classes of society elsewhere. Emancipated women nowadays, naturally, have much more personal freedom but less protection against unscrupulous males."[94]

Lacey's book had no immediate successors. While the 1970s and 1980s saw the publication of important studies of the ancient Roman family, of demographic realities, legal structures, and household relationships,[95] interest on the Greek side in those decades focused for the most part on the representations of women in Greek art and literature and on the ideological roots of those representations. The history of the family structures and gender relations standing behind those representations received little critical attention—and the nineteenth-century paradigm ruled unexamined. The historical framework, for example, of Sarah Pomeroy's groundbreaking *Goddesses, Whores, Wives, and Slaves: Women in Classical Antiquity* (1976) was still largely that of the evolutionary model, positing an essential decline in the position of women from the Bronze Age (which Homer is taken to depict) to the classical age in Athens. "Compared with subsequent Greek literature," wrote Pomeroy,

> epic gives a generally attractive impression of the life of women. They were expected to be modest, but were not secluded. Andromache and Helen walk freely through the streets of Troy, though always with escorts, and women are shown on the shield of Achilles helping to defend a city's walls. The rendezvous of a boy and girl outside the walls of Troy is referred to. Wives, notably Helen, Arete, and Penelope, may remain within the public rooms in the presence of male guests without scandal. Not only concubines but legitimate wives are considered desirable, and there is little trace of the misogyny that taints later Greek literature.[96]

Then, turning to classical Athens in three substantial chapters, Pomeroy presented an image of a society where women were in fact "secluded" and wives were not "considered desirable" in themselves but only as the legal bearers of citizen children. Despite careful presentation of the evidence of women's activities in classical Athens which might take them out of the house, even perhaps unescorted— for example, work or public religion—Pomeroy adhered to the solidly traditional notion of "oriental seclusion." She observed that "it seems likely" that women attended dramatic performances in Athens, yet claimed that "the women, absent or present, were not noticed by our ancient authorities."[97] Classical Athens is firmly fixed in its traditional position as the end of women's evolutionary decline, while .classical Sparta, as in Lacey's account, stands outside history, outside that decline, as a relic of an archaic and less misogynistic family structure.[98] Pomeroy is one of the founders of the late twentieth-century discussion of "women in antiquity"; the historical premise of her discussion, however, is rooted in the nineteenth century.

Twenty years after the publication of *Goddesses, Whores, Wives, and Slaves,* the field of "women in ancient Greece" continues to prosper and to produce results of increasing sophistication and depth, particularly as interdisciplinary methods and approaches have become more common. Unfortunately, the basic historical and evolutionary principles on which the discussion rests have remained to a large extent unquestioned. Two recent books bear witness. The multiple-authored volume *Women in the Classical World* contains an admirable range of artistic, literary, and documentary evidence but still assumes as "given" the familiar evolutionary model of women's decline to an excluded low in classical and democratic Athens. A revealing example occurs in introductory discussion of the grave relief of a certain Athenian woman named Mnesarete, on which appears the inscription:

> This woman left a husband and siblings, and grief to her mother, and a child and an ageless renown for great virtue.
> Here the chamber of Persephone holds Mnesarete,
> who has arrived at the goal of all virtue.

The authors emphasize the importance of interpreting the monument in the context of classical Athenian values, where the "relatively secluded wife avoided a public reputation and turned her energies above all to familial concerns, to producing children and to caring for her household." Their assumption of Athens' extremity and peculiarity in this regard leads to the odd comment that immediately follows: "yet the same monument, if it were dated to another time or place in the Greek world, might hint at greater public recognition of a living wife's virtues."[99] Similarly odd, and overtly ideological, is the heading "Silenced Women" for the section which begins with Pericles' advice to war widows to avoid being talked about (Thucydides 2.46) and ends with an account of the legal status of the heiress *(epikleros),* a figure with a reputation for anything but retiring silence. An awareness of the historical paradigm and its elements should make such unrecognized assumptions highly recognizable as they reappear throughout the book.

Similarly, Sue Blundell's *Women in Ancient Greece* presents a wealth of information about women's lives, drawing from recent specialized studies of the economic responsibilities and public activities of Greek women, including Athenian women. Nonetheless, the book's basic premise is that the "status" of women declined from the Homeric to the classical world, with a low in classical Athens, and includes statements such as the *kyrios* (male guardian) "acted as an intermediary between the private domain occupied by the woman and the public sphere from which she was excluded" and "though democracy needed them, [women] were excluded from its institutions." We hear of clans and lineages, and of Athenian women's exclusion from patrilineal inheritance as well as from the "public sphere."[100] Information is provided, however, that implicitly or explicitly disputes this image of an oppressive classical Athens. For example, Blundell comments that "it must be admitted that hippocratic doctors do not always insist on the beneficial effects of sexual intercourse for women" but "recognise that in some illnesses it is dangerous for women to become pregnant."[101] Her prefatory words "it must be admitted that" reveal the presence of the ruling paradigm. In fact Blundell's conclusion that "for Athenian women 'citizenship' meant only that they had a share in the religious, legal and economic order of the Athenian community" actually undermines her assumptions about the exclusion of women from the public sphere and the public institution of Athenian democracy.

Although the paradigm of Greek family history described here, with its emphasis on the progressive privatization (or seclusion) of the family (and women), remains dominant, there are a growing number of skeptics. Just as the nineteenth-century debate was broadly based in the intellectual circles of Europe and America, so also these new voices calling for an examination of the old paradigms are not monolingual. Marilyn Katz, Beate Wagner-Hasel, Josine Blok, and Pauline Schmitt-Pantel are among those calling for a greater awareness of the ideological basis of the topic "women in antiquity."[102] I offer this book as a further contribution to that challenge and call.

The "Otherness" of Greek Culture

Of the many problems inherent in the interpretation of ancient Greek family structure and history, perhaps the most difficult and the most persistent is determining on what basis, with what assumptions of strangeness or similarity, that interpretation is to be undertaken. Social history itself has seemed to some essentially "subjective" in that its subjects are not "laws, feasts or furniture" but "feelings."[103] But it is the subjectivity of the historian in attempting to understand the family structures and values of an assorted group of people we call "the ancient Greeks" that is by far the larger problem. How can we see "the familiar within the strange without losing the sense of either"?[104] How can we avoid the danger, evident in both old and new Greek family history, of creating a "strangeness" for the Greeks which is really just "us" seen through a "distorting mirror"?[105] And how do we cross what Virginia Woolf called the "tremendous breach of tradition" separating "us" from the Greeks?[106] These questions have no easy solutions: the Greeks are neither "us" in our cultural childhood nor so different as to be beyond our sympathy or understanding. But they are questions which I acknowledge even if we cannot answer them.

Virginia Woolf found the Greeks strange in their poetic clarity and in their laughter, but for the social historian the strangeness begins in the more mundane facts of premodern demography and subsistence agriculture. If the familial relations of ancient Greece—of parent and child or husband and wife—seem odd to us, as no doubt they sometimes do, the roots of that oddness often lie in the different life-expectancies and material realities of the ancient Greek family. Although the following chapters focus primarily on legal requirements and social customs rather than on demographic realities, a brief summary of those factors and their consequences for family experience is in order here.

The key determining factor in the structure of the ancient Greek family—or, more properly, the ancient Greek household—is clearly life expectancy. How long family and household members live affects not only the size of the household but also its structure and composition. Although it has seemed tempting to some to look for "solid" historical evidence in the small sample of available skeletal remains,[107] most historians have accepted the use of model "life tables" for a population with a life expectancy of twenty to twenty-five years as the basis for discussions of family size and composition. Such tables allow us to see the consequences of high infant mortality for completed family size (two to three surviving children) and the consequences of general mortality rates for the relative size of different age groups or of specific legally defined identities such as the "brotherless daughter" or heiress. The image of the ancient Greek family produced by the use of demographic models is one of small primary families, with the possibility of extension to include a living grandparent and the even greater possibility of fragmentation through the death of a parent or spouse. The literary record supports this image and adds the complicating details of practical response to these demographic realities: remarriage, adoption, and in general the creation of complex, mutable households. Such households and families differ significantly from modern norms and ideals. Their experience within the larger scope of Greek political and social history is nonetheless an important part of our modern understanding of that history. Realizing that no historical analysis is free of contemporary concerns and perspectives, but believing that there is no need to carry (unexamined) nineteenth-century concerns and perspectives with us, I turn now to the family in Greek history

2

THE FAMILY IN HOMER
AND HESIOD

The association of persons, established according to nature for the satisfaction of daily needs, is the household [*oikos*] . . . The next stage is the village, the first association of a number of households for the satisfaction of something more than daily needs . . . The final association is the polis. For all practical purposes the process is now complete; self-sufficiency has been reached and while the polis came about as a means of securing life itself, it continues in being to secure the good life.

Aristotle, *Politics* 1252b

These well-known lines from Aristotle's *Politics* underpin in one way or another most discussions of the rise and character of the Greek polis.[1] Aristotle states unambiguously that the polis is the last (and most perfect) of a progression of natural associations beginning with the association of persons in the household or oikos. He does not, however, claim that the household was in any way "defeated" by the emergence of the polis. For Aristotle the superiority of polis to oikos is a matter of teleology and natural development, not of winning or losing. Nor does this passage posit a hostile distinction or opposition between blood or kin relations and political relations, as do many reconstructions of early polis history. Rather, Aristotle traces a series (or expanding circle) of human associations organized around common interests or needs—household, village, and polis—in which the relationship of household and polis is teleological rather than antithetical. In this chapter and the next, I focus on the historical experience and interests of the first association, the household, amidst the emergence of the last, the polis. In particular I focus on the ways in which the interests of the early polis (or *poleis*—since no assumption is made that all were alike) intersected with household interests, and how this intersection was articulated in public law on family status, property, and inheritance. Because a prerequisite to this project is as clear an understanding as possible of the central relationships and structures of the early Greek family and household, I begin with the two poetic "parents" of Greek culture, Homer and Hesiod, and their images of the early Greek family.

The Early Greek Family

He has no dishonour when he dies defending
his country [*patre*], for then his wife [*alochos*] shall be saved and
    his children [*paides*] afterwards
and his house [*oikos*] and property [*kleros*] shall not be dam-
    aged.[2]

In this early appeal to civic patriotism, voiced by the Trojan hero Hector, we find not only an unmistakable connection between the well-being of the household and that of the larger community, but also a remarkably clear description of the Homeric family and household from the point of view of its male head: the hero dies to protect *alochos, paides, oikos,* and *kleros.* Of these terms, *paides* and *kleros* are perhaps the easiest to translate directly into English. *Paides* are one's children, including at least potentially both sons and daughters. Although at times *pais* (singular) might seem to refer specifically to a male child (the classic example is Herodotus 5.48: Cleomenes died *apais*, leaving only a daughter), this is also the general and inclusive word for "child," and there seems no reason to suppose that daughters are not implicitly included and protected here. Further, although Homeric society distinguished between legitimate and illegitimate children, that distinction is not articulated in this passage.[3] *Kleros* is also a relatively straightforward term: it is one's "portion" or "allotment" of land. The word does raise the historical issue of an "original" distribution of land—what was allotted, when, and by whom?—but for present purposes it is enough to emphasize that the word refers to a piece of land on which a household is built and so reveals clearly the agricultural basis of the early Greek family and community.[4]

The translation of *oikos* and *alochos,* on the other hand, though rendered by Lattimore simply as "house" and "wife," requires further discussion. First, is the *oikos* simply the physical house, or does it stand for something more inclusive, and perhaps cumulative, in this passage? The separate articulation of the four terms in these lines does not necessarily mean that they are conceptually discrete, and even in its most basic Homeric sense *oikos* was more than a physical structure. What also is the relationship of *oikos*—and indeed the relationship of all the elements evoked by Hector—to *genos,* a term not used here but very commonly assumed as the equivalent of "family" (either the immediate or extended kin) in modern discussions of ancient Greek society? Second, what sort of wife is the *alochos,* literally the "bedmate"? What distinguishes the *alochos* from and privileges her over any other woman, slave or free, the Homeric hero might take to bed with him? In short, what constitutes marriage in this society, and what makes a woman a wife?

The Homeric Oikos

A survey of Homer's usage reveals a strong spatial component: *oikos* refers to a place.[5] *Oikos* is, for example, the place to which Greek warriors think of returning, the place where Agamemnon would like to keep Chryseis, the place to which Telemachos tells Penelope to return and also that from which he refuses to force her.[6] On the other hand, *oikos* is also what Odysseus wishes for Nausicaa (along with a husband) and what Telemachos sees as being devoured by the suitors. Further, it is also the site of Trojan mourning for their dead.[7] Rather than simply "house" (mud-brick or whatever), *oikos* then would seem to have a larger, more inclusive, and more subjective sense of "home." Just as we do not imagine that the suitors are "eating away" the walls or roof of Odysseus' house, so we should not suppose that Odysseus wishes for Nausicaa merely a pleasant place to live (she had that already) or that the Trojan mourning took place only within the walls of their houses. And for Agamemnon to have Chryseis "at home" does not seem to depend on having her in a house.

Emphasizing then that the oikos was a place around which were focused experiences of living and dying, producing and reproducing, we might also justifiably understand *oikos* as meaning "household"—implying the connection between the physical house and the things and people held and produced within it.[8] Thus, *oikos* has an inclusive sense which could embrace both persons and property. And to the extent that the term does embrace both elements, Hector's use of *oikos* has a cumulative reference in the passage quoted at the opening of this section. But however we translate the word, the activities and emotions that cluster around the oikos argue for our seeing it as the conceptual center of the early Greek family. That is, early Greek family relations are essentially rooted in the relationships of house and household. This is not to say that there were not other kinds of family relations or structures of relevance in Greek society, but simply to emphasize the centrality of the household as the primary focus of both family loyalty and identity.[9]

Not everyone will readily agree with this conceptual centering of the early Greek family on the relationships of the oikos; some may identify instead a significant distinction between family and oikos, as is perhaps implied in Oswyn Murray's description of the Homeric hero, who stands "at the head of a group which can be viewed in two different ways: in terms of hereditary descent, as his *genos* or family, and in terms of its economic counterpart, the oikos (household or estate)." Here family is equated with descent, to which the term *genos* is applied without further comment. Although Murray goes on to emphasize that "the Homeric family is not a particularly extended group," that "beyond the immediate kin, the *genos* seems to have little significance," and concludes that "it is somewhat misleading therefore to translate *genos* as clan rather than family," he is in the end quite vague about just what "the *genos*" might be;[10] and given the long tradition of seeing early Greek society as clan-based or "gentile," Murray's construction of Homeric identity can easily be read in a traditional way. While he is cautious about the word "clan," other writers are less so. So Robert Littman, as recently as 1990, uses the term regularly in his discussion of Athenian politics of the late archaic and classical period.[11]

Because terminological vagueness is a significant problem in discussions of early Greek family history, it may be useful here to offer a few practical definitions. On the one hand, "family" is a word with many meanings but with an essential sense of "one's own." The very flexibility of the word is a key part of its power and usefulness. On the other hand, "clan" and "tribe" are terms with quite specific usages in social analysis, even though their definitions may not be universally agreed upon. I adopt here the standard definitions offered in the *Dictionary of the Social Sciences,* according to which "clan" refers to a unilineal descent group and "tribe" to a prepolitical or prenational social group whose solidarity is based on common territory, common language, and common culture.[12] Finally, there is one specific family term that should also be considered, since it will figure very significantly in the discussion to follow: the ego-based "kindred," which is "structurally shapeless," since "it comes in and out of existence as its focal egos are born and die."[13] When *genos* means "family" in Greek sources it often means this sort of kindred, whereas "clan" in its dictionary sense is for the most part out of place in both archaic and classical Greece.[14]

In recent years the traditional nineteenth-century view of early Greece as a primitive tribal or clan-based society has increasingly come under attack, and the usefulness of these terms is increasingly discounted—at least by those working directly in the field. It may in fact be possible to say that a "new consensus is emerging" which emphasizes the importance of the individual household in the midst of a fluid world of "expanding and contracting kin/client associations" focused on local "big men," and eventually (in central and southern Greece) of an emerging political/polis order.[15] Nonetheless, the implications of this changed perspective for understanding the character and experience of the Greek family within the broader scope of Greek history have not always been recognized. Murray is clearly aware of the problems with "clan" as a translation of *genos,* but his text nonetheless allows some uncertainty about what *genos* in fact might refer to or represent. What, for example, is implied by the statement that "marriages are arranged by the heads of the *genos*"?[16]

What, then, does *genos* denote? By far the most frequent Homeric use of the word is to indicate a person's or thing's origin or the natural group to which he, she, or it belongs. So both Glaukos in the *Iliad* and Odysseus in the *Odyssey* appeal to the need not to shame the *genos* of their fathers; Menelaos welcomes Telemachos as a youth clearly born of a *genos* of kingly men, while Athena (in disguise) urges Nausicaa, whom no one excels in *genos,* to prepare for marriage; and among the gods, Zeus and Hera, Zeus and Ares, and Zeus and Poseidon are linked by common *genos.* There are also the Chimaera of divine *genos;* Asteropaion, whose *genos* is of the river; and the Enetoi, from whose land comes the *genos* of wild mules.[17] It seems clear that *genos* does establish one's identity in the sense of answering the question "from where did you come?" (so Odysseus to Penelope, *Odyssey* 19.116), but it does not follow that it indicates the existence of a functioning group called "the *genos.*" When Telemachos says, *"ex Ithakes genos eimi"* (15.267), he means, on the most straightforward reading, "I was born in Ithaca." More examples could be added, but these should be enough to establish that *genos* in Homer does not refer to a lineage or corporate kinship group over which stood a "head" or patriarchal chief. Homer's *genos* was not a clan—and the society he depicts was not "gentile" in that sense. In sum, a man—a Homeric hero—was head and protector of his oikos but not of his *genos.*

Genos reveals a man (or woman's) identity, and appeals to *genos* often have a strongly rhetorical flavor, as characters urge or justify some future or past action: "You ought to do this because of who you are" (Odysseus to Telemachos, Athena to Nausicaa) or "You ought to do this because of who I am" (Hera to Zeus). But the *genos* was not a group to which one longed to return or for which one fought. *Genos* could be a matter of pride, but the oikos (and its members) was the focus of both sentiment and action. Although Hector's *genos* may explain why he died, he did not die for his *genos*—but rather for his *patre* (and polis) and, in its composite sense, his oikos and the family relationships rooted in that oikos.

Even though most late twentieth-century historians no longer hold extravagant and extreme views of early Greek society as a paradigm of matrilinear or patrilinear clan or "family" history, the view persists that in early Greece the most important family connections were those of lineage.[18] And with this view comes the corollary that family interests in this era, and indeed throughout Greek history, are essentially lineage or "blood" interests, distinct and often antithetical to the larger political interests of the community. Thus it is particularly notable that Murray summarizes his discussion of the political development of early (Homeric and Hesiodic) Greece with the following judgment: "Some features of the Homeric poems point to an earlier state; but as far as social and political organizations are concerned, despite the importance of the *genos* and the *oikos,* Homer and Hesiod show that the *polis* already existed in all essential aspects by the end of the Dark Age."[19]

Without the blinders of the family=lineage approach, however, we can appreciate with greater clarity the centrality and the political significance of the relationships contained within the oikos as depicted in the Homeric poems. The relationships which make the most difference to the poems' characters, and in which most is invested, are those of the oikos—husband to wife, parent to child, and also master to slave (a relationship omitted by Hector but one whose significance to the oikos is particularly evident in the *Odyssey*). To cite but one example, Odysseus depends in his successful return on his son, his slave, and his wife. This last is especially important if we see that Homer allows his audience to suspect that Penelope sets up the contest of the bow knowing, or at least strongly suspecting, that the beggar is in fact Odysseus.[20]

The Homeric Family outside the Oikos

Homeric society also recognized significant personal and familial connections outside the immediate oikos. Two passages, one from the *Iliad* and one from the *Odyssey,* illustrate their basic character:

> And now,
> when Hector reached the Scaean Gates and the great oak,
> the wives and daughters of Troy came rushing up around him,
> asking about their sons, brothers, friends and husbands [*paidas te kasignetous te etas te kai posias.*][21]

and

> "Tell me why you should grieve so terribly over the Argives and
> the fall of Troy . . .

Some kin of yours [*peos*] then died at Ilion
some first rate man, son-in-law or father-in-law [*gambros e*
   pentheros]
next to your own blood most dear [*kedistoi . . . meth' haima te*
   kai genos]?
Or some companion [*hetairos*] of congenial mind and valor?
   True it is, a wise friend
can take the place of a brother in our affection."[22]

Although the Homeric terminology is somewhat unfamiliar, the relationships are for the most part straightforward and familiar. In addition to children, brothers, and husbands, the Trojan wives and daughters ask about a group called *etai*, which Fagles translates as "friends" and others translate as "kin."[23] "Family friends" may be the closest English translation for a term that seems to partake of the character of both words. In the second passage, Alcinoos imagines that in addition to his immediate relatives "by blood and birth," Odysseus might be mourning a connection by marriage or again a companion, who indeed could be closer in affection than a brother. The Homeric sibling relationship, however, is a markedly intense one—as it continued to be in later Greek society. Meleager's mother curses her son because of the death of her brother *(phonoio . . . kasignetoio)*; her devotion is of the same order as Antigone's toward Polyneices.[24] The importance of sibling relationships reinforces the point that family relations outside the oikos are essentially those connections produced by marriage and the oikos itself—together with those assimilated thereto through close friendship or mutual dependence. From this perspective the early Greek family can be recognized as both a natural and a practical human association for the preservation of life and livelihood.

Even the exotic households of Troy and Phaeacia do not belie this point, for they are primarily exotic in the quantity not the quality of their household and extrahousehold relationships.[25] They are conspicuous and wealthy, and their material wealth is epitomized by their wealth in sons and daughters (and, for Priam, wives). In terms of basic structure, the households of Priam and Alcinoos are simply Ithaca writ large or multiplied for grand effect. The household relationships are not extended but multiple; the central relationships are still those appealed to by Hector: children, wife, and household property. The "primitive" family, the *genos* as a corporate and patrilinear clan, cannot be found in Homer. It is itself a mythical beast, in *genos* a chimaera.

Nonetheless, belief in a primitive Greek clan as the key form and focus of family in early Greece somehow persists and particularly doggedly so in discussions of "blood guilt" and "blood feud." So M. I. Finley, while otherwise rightly unconvinced by the historically fuzzy image of a "tribal" Homeric society, makes an exception in the case of murder. "I can find no evidence of clan authority at all in the poems," Finley comments, "outside of one clearly defined area, that of the blood-feud."[26] He does not, however, go on to elaborate just what that evidence is. So what do Homer's poems have to say about the family and the community's response to murder? Three passages from the *Odyssey* and one from the *Iliad* will establish the basic terms of the discussion:

"That is a good thing now, for a man to leave
a son behind him, like the son who punished
Aigisthos for the murder of his great father."[27]

"I too had to leave my home. I killed a countryman [*emphylos*].
In the wide grazing lands of Argos live
many brothers of his [*kasignetoi*] and friends [*etai*] in power,
    great among the Akhaians."[28]

"We'd be disgraced forever! Mocked for generations
if we cannot avenge our sons' [*paidon*] blood, and our brothers'
    [*kasigneton*]!"[29]

"Hard, ruthless man . . .
Why any man will accept the blood-price paid
for a brother [*kasignetoio*] murdered, a child done to death.
And the murderer lives on in his own country—
the man has paid enough, and the injured kinsman [the brother
    or father]
curbs his pride, his smoldering, vengeful spirit,
once he takes the price."[30]

It is quite clear that responsibility for punishing a murderer rested first with the victim's closest immediate male relatives—fathers, sons, and brothers. This responsibility is rooted in the household itself, not in membership in any larger clan or corporate family group. From there the responsibility extends, in ways which would be made more precise in later Greek law, to a larger group of "family/friends."[31] Thus, there emerges in these passages an expanding circle of persons with an interest in seeing that vengeance is taken on behalf of the victim, but these persons do not constitute an autonomous or corporate clan. Rather, they are this particular man's relatives and friends, whose connection to him derives (or extends) from the basic relationships of the oikos and so are properly understood as "kindred" not "clan."

Nor is the "blood guilt" extended to anyone, including any kin, beyond the murderer himself.[32] To a large extent, it seems, the punishment of a murderer depended on the sort of compensation—death, exile, or fine—the representative of the victim wanted or thought he could get. Although in its dependence on "self-help" for both vengeance and "blood price," and also in its lack of overarching public authority, this society might indeed be called "primitive," its primitiveness, if it be that, is not attributable to its family structure.

It is significant that the expanding circle of those with an interest in vengeance for an act of murder includes not only immediate "blood" relations but also "friends" (etai; Odyssey 15.272). Again, Homer imagines the interested group moving from fathers and sons, immediate members of family and household, to relatives (cousins), and then to what might be called an "extended family" of friends. The Homeric poems therefore do not support the assertion that "killing an outsider provoked the wrath of his victim's whole genos; against a killer the genos stood solid"[33]—if, that is, we understand genos as a clan or unilineal descent group. But, if we take genos in its common classical sense as a loose equivalent of "blood relations," the statement has some substance. Taking genos as a composite group of relatives including maternal as well as paternal connections, as in fact the bilateral kindred, it would be correct to say that a man's genos was responsible for his well-being during his life and after his death. In later Athenian legal terminology, anchisteia (or anchisteia tou genous) had this latter meaning: a web of relatives or

a "kindred," focused around one Athenian male citizen, with immediate responsibility, among other things, for prosecuting his (or his
daughter's) murderer. In Homer, *genos* has the simpler meaning of
birth or origin described earlier; and in neither Homer nor Plato is
genos a corporate clan. It may indeed be preferable to use the word
without the definite article.

The picturesque phrase "wrath of the whole *genos*" is taken from
a modern discussion of the famous trial scene represented on the
shield of Achilles in *Iliad* 18. But that scene is in fact a very important confirmation of the point just made, namely, that whereas
"blood price" was an important element of the Homeric way of
dealing with murder, blood feuds of clans were not. The scene also
introduces in an important way the community as a whole, or the
embryonic polis itself, into the field of conflict resolution. On the
new armor fashioned by Hephaestus for Achilles (at his mother's request), the god depicted two *poleis,* one at war and one at peace.
And in the polis at peace a very interesting public gathering just happens to be occurring:

> the people massed, streaming into the market place
> where a quarrel had broken out and two men struggled
> over the blood-price for a man just murdered.
> One declaimed in public, vowing payment in full—
> the other spurned him, he would not take a thing—
> so both men pressed for a judge to cut the knot.
> The crowd cheered on both, they took both sides,
> but heralds held them back as the city elders sat
> on polished stone benches, forming the sacred circle,
> grasping in hand the staffs of clear-voiced heralds,
> and each leapt to his feet to plead the case in turn.
> Two bars of solid gold shone on the ground before them,
> a prize for the judge who'd speak the straightest verdict.[34]

The system of justice depicted here is clearly rudimentary, but, as
was the case in later Greek litigation, judgment is sought by individuals not clans. What is particularly striking here, however, is the
emerging role of the assembled *demos,* which plays the part of a
proto-jury, indicating a public verdict on the judgments of the

elders/judges. Justice is in this way becoming a public concern; and its developmental course parallels that outlined by Aristotle for the polis as a whole in the *Politics:* vengeance taken by immediate household/kin or friends yields to trial and judgment delivered by the community as a whole (or its representatives).[35] There is no intermediate place for clan or tribal feuding, just as there is no intermediate place in Aristotle's progression for clan or tribe (in their dictionary senses). Family or household relationships here move naturally and progressively, not oppositionally, to political relationships. There is also no conflict here between the claims of family and state, but rather an appeal to the community to settle a dispute which traditional arbitration and an offer of payment have failed to settle. Still, "blood guilt" and "blood feud" of clan and tribe are an important feature of the modern image of early Greek society, and, looking ahead for a moment to the classical era, nowhere is this more noticeable than in discussions of Aeschylus' *Oresteia,* written some two and a half centuries after Homer's *Iliad.* So one critic and classicist writes when introducing this trilogy: "Because the single-family household had emerged relatively recently from a clan-based society, the polis only gradually gained the loyalty which had previously been paid to family and tribe."[36] So speaks the traditional paradigm.

   A different sort of antidote to the strong modern temptation to read the Homeric family in the light of an often romantic notion of the "primitive" and "gentile" might be to let Odysseus himself speak to what he and his world, and later Greeks as well, considered primitive in organization and social behavior: the Cyclopes and, even more, Polyphemus himself. As a group, the Cyclopes led a backward if somewhat idyllic life, without the benefits of an organized polis. They lived, so Odysseus tells his Phaeacian audience,

> without a law to bless them.
> In ignorance leaving the fruitage of the earth in mystery
> to the immortal gods, they neither plow
> nor sow by hand, nor till the ground, though grain—
> wild wheat and barley—grow untended, and
> wine-grapes, in clusters, ripen in heaven's rain.
> Kyklopes have no muster and no meeting,

no consultation or old tribal ways,
but each one dwells in his own mountain cave
dealing out rough justice to wife and child,
indifferent to what the others do.[37]

Polyphemus, however, was not even as socialized as the typical Cyclopes. If we can say that the Cyclopes are imagined here as constituting in their isolated household units a sort of pre-polis community,[38] then Polyphemus himself was pre-oikos. He had neither wife nor children to come to his aid when he was in trouble, and was accordingly undone by "NoMan/Odysseus," whose ruse tricked the other Cyclopes into staying at home. In its vivid negative image, Odysseus' encounter with Polyphemus reveals, for both polis and family, the dominant values of early Greek society. The oikos in this society was indeed more than a "house"; it was the household—the focus of relationships of both persons and property bound up with the primary emotions of loyalty and *philia* (love, family love) which underlay the emergence of the Greek polis. So we see that it is the lack of a family and an oikos that is "primitive" to Homer and his audience.

Inside the Oikos: Homeric Marriage and the Homeric Wife

If we now step closer and look within the Homeric oikos, what sort of relationship do we find between the hero and his *alochos,* that is, between husband and wife? What was Homeric marriage, and who was a Homeric wife? What does Homeric marriage tell us about early Greek society, the early Greek family, and the position of women in both?

First, there is no doubt that Homer's society distinguished between a concubine, generally "spear-won," and a wife, generally imagined as left "at home." The same descriptive or functional word, *alochos* ("bedmate"), could denote both women, but when need for clarity arose, the wife became the *kouridie alochos,* a term which seems literally to mean something like "virgin bride" but in context is closer to "wedded wife." (A Homeric husband could also be called *kouridios posis* to emphasize apparently his wedded status.)[39] So Agamemnon notes his preference for Chryseis over his *kouridie alo-*

chos Clytemnestra, and Briseis mourns the dead Patroklos, who, she claims, had promised to take her back to Phthia and make her Achilles' *kouridie alochos* by celebrating the *gamos* among the Myrmidons. This last example illustrates the way in which early Greek marriage (and later Greek marriage as well) was a socially recognized and marked relationship, whose significance the single words of physical relationship and union, *alochos* and *gamos,* do not necessarily fully capture. Briseis would still be an *alochos* in Phthia, and the physical reality of her union *(gamos)* with Achilles would not change, but by celebrating that union "among the Myrmidons" and acknowledging her privileged position, Achilles would have married her and established her status in that society as a wife not a concubine.

Once, however, we agree that marriage existed as a significant social relationship in Homeric society distinct from concubinage, there remain the problems of just how to understand the process of Homeric marriage and of what that process suggests about the character of Homeric society. Traditionally, the essential formal element of Homeric marriage, as well as the main obstacle to making historical sense of it, has been found in the complex system of gift-giving and property negotiations surrounding the celebration of marriage (or the marital *gamos*) in Homer's poems. Although M. I. Finley decisively refuted in 1954 the then widely held view that marriage in the Homeric poems was in a state of transition or evolution from a system of "bride purchase" to one of dowry, his own analysis of the problem has not met with general acceptance.[40] According to Finley, marriage was simply a "much-gifted" affair in a society in which gift-giving was the basic form of social, political, and economic "exchange." "Gifts of marriage" traveled in both directions—to and from the two households about to be linked by marriage—but neither dowry nor bride-price existed as a formal system of marriage. Of the several published objections to Finley's interpretation, the recent challenge from Ian Morris is particularly interesting in light of the issues raised earlier about family structure and terminology.[41]

Morris contends that Homeric marriage is neither a bride-wealth nor a dowry system but rather a "class in-marriage" system in which "women acted to some extent as *agalmata* [precious gifts] being exchanged between households in different communities in order to es-

tablish political alliances"; and that this system, though somewhat
anomalous in terms of its placement in a comparative anthropological analysis, is typically "aristocratic" and just as appropriate for
Greece in the eighth century as it was for either later or earlier eras.[42]
Although Morris' discussion raises important questions and refines
some points of the earlier discussion, his suggested solution, with ac-
companying terminology, has its own problems. The Homeric heroes, argues Morris, practiced "class in-marriage" as distinguished
from the "clan in-marriage" of the classical Athenians (and also apparently of the Homeric commoners).

But what is Morris' "clan in-marriage"? The term seems in fact to
be glossed by his earlier attribution to classical Athens of "a general
tendency toward lineage endogamy (marriage within a fairly restricted descent group, at Athens often the oikos group)"; later this is
referred to simply as "oikos-endogamy."[43] The meaning of this last
term is also difficult to grasp. In classical Athens marriages were
quite common between members of the same kindred—that is, the
family group formally called the *anchisteia* or *anchisteia tou genos,*
the people "closest in *genos.*" The *anchisteia,* however, was neither
an oikos (household) nor a lineage, and certainly not a corporate
clan. "Oikos-endogamy" does not make much sense for any period
of Greek history, classical or Homeric. Penelope, Eurykleia, and
Melantho, for example, are clearly part of Telemachos' oikos, but
none of them could ever be a prospective bride. On the other hand,
Morris' "class in-marriage," which he attributes to the elite class of
which Penelope is a member, is a perfectly understandable term: it
refers to the tendency to marry within one's social and economic
class. But that certainly can be taken as the general rule in most sec-
tors of society in most periods of Greek history. It does not say anything particularly interesting about Homeric marriage.

For present purposes then, the current state of the debate over
Homeric marriage (and marriage gifts), despite its promising appeal
to comparative anthropology, has in fact done little to clarify the
Homeric family and household. Instead of following the current line
of argument, I return to another point of Finley's influential discussion of Homeric marriage—his distinction between Homeric marriage within "an oikos-kinship world of status relations" and later
marriage understood as a "formal juristic act" in the "polis world of

transactions consummated under the rule of law." Finley suggests that the legal validity of a marriage was not of public concern in the Homeric poems, since in that society "there was no polis, no citizenship, no political problem of legitimacy."[44] Somewhat similarly, Lacey depicts Homeric marriage as an essentially "de facto state"—a "question of fact and not of law."[45] The distinction has become familiar and authoritative, but is it accurate? First, this approach implies that public concern is essentially a matter of formal law, something that is clearly not the case in ancient Greek society, whether early, middle, or late; and second, it assumes conversely that marriage was in fact a "juristic act" in the "polis world," and that was also not the case.[46] In Athens, as always the best-known example, there were laws having to do with who could marry whom, and who counted as a legitimate child and heir; but the transferral of bride from the house of her father to that of her husband was socially validated, just as in Finley's Homeric society, by the neighbors and relatives who attended and witnessed the wedding feast and celebration, or *gamos*. The social and also political (in the root sense of the word) significance of such a celebration is evident in the fact that it takes pride of place in the polis at peace, as the first scene described by Homer on Achilles' divinely wrought shield:

> With weddings and wedding feasts in one and under glowing torches they brought forth the brides from the women's chambers, marching through the streets while choir on choir the wedding song rose high and the young men came dancing, whirling round in rings and among them the flutes and harps kept up their stirring call— women rushed to the doors and each stood moved with wonder.[47]

Given the thematic centrality of marriage in both poems, it would seem unlikely that there was a complete absence of public (and polis) interest in recognizing the validity of a marriage, and perhaps "de facto" and "de jure" are misleading dichotomous rubrics under which to classify ancient Greek marriage rituals. *Kata nomon* ("according to custom or law") could apply, however, to marriages in both eras. Perhaps we stand to learn more about the Homeric oikos and its relationships by considering the importance of a communally recognized marriage.

It is clear that a marriage recognized by the community was a vehicle to "political" power and authority, as well as a communally approved way of transferring wealth and property. If Odysseus had accepted Alcinoos' offer of marriage to Nausicaa, he would have accepted a position of power as well, just as Penelope's acceptance of any one of her suitors would certainly have affected the political and economic position of Odysseus' household and the public order of Ithaca.[48] In a society in which personal and political authority were interlocked and in which the action of political institutions might depend on a personal assertion of control—as in Telemachos' calling of the assembly of the "citizens" of Ithaca after a hiatus of twenty years—public recognition of the basic oikos relationships around which the oikos was focused, including marriage, was highly significant.

It is also clear that in a communally recognized marriage, the wife had a vested interest. Odysseus' wish for Nausicaa, that she have an oikos and a husband, certainly implies that there is "something in it" for her. And Penelope's interest in the household which she has maintained over twenty years is evident in her persistent refusal to remarry—as well as in her plots to augment that household with the suitors' gifts (plots which warm the heart of Odysseus, newly returned and still in disguise).[49] Yet it is in the end the "oikos of Odysseus" which she has preserved, and it is not easy to discern what if any property rights Homeric women had in the *oikoi* of which they were a part. Penelope would seem to be a very independent woman of considerable authority; yet apart from several slaves whom she mentions as having been given to her by her father, there is little indication that she herself has any claim to property of her own.[50] Similarly, Queen Arete is explicitly said to be a powerful woman, who "dissolves disputes for those of whom she thinks well, even for men."[51] In rules articulated later in early Greek law, Arete would in fact have been recognized as an heiress—a woman who as her father's only daughter held an equal share of her paternal grandfather's estate together with Alcinoos, her husband and paternal uncle.[52] Yet Homer says simply that she is most honored of all women who "have a household [*oikos*] under men."[53] It seems that property rights or customs, particularly as they relate to women, may be just the sort of thing that the poet's "epic distance" led him to ignore. By contrast, women's virtues, character, and general status within the epic world, and within the household, were of interest to Homer and remain so to his modern readers.

The status of women in the *Iliad* and *Odyssey* has traditionally been an issue of signal importance, and also of debate, for the paradigm of the social evolution of the polis, which (particularly in its Marxist form) posited a necessary decline in women's status concomitant with the emergence of private property and the state. The question is usually seen as that of identifying just where on the evolutionary slope to place the Homeric woman. On the one hand, there are those who hold, with Lewis Henry Morgan, that in Homer's world woman's "dignity [was] unrecognized and her personal rights insecure,"[54] and on the other hand those who argue, with Friedrich Engels, that, though bad, women's lot in Homeric society was still better than in classical Athens. Sometimes indeed Homeric women sit at the very pinnacle of the historical status curve; there are those who might go so far as to agree with Thomas Day Seymour that in the *Iliad* and the *Odyssey* we find "the most wholesome and natural family relations in the whole ancient world."[55] More recently some interpreters have taken up the latter position and insisted that Homeric women were simply "more valued and more free" than women in the classical period, particularly again in Athens. So Sarah Pomeroy judged that "compared with subsequent Greek literature, epic gives a generally attractive impression of the life of women . . . Not only concubines but legitimate wives are considered desirable, and there is little trace of the misogyny that taints later Greek literature."[56]

The portrayal of women in the first texts of the Western literary canon is clearly a politically charged issue, but a few things can be said in response to the rosy view of Homeric women's lives and social position. To start with, "status" is hardly a simple concept, and in Homeric society, as in latter classical Greek society, there was more than one "status" for women.[57] Despite the poet's lack of concern for the practical details of women's economic or legal position, he makes it quite clear that Penelope's status was different from the slave maid Melantho's, and that Andromache's status would drastically change, as did Briseis', when her city was captured. Second, despite the significant roles women played within the Homeric oikos, caring for both persons and property, their personal vulnerability is clear. Personal "rights" are hardly an issue—they are nonexistent—

and walking the streets of Troy or eating dinner with the men pales in comparison to the experience of Briseis, Cassandra, Andromache, or the maids of Odysseus' household: enslavement, rape, exile, or ignominious death. Some Homeric women had extraordinary dignity and intelligence: Penelope is perhaps the best example, although Helen is hardly to be ignored. The end of the *Iliad* features prominently the laments of three women, Hecuba, Andromache, and Helen herself, over the death of Hector, an important reflection of the significant role women played in funeral ritual. These are elite women indeed, and others of course were considerably less well placed or well endowed. Perhaps the best summary is that the standing in society of Homeric or early Greek women—the authority and respect they enjoyed—was rooted not so much in legal rights as in social customs, which included the enslavement of women in war and the hanging of unfaithful female household servants as well as respected roles in royal households or public religion. However tempting it may be, the romanticization of early Greek "family values" on the basis of a sentimental reading of, for example, the parting of Hector and Andromache or the reunion of Penelope and Odysseus, and the setting up of simple paradigms of either progress or decline on this score, serve no real purpose. Homer's world in the *Odyssey* was one of goddesses, princesses, and queens—and also one of nursemaids, spear-won concubines, and household slaves. If an antidote to romanticization is still needed, Hesiod's *Works and Days* will provide a useful dose of hard "iron-age" reality, as well as important further evidence of the moral interconnectedness of oikos and polis in early Greek history.

Hesiod and Family Values

> Do not let any sweet-talking women beguile your good sense with the fascinations of her shape. It's your barn she's after.[58]

Hesiod is famous—or infamous—for his misogyny, and there is indeed no mistaking his view that woman is a "bad thing."[59] On second glance, however, this "badness" is distinctly bittersweet; because of a woman's desirability she is a "beautiful evil thing" and a "sheer deception," but because of her essential role in the oikos she is absolutely necessary and a man's only escape from "mournful old age."[60] What is also striking in Hesiod's misogyny is its flavor of economic competition. The wife is both a partner and a competitor: for Hesiod, "misogyny" is clearly directed at woman as *gyne*/wife. She has economic interests of her own (she's after the barn), and clearly a mind of her own. She has "the mind of a hussy, and a treacherous nature" but is also the vessel in which resides that ambiguous spirit, Hope. Who, in fact, can do without her?

Competition and "strife" are for Hesiod fundamental features of human life both within and outside the oikos; and like almost everything human, strife also has an ambiguous character, both good and bad, useful and destructive. So, Hesiod advises his brother Perses, who has taken off with more than his fair share of the family property: "get to work—don't let that 'strife who loves mischief' lead you to take your case to the 'bribe-devouring' judges!"[61] The *Works and Days* is formally Hesiod's lecture on good living to his brother Perses, and the upholding of "family values"—here essentially household values—is a key part of the lesson. As such, the poem reveals the tensions more than the sentiments of family life. Of the latter, there is only the rare gentle image of the young daughter,

> who keeps her place inside the house [*oikoi*] by her loving
>   mother
> and is not yet initiated in the mysteries of Aphrodite
> the golden, who, washing her smooth skin carefully, and anoint-
>   ing it
> with oil, then goes to bed, closeted in an inside chamber
> on a winter's day.[62]

More typical is Hesiod's practical advice on all agreements made between close relatives: "When you deal with your brother," says Hesiod, "be pleasant, but get a witness; for too much trustfulness, and too much suspicion, have proved men's undoing."[63] Hesiod's family is most prominently the oikos and its constituent relationships, and, like woman herself, it is a mixed human blessing and plague. Hesiod's "misogyny" is a strong indication of the wife's significant economic role in a household in which she had a vested interest. The extent to which that role and interest were based on formal property or inheri-

tance rights is again, as in Homer, difficult to judge. Despite tantalizing allusions to litigation and lawsuits, Hesiod provides little evidence
on the legal rules or customs governing the transfer of property upon a
man's death or upon his marriage. Hesiod's own legal dispute with his
brother over their inheritance makes it clear that in his mind the rule
was an equal division of property among sons (or brothers). Similarly,
his advice on "family planning," which follows the warning about the
barn, implies a system of partible inheritance yet leaves the status of
daughters unclear. One single son, says Hesiod,

> would be right to support his father's
> household [*oikos*], for that is the way substance piles up in the
>   storerooms;
> if you have more than one, you had better live to an old age;
> yet Zeus can easily provide abundance for a greater number,
> and the more there are, the more work is done, and increase in-
>   creases.[64]

On the basis of comparative anthropological analysis, we might
indeed expect to find a bilateral system of property devolution (one
including sons and daughters) in this plow-agriculture society, with
daughters' dowries functioning as a form of "pre-mortem" inheritance.[65] There is, however, no evidence for dowry, or for any kind of
marriage gifts (*hedna* or *dora*), in either the *Works and Days* or,
where it would be less likely, the *Theogony*.[66] There is just the barn
the would-be bride would like to get. In sum, despite the woman's
clear economic interest and role in the oikos (compare Penelope's behavior with the suitors), her position is not articulated in accordance
with, or connected to, formal rules of inheritance by either epic poet.

Nor does Hesiod give any support to the notion that a corporate
clan was recognized, formally or informally, as a corporate heir to a
man's property. The passage often used to support such an idea,
Theogony 606–607, laments the fact that if a man does not marry and
have children, the "widow-inheritors" (Lattimore's literal translation
of *cherostai*) will divide up his property.[67] There is no implication that
these people, whoever they may be, have a legal right to dispose of his
property. As Hesiod's own case shows, the next level of authority and
arbitration for property disputes, beyond the immediate relationships

of the household, is the polis, with its "bribe-devouring" *basileis* (kings). As with the Homeric trial scene, the system may be rudimentary but is hardly evidence of a "primitive" family order. "Widow-inheritor" is of course a somewhat odd term here in that the man in question is specifically said not to have married and so would have had no widow. Perhaps the term had already been generalized to refer to all those relatives or neighbors who, reminiscent of Penelope's suitors, might try to get for themselves a piece of an heirless or headless estate. Or perhaps the oikos itself was thought to be "widowed." But whoever these "widow-inheritors" might be, they are not a clan; they are not a family at all in any sense of the word.

The word *genos* is frequently used in discussions of Hesiod's world as the equivalent of "clan." It may be useful to look briefly at just how the poet uses the word. In Hesiod's poems, *genos* refers most often to origin, or natural kind. For example, the *Theogony* speaks of the *genos* of immortal gods and of women (21, 33, 590); the *Works and Days*, of the *genos* of mortal men (109). It is an important way of connecting or identifying people or animals or things, but has little to do with defining or motivating family relations as they appear in Hesiod's poems (particularly the *Works and Days*). Hesiod offers no sign of "the *gentes* worshipping their ancestors,"[68] one of the traditionally assumed activities of the early Greek clan along with the blood feud. The hearth is a place of purity: "Do not, when in your house, ever show yourself near the hearthside when you are physically unclean."[69] But it is hardly a god or an ancestor. Nor is there any sign of hallowed "family tombs" or inalienable "family lands" on which those tombs lay, again both regular features of the modern image of primitive Greece and its families most memorably articulated by Fustel de Coulanges. There were tombs where members of the same family were buried, and care of parents' tombs was certainly an important responsibility for ancient Greeks; but there is no evidence for clan or lineage groups maintaining a sense of corporate identity through burial rites.[70] Self-conscious attention to lineage and ancestors seems more typical of elite families striving for preeminence in an increasingly democratic society than of earlier archaic Greek society in general. (A particularly good example of this early classical development might be found in Pindar's victory odes celebrating the family lineage of the victorious athlete.)

Genos (birth or heritage) is not the focus of worship or cult in Hesiod's society; however, looking at the question of religion from the point of view of the oikos and its relationships (husband/wife, parent/child, as well as brother/brother and guest/host), we could say that there is indeed in Hesiod a sense of "family religion" and definitely of "family values." Rather than Fustel's ancestral shades, this religion features the "gods" Nemesis (retribution) and Aidos (shame and reverence), who protect the basic household relationships, thereby making even the Iron Age livable for men. As an illustration of the importance of these values, and of the way in which the oikos stood at the moral center of the early Greek family, two passages from the *Works and Days* are especially vivid. In the first, the two gods appear (and disappear) as Hesiod issues a prophecy worthy of Jeremiah:

> But Zeus will destroy this generation [*genos*] of mortals also,
> in the time when children, as they are born, grow gray on the
>   temples,
> when the father no longer agrees with the children, nor children
>   with their father,
> when guest is no longer at one with host, nor companion to
>   companion,
> when your brother is no longer your friend, as he was in the old
>   days.
> Men will deprive their parents of all rights, as they grow old,
> and people will mock them too, babbling bitter words against
>   them,
> harshly, and without shame in the sight of the gods; nor even
> to their aging parents will they give back what once was given.
> Strong of hand, one man shall seek the city (polis) of another.
> There will be no favor for the man who keeps his oath, for the
>   righteous
> and the good man, rather men shall give their praise to violence
> and the doer of evil . . .
> and at last Nemesis and Aidos, Decency and Respect, shrouding
> their bright forms in pale mantles, shall go from the wide-wayed
> earth back on their way to Olympos, forsaking the whole *genos*
> of mortal men, and all that will be left by them to mankind
> will be wretched pain.[71]

The second passage is Hesiod's bitter warning on the effects of "shamelessness"—the result of the disappearance of Aidos—in both the public and the private realm:

> If any man by force of hands wins him a great fortune,
> or steals it by the cleverness of his tongue, as so often
> happens among people when the intelligence is blinded
> by greed, a man's shameless spirit tramples his sense of honor;
> lightly the gods wipe out that man, and diminish the household
>   [oikos]
> of such a one, and his wealth stays with him for only a short
>   time.
> It is the same when one does evil to guest or suppliant,
> or goes up into the bed of his brother, to lie in secret
> love with his brother's wife, doing acts that are against nature
>   [parakairia];
> or who unfeelingly abuses fatherless children,
> or speaks roughly with intemperate words to his failing
> father who stands upon the hateful doorstep of old age.[72]

There is no clearer image of the early Greek family and early Greek family values than that produced by these lines. Certainly nothing is said in the *Works and Days* about "birth" or parentage that can match these passages in intensity. This point is of central importance for the thesis of this book: the most important family interests in early Greece were those of the oikos and of its members bound together in the central relationships of husband/wife, parent/child, and master/slave. We need to recognize the importance in early Greece of a strong sense of "family" based not so much on "blood" or "bloodline," which at its most basic levels was always recognizable and important, as on a common practical and productive interest which might properly be called "economic" in the root sense of the word. Family members were connected to one another by their common membership in the productive and reproductive household. The polis grew in positive connection with the formal protection of these household relationships, and Hesiod leaves little doubt that the strength of the polis community was rooted in the strength of the oikos and the protection of its essential relationships. Finally, despite the prevalence of hierarchy in household relationships, it is undeniable that within those crosscutting hierarchies women played a significant role. Hesiod did not rail against a resourceless female cipher.

Thus the interests of the early Greek family are best understood as rooted essentially in the household. Nor does Hesiod leave any doubt that those interests were inseparable from the interests of the community and the polis as a whole. In light of the evidence discussed here, it is puzzling to recall the persistence of the view that the family must lose and be enclosed in the private sphere in order for the polis to emerge preeminent in the public sphere. In contrast, I would argue, with Aristotle, that the oikos was the social precondition of the emerging polis, and also, with Hesiod, that the integrity of oikos relationships was the moral precondition of the healthy polis.

The extent to which this emerging polis of Homer and Hesiod can properly be called a "state" is a much-debated question.[73] Murray is certainly correct in saying that the basic elements of the polis already exist, such as the basic settlement pattern, the traditional two deliberative bodies of assembled *demos* and council of elders, and to a lesser extent the civic character of religious ritual.[74] On the other hand, the highly personal character of polis government in both Homeric and Hesiodic society, and the lack of formal structures of justice or administration, weigh against considering these poetic *poleis* as genuine states in a modern sense. On those same criteria, however, the claim of the classical polis to the name "state" could also be challenged—and the makeshift term "city-state" is equally open to criticism.[75] In any event, Murray and Kurt Raaflaub are surely right in maintaining that the polis makes an appearance in the Homeric poems—that the basic institutions and character of the polis are evident in Homer.[76] And central to the well-being of the larger community—the polis or what might be called the ancient Greek state—was the oikos as household, as the focus of family organization and identity in the early Greek world.

When the Greek polis did begin to articulate its rules and institutions through formal law, the oikos was one of its earliest beneficiaries. The material and moral integrity of the family as household was one of the earliest topics of early Greek polis law as it emerged in the seventh and sixth centuries, soon after if not during Hesiod's lifetime. Family law is thus an important indicator of both the early de-

velopment of political institutions and the interaction of those institutions with family and household. In the next chapter, I counter the
traditional paradigm of "state over family" through a close examination of early Greek family law. I suggest that, instead of winning or
losing, polis and family developed in a relationship of creative and
productive partnership.

3

EARLY GREEK LAW AND
THE FAMILY

Homer speaks of a king who gives good judgments (*Odyssey* 19.107–114) and Hesiod of numerous "kings" who give crooked ones (*Works and Days* 38–39), but neither epic poet suggests the existence of formal, written or codified law. That was the achievement of the next generation, and is a clear indication of the growing complexity of Greek society and also of the growing self-consciousness of the polis. If there was any doubt of the polis' presence in the world of Homeric epic as an early form of state, there is no ignoring it now. In the seventh century Greeks roamed the Mediterranean, establishing from *metropoleis* (mother cities) at home permanent new polis "offspring" in the west and northeast, and opening up new economic routes and cultural connections both with the old civilizations of North Africa and western Asia and with the newer ones of southern Europe. The polis was the protagonist of this adventure, and political institutions of officeholding and decision-making emerge more clearly during it. The tensions and excitement of the age are revealed in the new genre of personal lyric poetry, as for example Alcaeus' poem "Storm in the State":

> I cannot understand how the winds are set
> against each other. Now from this side and now
> from that the waves roll. We between them
> run with the wind in our black ship driven,

hard pressed and laboring under the giant storm.
All round the mast-step washes the sea we shipped.
You can see through the sail already
where there are opening rents within it.

The forestays slacken . . .[1]

The polis had embarked on a turbulent voyage.

Another new genre, equally revealing of the society in which it was created, was written *nomoi*—formal laws and law codes. By common Greek tradition, Zaleucos of Locris and Charondas of Catana, both from "colonial" western Greece, stand at the head of the first group of Greek lawgivers *(nomothetai)*. Apart from their names and their *poleis,* however, not much is known of either one. But although their historical achievement is shadowy, the western Mediterranean identity of Zaleucos and Charondas makes clear the connection between the unsettled, uncertain conditions of the expanding Greek world of the seventh century and the emergence of written or codified law. The first lawgivers appear in the new *poleis* of the west, where immigrants from several "old world" *poleis* frequently merged into one polis, and in doing so were forced to come to terms not only with the manners and customs of the indigenous population but with their own differences as well. In such circumstances it is hardly surprising that a primary focus of early law was property and status—who was who and what was whose? In addition to Zaleucos and Charondas, Aristotle mentions a certain Androdamas of Rhegion, who legislated on homicide and heiresses for the city of Chalcis in Thrace; and also Philolaus of Corinth, who gave the Thebans laws on the begetting of children and on adoption which were "designed to keep fixed the number of *kleroi* [lots]."[2] Apart from these tantalizing bits of tradition, however, the "family law" of early Greece is best seen in three *poleis,* Sparta, Gortyn, and Athens—none of which was a colony or in any sense "typical," but each of which turned to law or the lawgiver for the articulation of the social order. Together these three *poleis* and their laws illuminate key themes in the historical experience of the early Greek family.

Polis Law and the Family in Sparta, Gortyn, and Athens

The first issue to be confronted in a discussion of the intersection of polis law and family interests in these three *poleis* is the differing character of the historical sources and of the laws themselves, the *nomoi*. Although the early development of each polis is illuminated by its laws, our knowledge of both the laws and their context is profoundly different for the three. For Sparta there are the problematic traditions of the semimythical lawgiver Lycurgus, who is placed anywhere from the ninth to the sixth century and whose "lawgiving" is acknowledged by Herodotus (1.65) and Thucydides (1.18) but receives its fullest description in the highly moralizing later Hellenistic accounts used by Plutarch. It is also important to note that although Plutarch claims that Lycurgus did not put his laws into writing, he also appears to quote the text of the most famous Spartan law, "The Great Rhetra" (the legal "oracle" traditionally brought from Delphi to Sparta by Lycurgus). Furthermore, he observes that the kings Polydoros and Theopompos "wrote in" a rider to the rhetra limiting the political power of the people. Here I will follow the path of agnosticism on the historical status of Lycurgus and on the written status of his laws and focus instead on the character of those rules and *nomoi* (some written and some probably not) which can reasonably be taken as defining the early Spartan state and the "Lycurgan order" from the seventh through the early fifth centuries.

In addition to the oracle at Delphi, Lycurgus was said to have visited Crete and adopted Cretan laws for his new Spartan order. Whatever the reliability of such traditions,[3] it is true that Crete was the home of the mythical lawgivers Minos and Rhadamanthos, and also the historical home of some of the earliest inscribed Greek law; somewhat later, in the early or mid-fifth century, the Cretan city of Gortyn produced the most complete inscribed code of law now extant from any Greek city, the "Great Code of Gortyn."[4] Although the Gortyn Code is relatively late in date and is also without clear historical author(s) or much historical context, it stands in a tradition of earlier local lawgiving and is therefore a rich and complex—if often frustratingly obscure—source for the study of early Greek family law.[5]

Finally, unlike Gortyn but like Sparta, early Athens had a lawgiver with a name. What is more, in Athens that lawgiver's historical status is unquestioned. Solon, poet and lawgiver, is rightly considered the first historical Athenian. Chosen by his fellow Athenians as archon and mediator in 594, he left behind a historical record, the poems with which he counseled his fellow citizens and which stand as Athens' first literature. The interpretation of Solonian law is, however, not without its own difficulties, for whereas fragments of his poetry survive, the code of laws does not. The laws themselves are known primarily through later rhetorical citation in speeches delivered in the popular courts as well as from Plutarch's useful if not completely reliable quotation, direct and indirect, in his life of Solon.[6] Thus, the historical interpretation of family law in each of these *poleis* has distinctive problems. I begin with the always difficult case of "Lycurgan" Sparta.

Sparta

On the traditional reading of early Spartan society, the experience of Sparta might seem to be a straightforward example of the "dismemberment" of the family by the emerging polis. According to the common account, based primarily on Xenophon's *Politeia of the Lacedaemonians* and especially Plutarch's *Lycurgus,* the Lycurgan system significantly transformed the basic household relationships of husband/wife, parent/child, and person/property in ancient Sparta. For the most part, the elements of this system were assumed by contemporaries (as well as by modern historians) to have been in place by the time the Spartans joined the Athenians and other Greeks in the war against Persia in 480/79. Both Herodotus and Thucydides considered the Spartans in the fifth century as living and preserving a much older social system. In general, then, the Lycurgan order known from the fifth and fourth centuries can reasonably be taken as revealing an archaic or preclassical response to the common need for political rules and order.

Throughout his treatise Xenophon insists that Lycurgus established institutions different from those of most Greek states,[7] beginning with marriage and childrearing. "If a man did not wish to live with a wife, but wanted children worthy of note, Lycurgus made it legal for him to select a woman who was noble and the mother of fine children, and, if he obtained the husband's consent, to have children by her" (1.8).

Then, instead of leaving the education of children to the discretion of parents, he established a public official, the *paidonomos,* with the "authority to assemble the children, inspect them and punish any faults severely" (2.2). Further emphasizing the public character of Spartan education, Xenophon notes that Lycurgus "laid it down that any citizen who was present could give the boys whatever instructions seemed necessary, and punish any misconduct" (1.10). He reiterates the point somewhat later with the general comment that "in other cities each man controls his own children, servants, and property, but Lycurgus, because he wished the citizens to benefit from each other without doing any harm, gave fathers equal authority over all children, whether their own or those of others" (6.1). Similar in spirit, according to Xenophon, was the institution of public messes: "The Spartiates were in the habit of living at home like the other Greeks, and [Lycurgus] realised that this led to considerable neglect of duty; he therefore instituted public messes, believing that this would be the most effective check on disobedience"(5.2).

In his *Lycurgus,* Plutarch expanded some 450 years later upon these points of communal education and dining, and added to them the assertion that Lycurgus' boldest innovation was the redistribution of land, with the implication that each Spartiate was given an inalienable lot, or *kleros.*[8] The authority of the public state over the private household, both persons and property, in Plutarch's image of Sparta is epitomized in his description of the Spartan (or Lycurgan) procedure after the birth of a child:

> The father did not have authority [was not *kyrios*] to rear the baby, but he took it to a place called a *lesche,* where the eldest citizens sat and inspected the child. If it was well-built and strong, they ordered him to rear it, allocating to it one of the 9,000 lots, but if it was ill-born and unshapely, they sent it away to the so-called Apothetai, a place like a pit near Taygetos, believing that it was better both for itself and for the city that it should not live if it was not well-formed for health and strength right from the start.[9]

All the traditional responsibilities of the oikos and its members would seem then to be usurped by the Lycurgan polis as portrayed by Xenophon and elaborated by Plutarch. Indeed, what could be left of the Homeric or Hesiodic family in such a polis? Lycurgan Sparta as depicted by Plutarch was undeniably hostile to, and disruptive of, the interests and traditional relationships of the Greek household. This conclusion, however, and all the colorful Plutarchian details which seem to give it historical substance (for example, the transvestite marriage by capture or the rituals of Artemis Orthia in which "many" young Spartans died; *Lycurgus* 15 and 18) are heavily dependent upon the mythologizing perspective of historically remote sources, for whom Sparta was more of a cause célèbre or a philosophical paradigm than a historical community. Xenophon, on the other hand, is describing a contemporary society which he clearly admires and idealizes but does not mythologize. When Xenophon's account is put together with the more scattered testimony of Herodotus, Thucydides, and Aristotle, it is apparent that the public rules and regulations that Xenophon finds so distinctive overlay but did not eliminate traditional household structures of property, status, and inheritance; that is, in classical Sparta, children inherited the property of their parents, marriage was the basis of legitimate inheritance, and social status varied with private wealth.

The particular importance of source criticism in the untangling of the early history of Sparta and the history of the Spartan family has been effectively demonstrated by Stephen Hodkinson. After carefully sifting through the ancient testimonia on Spartan landholding and property institutions, Hodkinson argues that the basic economic and family relations of Spartan society are most reliably seen through the critical analysis of Aristotle, with some help from Herodotus and other earlier accounts.[10] A painstaking comparison of classical sources with later accounts, especially that of Plutarch, leads to the conclusion that the Aristotelian view, which emphasizes the freedom of gift and testament in Sparta, is the more historically reliable and that "Spartiate land tenure was not markedly different in quality from that of private property in other Greek states" and was "a system which was pre-eminently one of private estates transmitted by partible inheritance and diverging devolution and open to alienation through lifetime gifts, testamentary bequests and betrothal of heiresses."[11]

Hodkinson's argument on these points is worth summarizing here because it has interesting implications for the interaction of polis and household interests in early Greek law. Hodkinson first challenges head-on the myth of the allotment of equal, inalienable, and indivisible portions of land to Spartan citizens, showing that the idea cannot be reliably traced back further than the Hellenistic era, and most likely is a product of propaganda during the Spartan revolution of the third century.[12] Even granting the existence of a type of property called "ancestral" whose sale or division was restricted, "marked differences in wealth" among Spartan citizens are part of the historical record "from the sixth century down to Aristotle." Further, the Spartan rules of adoption of children and betrothal of heiresses which are assumed or described in historical sources not intent on mythologizing the system (for example, Herodotus 6.57) all depict a system in which the individual Spartan had control over the disposal of his own property and in which children, however communal their upbringing, belonged to the household of their fathers. Xenophon's comment that Lycurgus made it legal for a man to select a woman who was noble and the mother of fine children "and, if he obtained the husband's consent, to have children by her," reinforces rather than contradicts the argument. For the point is clear that such children are regarded as legitimate offspring of the "bachelor father"— and thus as heirs of his own private property.[13]

The second feature of Hodkinson's reevaluation of Spartan society is an analysis of the place of women in the propertyholding system of Sparta. Beginning from Aristotle's statement that in his time women owned two-fifths of all Spartan land (so depriving would-be Spartiate soldiers of their necessary economic base), and employing quantitative/demographic evidence on the probable consequences of female inheritance in Sparta together with anecdotal evidence on marriage strategy among the Spartan elite, Hodkinson argues that in the Spartan system of partible inheritance women did not simply receive a dowry as their portion of the family property but were heirs (though perhaps not equal heirs) alongside their brothers. Given the demographic realities of ancient Greece, such inheritance of land by daughters could very well have resulted in the situation described by Aristotle—and also in the royal marriages described most frequently by Plutarch.

Hodkinson concludes by pointing out two important contradictions within this portrait of Spartan society:

first, between the facade of a seemingly stable society marked by an unchanging system of government and the reality of an unceasing movement of significant tracts of landed property and continual shifts in the fortunes of a declining number of citizen households; and, secondly, between the narrowly political demands of the male-centred hoplite polis, which overtly minimised the importance of material considerations, and the fundamental economic needs of female-influenced households upon whose survival the polis depended.[14]

One might also note the obvious tensions produced by women's property status and military uselessness in classical Sparta, the professional hoplite state. What was the function in and the contribution to the polis of a Spartan woman, and especially of a wealthy Spartan woman? The fabled "liberation" of Spartan women may be appealing to (some) modern eyes, but it clearly created tension and some instability in the ancient society.[15] Thus, the Lycurgan system produced a model military state resting somewhat precariously upon a traditional economic foundation; the historical record preserves the evidence of military successes until the early fourth century, but that same record suggests that military success did not foster oikos and economic (in both its root and modern senses) stability.

Finally, a question on Spartan marriage: was it primitive or enlightened—or perhaps neither but rather, once again, a traditional institution overlaid with the peculiar needs of the military state? Plutarch's image of Spartan marriage is an inherently contradictory and unhistorical one.[16] On the one hand he describes a form of "marriage by capture" and on the other an open relationship in which men borrow one another's wives, supposedly free of both jealousy and even the concept of adultery (see *Lycurgus* 15). Plutarch's often-cited account of the clandestine abduction of the transvestite bride, however, is not supported by classical authors, who seem to imply the existence of ordinary marriage arrangements, at least among those elite households of which we have record. Similarly, the "free" Spartan marriage seems somewhat less so when it is properly noted that the husband fully controls the "loan" of his own wife to another man. Xenophon stipulates that a man must get permission to produce heirs with another man's wife. Despite some modern views to the contrary, Sparta was not a society which fostered the sexual independence and self-expression of women. On adultery, Plutarch cites the Spartan Geradas' "proof" that there could be no adulterers *(moichoi)* in Sparta and seems to give its conclusion more credit than he as a well-trained philosopher should.[17] Just as there was marriage in Sparta, even if it might be manipulated and distorted in accord with the needs of the military state, so also there was the possibility of adultery (note the adulterous affair of Alcibiades and the king's wife recounted by Plutarch in his *Alcibiades*).[18] Though certainly constrained by the military needs and values of Spartan society, in which the role of a woman was to produce warriors, or by the peculiar needs of the royal household, Spartan marriages were apparently the result of traditional household strategy—within an inheritance system in which property ordinarily devolved to legitimate children of a recognized marriage and household.

So it seems possible to conclude that the oikos in early Sparta provided the initial material and personal basis of a citizen's status, as it did in the more fluid world of Homer and Hesiod. Spartan men were sons and heirs of households which redistributed their wealth to the next generation according to traditional rules of partible inheritance. Those rules included daughters, despite the clear exclusion of women from the military life that was the preeminent focus of Spartan citizen life. What made Sparta distinctive, then, was not the absence of private ownership and personal inheritance, but the state apparatus and extreme military ethic that separated the Spartan male from his household and valorized the experience of the hoplite who stood as an equal in a line of "equals" fighting for the polis. So the Spartan female held the highly ambiguous position of economic shareholder within the privileged citizen elite who was nonetheless excluded from actively participating in the public activities most highly valued by the citizen elite. Even more than in other Greek *poleis*, the Spartan polis celebrated women for producing sons—and, judging from the "Sayings of Spartan Women" collected by Plutarch (*Moralia* 240c–242d), may have succeeded in fostering in many a total commitment to the public military life in which they had no direct part.

Thus early or "Lycurgan" Sparta fashioned an uneasy relationship between polis and oikos which left the members of the individual household in charge of household property, and indeed reinforced the particularism of that household by allowing free choice of heir over the claims of family or kin, yet also glorified the purely male community of warriors as the true citizens of Spartan society.

Gortyn

In untangling the Spartan inheritance system, and particularly the propertyholding status of Spartan women, Hodkinson frequently cites the Gortyn law code for supporting evidence. On such issues as the inheritance rights of daughters, that code is satisfyingly specific: "the daughters, no matter how many, shall each receive one part [while the sons receive two parts]."[19] Unfortunately, the overall structure of Gortyn's propertyholding system and its social and political classes is less easy to decipher.[20] The code assumes the existence of a highly stratified society at the top of which were free citizens. Beneath these were the group called the *apetairoi,* apparently negatively defined as those who were not members of associations called *hetairiai.* Still lower were at least two servile statuses, one apparently that of the unfree agricultural laborer *(woikeus),*[21] the other of the chattel slave *(doulos).* The hierarchical relationship between these statuses is particularly clear in the penalties set down for rape (or "intercourse by force"). If a free person rapes a free man or woman, he pays 100 staters; if he rapes an *apetairos,* the penalty is 10 staters. If a *doulos* rapes a free man or woman, the penalty is double (that for a free man?), and if a free man rapes a *woikeus* (male or female), the penalty is five drachmae (= 10 staters). If a *woikeus* rapes another *woikeus* the penalty is half that, or 5 staters. And at the bottom of the pile: "If a person would forcibly seduce a slave belonging to the home, he shall pay two staters; but if she has already been seduced, one obol by day, but if in the night, two obols."[22] It is considerably less clear, however, just how these different groups constituted together a functioning society, and my emphasis here will be on the formal logic of the code without any assumption that it adequately describes a historical society. We do not know historical Gortyn.

It is notable that even amidst the unfamiliar terminology and categories,[23] the oikos/household and its recognizable relationships of persons and property sit squarely at the center of the social and economic order. Despite Ronald Willetts' strong belief that the code can and should be read, with Lewis Henry Morgan as an interpretive guide, as a historical example of a society in the process of evolving from a clan-based tribal order to one based on private property and the more narrow construction of kinship typical of the historical polis, there is little here that can substantiate such a view. Upon examination, what are claimed as vestiges of the power of matrilineal clans, such as required exogamous marriages of clansmen, simply are not there.[24] The operative social groups of the code are the *oikoi* and *pylai* [= *phylai*]. The latter were most likely here, as in other Greek *poleis,* political subdivisions of the citizen population into which recruitment was hereditary through the father. There is no adequate reason to consider them as in any sense real kinship groups.[25] Similarly Willetts' suggestion that the term *startos,* used only once in the code, refers to a ruling Gortynian clan is likewise rooted in his larger evolutionary image of Gortynian society.[26] The complexities and peculiarities of Gortynian society, however, seem to be essentially those of economic, social, and political class rather than of kinship and family structure.

The code's rules of inheritance are significantly complicated by the presence of the intermediate servile status of the *woikeus,* who in certain circumstances apparently had rights of use or ownership over buildings and livestock. Nonetheless, it is quite clear that the individual household/oikos is the locus of propertyholding and the definer of propertyholding status. The code prescribes that

> the father shall be in control of the children and division of the property and the mother of her own property. So long as they are living there is no necessity to make a division . . . and in case (the father) should die, the city houses and whatever there is in those houses in which a *woikeus* living in the country does not reside [*enwoikei*], and the cattle small and large, which do not belong to a *woikeus,* shall belong to the sons; but all the rest of the property shall be fairly divided and the sons, no matter how many, shall each receive two parts, while the daughters, no matter how many, shall each receive one part. The mother's property too, in case she dies, shall be divided in the same way as is prescribed for the father's.[27]

Then the general rule of inheritance, including that of a childless household, is prescribed:

When a man or a woman dies, if there be children or children's children or children's children's children, they are to have the property. And if there be none of these, but brothers of the deceased and brothers' children or brothers' children's children, they are to have the property. And if there be none of these, but sisters of the deceased and sisters' children or sisters' children's children, they are to have the property. And if there be none of these, they are to take it up to whom it may fall [*ois k'epiballei*] as a source of property. And if there should be no *epiballontes* then those of the household [*woikias*—genitive case] composing the *klaros* [= *kleros*] are to have the property.[28]

Willetts, again without any apparent or stated justification, interprets the term *epiballontes* in the latter passage as meaning "belonging to the same clan,"[29] presumably because of his assumption that the clan still retained some authority over the property of the newly emerging independent oikos family group. The word, however, seems quite neutral in its meaning, with a clear derivation from the verb *epiballei* ("[the property] may fall"). The code does not specify by what rules the "falling" occurs. The fact that the servile dependents of the household are apparently the final recipients of the household property "if there should be no *epiballontes*" strongly suggests that property devolution in Gortyn was closely and firmly tied to the household itself and to a set of relatives centering on it—and not to a corporate clan, which is not recognizable in the code.[30] The *phyle* does play a role in the disposition of the Gortynian heiress, but as a patrilineally recruited subdivision of the citizen population, not as a kinship group.

In addition to the possible inclusion of the nonfree *woikeus* in the circle of heirs, even if in the most remote degree, there are two features worth emphasizing in the inheritance structure outlined in the passages quoted above. First, paternal and maternal property are clearly distinguished and inherited separately. Although the household was a cooperative productive unit during the life of a husband and wife, the partnership dissolved upon their death, and the property of each partner was inherited separately according to parallel rules. Second, these rules of inheritance, outlined in the second passage quoted above, create a sequence of potential heirs focused uniquely and directly on each male or female property owner and thus reinforce the separate status of the property of husband and wife. A man's heirs are first his children, grandchildren, and great-grandchildren, and then his brother's children and grandchildren, and finally his sister's children and grandchildren. Likewise for a woman. The system is complex but clear. It is not easily fitted into an evolutionary schema, since both male and female property are securely recognized and inherited through a nonagnatic sequence. Finally, it is important to note that the system does not envision a role for the clan but rather for the ego-centered kindred, as uniquely defined for each (male or female) member of the community.

One interesting feature, then, of Gortynian law is that it did not merge the property of husband and wife in a "conjugal estate." Although the Gortyn Code recognized the oikos as the focus of economic life, and a person's position within the oikos (for example, son, daughter, or *woikeus*) as an essential criterion for heirship, it did not recognize property as belonging to the oikos itself. Rather, property belonged separately to the man and the woman who had created that oikos and was inherited separately by their male and female descendants. As in Sparta, women's relation to property, as daughters or wives, was independent and discrete. In contrast, the Athenian woman's property in the form of dowry was tied to the household of which she was a part, either as wife and mother (it was inherited by her children) or as daughter (if the marriage were dissolved it returned to her natal household). Similarly, the sequence of potential heirs to an intestate estate in Athens (the *anchisteia*) included maternal relatives (to the degree of sons of cousins) after paternal kin (to the same degree), so producing a web of legal right and responsibility that recognized the household as formative of essential family relationships (see Figure 1). The different relation of women to property in Sparta and Gortyn as opposed to Athens thus had more to do with the differing status and character of the household than of "women" by themselves. In the basic Greek system of partible inheritance and bilateral devolution of family property, women's relation to property presents a problem which is solved differently in Athens than in Gortyn and Sparta. That women did have, as members of the community and its households, a share and an interest in family property is common to all three *poleis*.

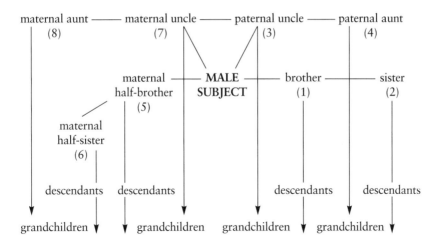

Numbers indicate sequence of claim to intestate estate; arrows indicate the claim continues through succeeding generations.

Figure 1. The *anchisteia* in Athens (for intestate estate)

In sum, when the Gortyn Code is read without the assumptions of the evolutionary paradigm, Gortyn loses its "missing-link" status as a semiprimitive tribal order in the process of giving way to the new oikos-based polis system;[31] and its family structure is shown to be essentially, like that of Sparta as well as Athens, the Aristotelian household based on relationships of husband/wife, parent/child, and person/property (including master/slave). But the specific ways in which the Gortyn Code articulated this household structure (for example, the apparent presence of nonfree heirs and discrete paternal and maternal property) are distinctive as well as historically obscure. They make Gortyn, like "Lycurgan" Sparta, an important piece of the polychrome puzzle of early Greek family history.

Athens

Despite the interest and importance of the history of the family in Sparta and Gortyn, there is no denying that the experience of Athens holds a privileged historical place. The effect of the rise of the polis and the growth of polis institutions has traditionally been viewed on

an Athenian stage, literally and metaphorically. Indeed, it is probably fair to say that the most significant source and support for the established view that family and state, oikos and polis, were antithetical historical players is fifth-century Athenian drama. So from
Bachofen to the present day, the *Oresteia* is read as the story of the
defeat of women, the matriarchal principle, and "the family" by the
rising patriarchal polis. The polis takes over from the family and
from the female Furies/Eumenides the responsibility and jurisdiction
in cases of homicide, thereby illuminating through this one central
social issue the larger course of Greek history.[32] Similarly, the story
of *Antigone* has become so much a pillar of the oppositional, evolutionary interpretation of Greek family history, a story of "family versus state," that it is often necessary to remind readers that Antigone
in fact struggles against her own family as well as the polis (Creon is
her uncle) in her determination to carry out her public responsibility
to see to the burial of her brother, and that in doing so she is noticeably dismissive of any other family or household relationship. In addition, it is necessary to remind ourselves that these plays were written for a fifth-century audience and are not historical documents
from the archaic world of the emerging polis. The conflicts they
record have therefore presumably more to do with the history of
family/state interaction in the fifth than the seventh century. For the
interpretation of early Athenian family history, we are better served
by looking in detail at the career of that first historical Athenian,
Solon, and at the laws which are attributed to him. Drama is reserved for later chapters.

According to Aristotle, the *nomothesia* of Solon was precipitated
by a severe economic and social crisis, the most prominent feature of
which was that "the many were enslaved to the few" or, in other
words, "the poor were enslaved to the rich" (*Athenaion Politeia* 5.1;
2.1). The exact nature and background of this "enslavement" are
unclear and have provoked considerable scholarly debate;[33] but that
it threatened the essential integrity of the oikos and oikos relationships seems undeniable. Children were no longer heirs, but were de-
tached from the household and seized as payment for debt. The
household land, or *kleros,* the essential material component of the
oikos, was bound by debt and itself "enslaved." In response to this
situation, which recalls some of the dire predictions of Hesiod and

certainly was as much an economic (in its root sense) as a political crisis, Solon promulgated a broad-based code of laws. These included most prominently the relief of present debts (the *Seisachtheia*) and the prohibition of any future enslavement for debt.[34] The centrality of this reform for the larger well-being of the community emerges in Solon's own words as quoted by Aristotle:

> "I took up the markers fixed in many places—previously she was enslaved, but now is free. Many I brought back to Athens, their divinely founded city, who had been sold abroad, one unjustly, another justly and others who had fled under compulsion of debt, men who no longer spoke the Attic tongue, so wide had their wanderings been. Those at home, suffering here the outrages of slavery and trembling at the whim of their masters, I freed. This I achieved by the might of law, combining force and justice. I carried it out as I promised."[35]

From this moment in Athenian history, the protection of the person and the freedom of the oikos, both persons and property, are the central interlocking privilege of Athenian citizenship—of "having a share in the polis" of Athens."[36] Aristotle's account reveals the centrality of this principle of Solon's lawgiving, but Aristotle himself is typically more interested in the constitution *(politeia)* which Solon put in place, including the new census classes and their privileges and the structure of the "tribal" council chosen from the four *phylai*. Modern commentators have generally followed Aristotle's lead in emphasizing Solon's role as a political and protodemocratic reformer.[37] For present purposes, however, the "laws on inheritances and heirs," whose lack of clarity Aristotle commented upon (*Ath.Pol.* 9.2), and the many related rules of family and household behavior which are variously attributed to Solon by Plutarch and the orators are more important than the better-known constitutional arrangements. Solon's laws on the family and household reveal not only the oikos as the economic and social foundation of the polis, as in Sparta and Gortyn, but also the distinctive way in which Athenian law, Solonian in spirit if not always genuinely his, went beyond those other *poleis* in articulating and protecting the oikos and its essential relationships.

Public and Solonian interest lay in the security and "freedom" of citizen propertyholding. Debt and debt bondage, however, were not the only threats to the integrity of the oikos as such. Just as dangerous was the possibility foreseen by Hesiod that a man would die childless and heirless, so allowing the "widow-inheritors" or other such claimants to carve up the oikos. Against this danger, Solon instituted the formal right of testament for those without legitimate children. According to Plutarch:

> [Solon] is likewise much commended for his law concerning wills; for before him none could be made, but all the wealth and estate of the deceased belonged to his family [genos]; but he, by permitting them, if they had no children, to bestow it on whom they pleased, showed that he esteemed friendship a stronger tie than kindred (syngeneia), and affection than necessity; and made every man's estate truly his own.[38]

To this important but not unproblematic statement can be added various references in the orators to the right of testament, for example the extended "quotation" of the law by Demosthenes:

> Any citizen with the exception of those who had been adopted when Solon entered upon his office, and had thereby become unable either to renounce or to claim an inheritance, shall have the right to dispose of his own property by will as he shall see fit—if he has no male children lawfully born and unless his mind be impaired by one of these things: lunacy, old age or drugs or if he is under the influence of a woman.[39]

The attribution of some such law to Solon is generally accepted and traditionally seen as a move in behalf of the private rights of the individual or the individual household against the claims of lineage or clan.[40] Plutarch's use of genos ("all the wealth and estate of the deceased belong to his genos") refers then, on this view, to a clan. But as in the world of Hesiod's Works and Days, historical evidence for clans in pre-Solonian Athens is lacking. There were groups called genē in historical post-Solonian Athens, but like the phratries with which they were often associated, these were clearly fictive kin groups. They were recognizable corporate groups with specific social and religious roles who used the language of common kinship as a form of group identity. The Eumolpidai, or "sons of Eumolpus," provided the cult of Demeter at Eleusis with its priestess; and the Eteoboutadai, or "original sons of Boutes," did the same for Athena Polias on the Acropolis. Apart from any claims based on true kinship ties through the *anchisteia,* such *genē* had no claim to the property of their members. There is no justification for reading these *genē* backward in Athenian history as in origin true clans which did have such rights.[41]

The use of the suffix *–idai* in Athenian sources, then, does not guarantee actual descent or kinship among those so described, a fact which should also discourage the use of clan as a descriptive term for other such groups in other Greek cities. According to Herodotus, the early government of Corinth had been an oligarchy in which those "who called themselves Bakchiadai" ruled the city, intermarrying only with one another.[42] Such a group was clearly a closed governing elite and might therefore be called a caste, but it was not a clan. The same should probably be assumed for the ruling group in Mytilene called the Penthilidai. In Athens, the Eupatridrai are often assumed to have held the same monopoly of power in pre-Solonian Athens, but there is reason to doubt both that this was a recognized political caste and that these "sons of good fathers" were anything more than a self-styled Athenian elite.[43] The Eupatridai have also been identified as constituting all the Athenian *genē* together as a recognized ruling class or nobility. This claim too has little to support it—and also takes us quite far from the issues of family structure and inheritance. There is no question that the Eumolpidai and other such recognized and named *genē* were not true unilineal descent groups.[44]

We can assume that Plutarch knew of the specialized meaning of *genos* as corporate/fictive kin group, but not that he was using the word in that sense in the passage on Solon. The context is quite general: he is speaking of the property rights of all Athenians, not specifically those of any particular groups. More significantly, his use of *syngeneia* later in the passage suggests that he has real kinship in mind, not fictional; the members of a fictive *genos* inherited that membership from their fathers but were not necessarily connected to one another by *syngeneia.* Thus it seems most reasonable to take Plutarch's use of *genos* here as referring broadly, in good classical usage, to a man's closest relatives, his "kindred," and perhaps more specifically to the *anchisteia tou genous*. This was Plato's standard usage in the *Laws,* and Plutarch as a Platonist (among other things) is likely to have adopted Platonic terminology on these issues.

Plutarch here emphasizes the right of testament, but Athenian law (also associated with Solon) prescribed as well that if a man died without a will (intestate) then his kindred, Plutarch's *genos* and the law's *anchisteia tou genous,* continued to be the designated heirs to his property, following the prescribed sequence. The formal definition of the *anchisteia,* as well as the formal right of testament, seems to have been an important element of Solon's law code.[45] Thus, Plutarch should not be read as attributing to Solon the exclusion of *genos* and *syngeneia* as criteria of inheritance, but simply the recognition of a man's legitimate right to make a will to establish an initial heir, who often might be a relative in any case, before turning to a now formally defined "default" category of the *anchisteia tou genous*—the web of closest relatives.

From a broader perspective, it could be argued that the significance of Solon's law establishing the right of testament lies more in the fact of its public recognition of the validity of the will than in the exclusion of any particular interested party from making a claim. Thus the polis itself asserted its authority and interest in the orderly transmission of property, property which—as a result of the Athenian tendency to adopt, as well as marry, their own close kin (within the *anchisteia*)—still might end up in the hands of a relative. Theoretically, at least, the property would not be torn apart by property scavengers such as Hesiod's "widow-inheritors," provoking the potential for public disturbance. As is clear throughout the Greek historical record, security of property was a volatile and persistent political issue.

The character and function of the Athenian *anchisteia,* the formally defined "nearest" relatives, provided a theoretically orderly sequence of claim to an intestate estate.[46] Its structure also speaks strongly against the traditional linear view of the Athenian family and family interests. Like the Gortynian sequence of potential heirs, the *anchisteia* was not a corporate group of any sort, but rather a kindred, a unique web of kin, constructed around a male Athenian and not outliving that Athenian, and defined for the purpose of assigning responsibilities or protection to persons and property. Though focused on the male citizen, the Athenian *anchisteia* was nonagnatic, including females and their descendants after males and their descendants in each degree of relationship to the degree of "children of cousins" (see Figure 1). It was also bilateral, moving to maternal kin through the degree of children of cousins when the paternal side was empty. It should be clear that this system created a complex legal definition of family identity and responsibility focused more on household than on lineage.

The Draconian homicide law (the one law said to have been left in place by Solon) provides another function of the kindred in early Athens beyond that of inheritance, and also illustrates the relationship of the kindred (or *anchisteia*) to the Athenian phratry, the more broadly based Athenian fictive kin group with a clear corporate status and substantial social significance.[47] As reinscribed in the late fifth century, Dracon's law assigns the responsibility for the prosecution of homicide first to the victim's immediate male relatives, his father, brothers, or sons, and then (sequentially) to those within the limit of "sons of cousins."[48] So we see the *anchisteia* in action. After the *anchisteia,* the responsibility devolves upon the son-in-law and father-in-law (*gambros* and *pentheros*) and finally upon the members of the man's phratry, that wider but still often quite local community through which an Athenian participated in the larger organization of the polis. The Athenian phratry is actually better known in classical sources for the role it played in supervising issues of status, inheritance, and property, where it played an important role in bridging the gap between household and polis, protecting the interests of the former in behalf of the latter.[49] Although the phratry was not necessarily equivalent to a village, it does seem to have been often locally based, and so serves to illustrate for early Athens the progression of expanding social organizations outlined by Aristotle in the *Politics*— from household to village to polis, with, however, no clan in sight.[50]

A public and Solonian interest in the protection of household property and persons from the dangers of disintegration and also from internal dissension is likewise apparent in rules on bastards and, more generally, on the relationships of parents and children within the Athenian household. The *nothos/nothe,* or "bastard," is a figure known from the Homeric poems, where he or less often she is

typically the child of a hero and his concubine. The *nothos/e* is
clearly distinguished from the *gnesios,* or "legitimate" child, but yet
maintains a connection with his (her) father through the use of the
patronym (for example, Teucros *nothos* son of Telamon).[51] The material claims of the Homeric *nothos* to a share of his father's property seem to have been traditionally inferior to those of the *gnesios,*
although there is little evidence of formal rules or law. The term
nothos is not used in the *Odyssey,* but it is suggestive that when
claiming to be the son of a certain Cretan and his bought concubine,
Odysseus complains that he received from his legitimate half-
brothers a "wretched portion, a poor house." He was not, however,
excluded completely (14.203–210).

   Although the full details of Solon's laws on *nothoi* are open to debate, it can at least be said that Solon attempted formally and legally
to cut the *nothos* off from the household and its protective *anchisteia.* According to Plutarch, who cites as his source Heraclides Ponti-
cus, bastard sons *(nothoi)* were not required by Solon to support
their fathers—so eliminating in their case one of the primary moral
and economic responsibilities of the early Greek household. Then,
turning the point the other way, a notorious Aristophanic quotation
of Solonian law on *nothoi* in the *Birds* establishes, at the least, that
Solon formally limited the amount a *nothos* could inherit, and perhaps excluded him altogether from his father's estate.[52] As cited
more reliably by later orators, the law stipulated that "for *nothos*
and *nothe* there is no *anchisteia*" (Isaeus 6.47). In this way, the disruptive effects of bastards' claims, and perhaps of concubines as
well, were limited, and the Athenian household focused more
closely, morally and economically, on the basic relationships of hus-
band/wife and parent/(legitimate) child.

   A strong moral investment in oikos relationships is also evident in
the law that made killing a man who entered the interior spaces of
the household, for the purpose of sexual intercourse with one of its
female members, a case of justifiable homicide.[53] It is likewise clear
in the exception made by Solon in his law against the selling of free
Athenian children. Such sale is forbidden, except for the case of the
daughter or sister who, as an unmarried virgin, has been caught in
sexual intercourse with a man (*Solon* 23.2). The same interest is apparent in the several laws regulating the marital relations of the

heiress and her husband. All these regulations emphasize the public and political interest in the integrity—economic, moral, sexual—of the polis' constituent households as essential to the stability of the polis as a whole.[54] In particular, the rules on the marriage of the heiress are an essential key to understanding the structure of the Athenian family and its relation to the polis community. They can also be usefully compared to the legal status and marriage of the heiress in both Sparta and Gortyn, and to the philosophic legislation of Plato. Plato's attention to the heiress in the *Laws* elucidates the basis of the public interest, and also implicitly criticizes the contemporary law of both his native Athens and of Sparta. A comparative analysis of the legal treatment of the heiress provides a useful case study for my thesis that the Greek polis rose in a relationship of creative interaction with its constituent households—with not all *poleis* necessarily acting and interacting in the same way.

The Heiress in Early Greek Law

The legal persona of the heiress is a creation of the emerging polis and as such an indication of polis interest in establishing rules for the transfer of property. Although the Homeric world was certainly filled with influential female characters, that influence is not directly connected by Homer with property rights. From a later Greek legal point of view, queen Arete of Phaeacia can be considered a classic example of the heiress, an only daughter married to her father's brother, Alcinoos (*Odyssey* 7.54–66). She and her uncle Alcinoos are, or would have been in later inheritance law, heirs to equal shares of the property of her paternal grandfather Nausithoos. Arete's remarkable authority would then from this perspective be that of the heiress—a woman who in classical times was at times caricatured as the monstrous ruler of both husband and household.[55] Homer, however, leaves the source of Arete's distinctive authority somewhat mysterious and exotic, allowing Bachofen and others to imagine that her power is a relic of early Greek matriarchy.[56]

The early Greek lawgivers, on the other hand, could not overlook the economic role played by women within the household. Although Hesiod provided clear, if somewhat embittered, testimony to the general importance of that role, the rules expressing and defining

women's relation to property and household were first articulated by
the early law codes and lawgivers. Despite the distinctive problems
noted earlier for interpreting family law in Sparta, Gortyn, and
Athens, enough evidence exists for the rules governing the marriage
of the heiress in each to make possible a comparative analysis of her
legal status in these three *poleis* and in Plato's *Laws*.

Who Is an Heiress?

First, there are some prior questions of terminology and definition.
Who is a Greek heiress? A straightforward (if somewhat tardy) descriptive definition appears in the Gortyn Code, as the legislator
pauses in the midst of his regulations on the marriage of the *patroiokos* to note that the *patroiokos* was "the woman who has no father, or brother by the same father." The literal meaning of the term
patroiokos—"having the father's property"—suggests, however, a
more basic underlying structural definition, as do also the Spartan
term *patrouchos* (= *patroiokos*) and the Athenian term *epikleros*
("upon the [paternal] estate"). The distinctive thing about the heiress
then in her Greek context is that she stayed with or held onto her father's property instead of being married "out" into another household. The latter situation was the social and iconographic norm, as
the bride's rite of passage from one household to another, one life to
another, was commemorated in wedding scenes on vases or in literature.[57] But the fact that such movement at marriage was the norm
for Greek women does not affect the important point that both the
daughter who married out and the heiress who remained with the
paternal property were part of their natal family's inheritance and
kinship network. The wife, in contrast, was not a part of her husband's *anchisteia,* not legally a part of his kindred. Her children,
however, male and female, were part of the *anchisteia* of their maternal relatives as well as that of their father; thus although she herself
had no claim to the intestate estate of her husband, she provided the
link which gave her children claim to inheritance on both the paternal and maternal sides.

The distinguishing feature of the Greek heiress should be understood then as more structural than functional: she was distinctive not
in being a female heir but in being a female heir who remained with

or upon her paternal estate. The archaic and classical Greek property and inheritance systems did not in general exclude females, but the specific ways in which women were included and connected with property varied considerably—as will be seen in the regulation of heiresses in Sparta, Gortyn, and Athens.

Before looking in detail at those regulations, one final demographic point should be made about the position of the heiress in Greek society: although she was distinctive, she was not rare. One of the most persistent misconceptions in discussions of the legal treatment of the heiress is that it was highly unusual for a household to have only a daughter (or daughters)—indeed, that such a situation called for emergency or crisis measures.[58] Demographic probability, however, suggests that a significant share of Greek families—perhaps 20 percent—would have had only daughters, while almost as many would have been childless.[59] Many such families would certainly have attempted to solve their childlessness (or their lack of a son) with adoption, but the key point here is that the heiress was a significant presence in the ancient Greek family. In her close connection to the paternal estate, the heiress illuminates the public interest in female inheritance in each of these Greek *poleis*.

Who Marries the Heiress?

The basic features of the Gortyn Code's impressively detailed regulations on the *patroiokos* (columns VII–VIII) are as follows (see Figure 2):

1. The *patroiokos* is given in marriage to the oldest brother of her father. If there is no brother, she is given to the brother's son. If there are more than one *patroiokos* or more than one son of the brother, then order of age rules. And the *epiballon* shall have one *patroiokos* and not more.[60]

2. If the marriage cannot be concluded for various reasons, the law has various responses:

A. If the *epiballon* is underage, the *patroiokos* receives the house and he receives half of all revenue.

B. If the *epiballon* is of age but is unwilling to marry, he can be taken to court. If he still refuses, the *patroiokos* keeps the prop-

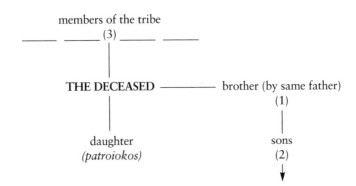

Figure 2. The *patroiokos* in Gortyn

    erty and looks for the next *epiballon.* If there is none, she mar-
ries whomever she wants from her father's *pyle.*

C. If the *patroiokos* does not want either to wait to marry an underage *epiballon* or to marry one who is of age, she takes the
house, its contents, and half of any other property—and is married to the man of her choice from [her father's] *pyle.* The
epiballon gets the other half of the property.

D. If there are no *epiballontes,* the *patroiokos* takes all the property and can marry the man of her choice from the *pyle.* If there
is no man willing, she can marry whomever she can find (after
the relatives ask publicly: does no one wish to marry her?).

    3. If a woman is already married when she becomes a *patroiokos,*
she apparently is not required to divorce her husband and remarry.[61]
But if she chooses to remarry and claim the estate and if she already
has children, she marries a man of her father's *pyle;* if she does not
have children she must marry the *epiballon.* Finally, if a *patroiokos*
who has already borne children to the *epiballon* becomes a widow,
she is not required to remarry.[62]

    For present purposes the most notable features of these complex
rules are the initial limiting of claimants to the heiress' father's
brothers or brothers' sons, and the subsequent opening of candidacy
to all males of the *pyle* if there are no such *epiballontes* (brothers or
brothers' sons). The *epiballon* is the marriage candidate prescribed
by law. The interesting implication is that the code's logic is more

concerned with the continuity of propertyholding within the patrilineally recruited *pyle* than with "family" or "lineage" continuity per se. A Gortynian belonged to the *pyle* of his father, even though he could inherit from his mother and might therefore have numerous kin and more distant inheritance claims outside that *pyle*. These regulations stipulate, however, that the *epiballon* must belong to the *pyle* of the *patroiokos'* father. The heiress must marry (except in the case of last resort) within her father's *pyle*.

In contrast to the rules for marrying a *patroiokos*, the regulations for an intestate estate included sisters of the deceased, sisters' children, and children's children as claimants after brothers, brothers' children, and so forth.[63] Why the difference? Perhaps the explanation here is political rather than familial—the heiress was a highly visible and lonely figure evoking the protective response of both the polis and her father's *pyle*. Sisters' sons are excluded from the pool of *epiballontes*, since they would belong to their father's *pyle* (which might but would not necessarily be the same as their maternal uncle's *pyle*), and the next class of candidates logically becomes the male members of the *pyle* itself. Or perhaps the difference reflects the presence of different strata within the single law code as it survives now. In any case, by insisting on either a brother or brother's son or a member of the father's *pyle* as husband for an heiress, the code seems to be insisting that in this situation the patrilinear recruitment of both persons and property should continue within the *pyle* and that tribal membership and property should be maintained with some degree of equilibrium.[64] In general, the concern for stability in property ownership is a notable feature of Greek legislation and political science, and would seem to be typically evident here in these rules for the marriage of a *patroiokos*.

The *patroiokos* could, however, refuse to marry. But if she had not produced an heir for the *pyle* she would then forfeit a portion of the property—which would duly go to the rejected *epiballon*. Throughout these regulations, the *patroiokos* is never excluded from being her father's heir; her right to the property is never questioned. In fact, if she does give up some property by refusing the *epiballon*, she still retains the "house in the city" that in other circumstances seems to have been reserved for sons.[65] Though still opaque in some respects, the Gortyn regulations can be explained as a well-crafted

compromise between the polis' administrative interest in stable recruitment in the tribes and the daughter's traditional and rightful position as her father's heir.

In his discussion of these complex rules, David Schaps argued that
the Gortynian regulations were a system "by which the larger oikos—
the descendants of the dead man's father—took care of the smaller
oikos, in which now only a daughter remained."[66] Schaps's double use
of the word *oikos* is typically problematic here, especially in that it is
not at all clear that descendants constituted an oikos in the Gortyn
Code or in any other Greek source.[67] Similarly his claim that the "rules
of Gortyn show concern for the family and for the tribe" employs the
former term without clear explanation or reference.[68] Once again, it
seems that a loose association of *oikos* with English "family" in all its
many senses, large and small, has produced substantial confusion. If
we speak of the initial candidates for the heiress' hand (her paternal
uncle and male cousin) as members of her "family," as certainly we
could, then it would be more proper to say that her family has a legal
concern for her than that the law has a concern for family. In any case,
the code does not articulate two distinct family groups that could be
called *oikoi* in these regulations, but uses two basic categories: immediate close kin (uncles and cousins) and the tribe.

As noted earlier, maternal and paternal properties (*patroia* and
matroia) in Gortyn were inherited separately by the children of the
household, and if there were no children, each separate property
could be claimed in sequence by its own unique web of secondary
heirs. Similarly, the two properties were separately liable to debt.[69]
Despite this apparent symmetry between the treatment of male and
female property, however, only the *patroiokos,* the brotherless
daughter holding her father's property, receives special additional attention in the code. This special interest, along with the modification
of the customary rules of inheritance (that is, the exclusion of sisters'
sons) in the regulation of her marriage, seems to speak to the public
and political importance of the *patroiokos,* the woman without father or brother, to whom the polis itself becomes a surrogate father.
The *patroiokos* is a high-profile problem, and the polis thus undertakes to find her a husband, so completing what would otherwise be
a "single-yoked" household and allowing that household to continue
to be a productive part of both *pyle* and polis.

*   *   *

The public interest in the marriage of the heiress, or *epikleros,* is also clear in early Athens. According to Aristotle, the only circumstances under which an ephebe could leave his post and enter into the public realm were "to deal with matters of inheritance or an *epikleros,* or to take up an hereditary priesthood" (*Ath.Pol.* 42). Earlier in his treatise, Aristotle has attributed to Solon laws on the first two topics, noting that Solon's laws on *kleroi* and *epikleroi* (and others as well) were not "drafted simply or clearly" and so had contributed to the public courts' having to "decide everything, public and private" (9). However, since Aristotle does not quote these laws specifically, but has left us the task of extracting their substance from the rhetorical arguments in the law courts and the moralizing citations of Plutarch, we will never know if Aristotle was right in his estimation of Solonian clarity. Although there are puzzles and problems, a straightforward account of the Athenian (and very likely Solonian) rule on the *epikleros* is provided by Isaeus, a fourth-century specialist in family law: "For we consider that those closest in *genos* [*ton engytato genous*] ought to marry this woman [the *epikleros*] and that the property ought for the present to belong to the *epikleros,* but that when there are sons who have completed their second year after puberty, they should have possession of it."[70]

There are other citations of and references to the laws affecting the Athenian *epikleros,* but the fragment just quoted covers the main issues in an unusually concise manner.[71] The phrase *ton engytato genous* is equivalent here in meaning to *anchisteia tou genous,* the bilateral, nonagnatic web of relatives responsible for the well-being of an Athenian—and also heir, in sequence, to his property if he were to die intestate (see Figure 3). Thus it is immediately apparent that one important difference between the Athenian and Gortynian rules for the marriage of an heiress lay in the definition of the pool of candidates. In contrast to the Gortynian rules, the same sequence of claimants (including sons of sisters and eventually maternal relatives) obtained for marrying the Athenian heiress as for inheriting an intestate and heirless estate. Keeping the property within one patrilineal line—or one deme, phratry, or tribe, membership in which was inherited patrilineally—cannot have been the primary interest of the Athenian system.

It seems that in Athens the patrilinear recruitment into basic political divisions of the polis coexisted with a property and kinship sys-

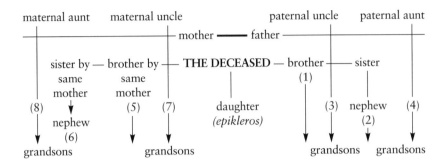

Numbers indicate sequence of claim; arrows indicate the claim continues (in theory) through succeeding generations.

Figure 3. The *epikleros* in Athens

tem, best seen in the structure of the *anchisteia,* that continually crossed those linear relationships and envisioned a branching web of relationships rather than a "line." And although there is no doubt that the Athenian public interest lay in securing the heiress an appropriate husband and so preventing the dead-end "single-yoked" household, unlike in Gortyn this interest was not articulated through the political subdivisions of deme or tribe but through the structurally distinct "ego-focused" *anchisteia.* According to Athenian rules, it would seem to be just as likely that the heiress would marry without as within her father's deme and tribe. The legal institution of the "epiklerate" in this way presents noteworthy evidence of the dual character of Athenian civic identity, one based both on a bilateral family structure and on patrilineal political recruitment.

If we look now beyond the specific structural rules for claiming an *epikleros* to what might be called "moral rules" for living with her in marriage, we find that Solonian law presents a few twists—some that Plutarch, writing 700 years later, found puzzling, and others that modern readers might consider an egregious invasion of privacy. "It seems an absurd and foolish law," wrote Plutarch,

> which permits an heiress [*epikleros*], in the event of her lawful husband's proving impotent, to marry one of his next of kin. Still there are some who say that this was a sound provision against men who

are incapable of fulfilling the duties of a husband, but marry heiresses for the sake of their property and so exploit the law to do violence to nature. When such men see that the heiress may consort with whomever she chooses, they will either put an end to the marriage or, if they persist in it, suffer disgrace for their greed and presumption. It was also wise to stipulate that the heiress should not be completely free in her choice of a consort, but should be limited to her husband's relatives [*ton syngenon*], so that her child may be *oikeios* and share in the same *genos*. The same purpose, too, is served by Solon's direction that the bride and groom should be shut in the bridal chamber and should eat a quince together, and that an heiress' husband should have intercourse with her at least three times a month.[72]

This passage in Plutarch's *Solon* is interesting for a number of reasons—in addition to the suggestion of some independence of choice on the heiress' part. First, it suggests that there was not simply one Solonian law regulating the marriage of an heiress, specifically putting her into the hands of the man "nearest in *genos*," but rather a cluster of rules intended to ensure that that marriage would be a beneficial one for the oikos of her father. She ought to produce children. The central concern of these rules was clearly that the household would continue to be a productive and reproductive unit. *Epikleros* and *kleros* were two necessary but not sufficient elements of an oikos; a husband was the third, and children a fourth.

Second, the selection of the husband from the father's bilateral *anchisteia*, and of the replacement husband from the first husband's *anchisteia*, which would overlap but not be coextensive with the father's, suggests once more that collective responsibility for the well-being of households and not lineage continuity was the motivating concern. The insistence on a "family member" as the heiress' husband has seemed inexplicable to some. If lineage is not the motive, what then is the point? But when the rule is put in the context of other responsibilities of the members of the *anchisteia* toward their focal Athenian, such as prosecuting his murderer or mourning at his funeral, then this responsibility toward his daughter fits in quite well. It should also be remembered that this system is a backup. Preferably, before he died the father would have found his daughter a husband, and perhaps adopted that man as his son.

Because of the prevailing assumptions about the lineage interests of the Greek and Athenian family, however, discussion of the Athenian heiress has focused on the effects the rules would have on the paternal line rather than on the household itself. The result has been general confusion. The difficulties presented by this approach were pointed out by David Schaps, who, as in his analysis of the Gortyn Code, speaks of two *oikoi* with an interest in the fate of the *epikleros*: "For there were in fact two *oikoi* involved: the immediate *oikos* of the deceased—that is, his descendants—and that of his parents or grandparents, of which his collaterals were a part."[73] On his argument, neither of these *"oikoi"* was preserved by the heiresses' marriage. It was apparently not legally required that the son of the *epikleros* be posthumously adopted as his maternal grandfather's heir, although that was in fact often done. Thus Schaps argues that the father's oikos was not legally preserved and that it would cease to exist when the daughter married and joined her new husband's oikos. On the other hand, Schaps's second *"oikos"* was not in any danger as long as it had "surviving males." By now it should be apparent that the argument represents the oikos as a lineage. There are other ways to look at the logic of the law and its consequences.

First, if the *epikleros* and her husband simply gave a son his maternal grandfather's name, as was quite common,[74] a formal adoption may have seemed superfluous. The son would have the grandfather's property (or part of it) and also his name, which would be a significant acknowledgment of popular sentiment for household continuity. That son might belong to a different deme or phratry than had his maternal grandfather, but that need not have been a problem. Demes and phratries were political, not kin organizations, despite the frequent use of the language of kinship.[75] Second, if by marrying the *epikleros* the father's close relative (or *anchisteus*) thereby combined two estates, it should be remembered that such a marriage might also have been reuniting what had previously been one, in a property system that typically produced continual fission and fusion of property. Third, if *oikos* is properly understood as a practical and productive composite of persons and property, then a focus on linear continuity is misleading. The oikos and its relationships are continually recreated, not transmitted. Note that Plutarch suggests that the motive behind the "intrafamilial" marriage of the heiress is "that the child may be *oikeios* and share in the same *genos*."

In sum, Solon's concern in the early Athenian laws credited to him seems to be the maintenance of productive households within a complex system of property devolution in which the property rights of women were subordinated to those of men or to the household as a whole, but not eliminated. The heiress did inherit and "have" the property (and the evidence on women's management and use of property indicates that this was not necessarily a token ownership), but she was not free to allow the oikos to become extinct, and when her heir came of age the norm of a male head of household was restored.[76] The benefits of such a system may be evident in the relative economic stability of post-Solonian Athens. This stability becomes even more apparent in contrast to the weakness of the Spartan property law in dealing with this same issue.

According to Herodotus, our earliest source on Spartan family structures and history, the Spartan kings "alone judge concerning the unmarried *patrouchos* to whom it pertains to have her, if her father has not contracted her marriage" (6.57).[77] This evidence is certainly minimal, even by early Greek standards, but it seems significant that the king's decision was apparently not governed by set rules. Herodotus specifies no formally defined group of candidates from which the king would choose, as was the case in Gortyn and in Athens. Like the archon in Athens, the Spartan king acted in the role of surrogate father, but he apparently had considerably more freedom of action (see Figure 4). Perhaps the near relatives or kindred had a traditional claim to the *patrouchos*' hand. Gorgo, for example, the only child of King Cleomenes, was married to the king's brother Leonidas. Other testimony, however, particularly that of Aristotle, suggests that, unlike in Gortyn and Athens, the marriage of the heiress was not carefully monitored by public law. In his well-known criticism of the Spartan property system in the *Politics* (1270a), Aristotle draws particular attention to this neglect:

> approximately two-fifths of all the land is possessed by women. There are two reasons for this: *epikleroi* [Aristotle uses the Athen-

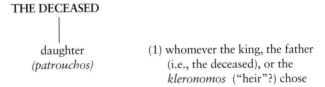

THE DECEASED

|

daughter   (1) whomever the king, the father
(*patrouchos*)   (i.e., the deceased), or the
                          kleronomos ("heir"?) chose

Figure 4. The *patrouchos* in Sparta

ian term] are numerous and dowries are large. It would have been better to have regulated dowries, prohibiting them altogether or making them small or at any rate moderate in size. But, as it is, an *epikleros* may be given in marriage to any person whatsoever; and if a man dies without making a will, then whoever is left as *kleronomos* gives her to whom he likes.

Aristotle's point is clearly that there was a consolidation of property in Sparta as a result of the lack of regulation of the marriages of wealthy women—either heiresses or those with large dowries. His terminology, however, is less than clear. Not only does Aristotle use the Athenian term for "heiress," but by speaking of a *kleronomos*—which ought to mean "heir" or "one who takes the *kleros*"—he confuses the real position of that heiress in relation to her father's property. Just who was this *kleronomos,* and what was his relation to the *kleros?* Perhaps he is the Spartan equivalent to the Gortynian *epiballon.* Still, whatever the answer to those questions, Aristotle was not mistaken about the demographic crisis of classical Sparta. There were only some 1,000 Spartiates by the early fourth century, in a polis that had once had as many as 9,000 citizen "equals" and in a land which, according to Aristotle, could support 30,000 hoplite soldiers (*Politics* 1270a30).[78] Whether or not rich Spartan heiresses were in fact sitting on all that property we will never know, but the potential consolidation of property ownership produced by the unregulated marriage of wealthy heiresses with wealthy Spartans is undeniable.

Like other students of Spartan history and society, Aristotle would have found it difficult to get accurate information about the polis and most likely relied on his own theoretical principles in analyzing what data he did have. Similarly going out on a limb, I suggest that the family structures most weakened by the "Lycurgan order" as it emerged in the sixth century were not the traditional household relationships and inheritance practices per se (private property existed and was inherited by legitimate children of a recognized marriage) but the traditional network of related kindred, such as the Athenian *anchisteia,* that might have acted, here and elsewhere, to protect the health and welfare of the individual Spartan oikos. (The starkness of the Spartan situation is represented schematically in Figure 4, presenting a clear contrast with Figures 2 and 3, Gortyn and Athens.) In sum, the Spartan polis failed—at real cost—to institutionalize an adequate support system for household stability, thus allowing the concentration of wealth in the hands of a few and the general impoverishment of the Spartiate class apparent in the historical record. Classical Sparta displays a notable tension between the supposedly equal, male military public state and the clearly unequal, and frequently female-focused, private households.

Plato's Philosophical Solution

Plato was surely no less aware of the failures of the Spartan property system than was Aristotle, and in book 11 of the *Laws* he presents his own solution to the traditional and common Greek problem of the heiress and her marriage. His Athenian, Spartan, and Cretan interlocutors create in their conversation the blueprint for the "second-best" city, in which the preservation of a stable property system is a key concern. The differences from, and implicit criticism of, the laws of the historical lawgivers are striking, and reveal Plato's distinctive view of the place of the family within a philosophic polis.

Before coming to the issue of the heiress, Plato has already in book 5 established two important principles of his property-owning system: the inalienability and the indivisibility of exactly 5,040 *kleroi.* Neither principle was typical of Greek *poleis* in his day. As was argued earlier, the Spartans may have preserved an "ancestral" portion of land as an inalienable allotment, but the large majority of land in Sparta could quite evidently be given and bequeathed, if not sold. Certainly sentiment favored keeping property among close kin, but in making it a matter of law Plato parted company with his own society. Even more at odds with his contemporary society was Plato's insistence on the indivisibility of the *kleros*. Partible inheritance was a way of life in the Greek family, no better illustrated than in Hesiod's advice to rear only one son or to hope that many children would also be many workers. Given his strong commitment, however, to as near unchanging stability as was possible in the mortal realm, Plato's logic was unimpeachable. If the same 5,040 lots were to remain the unchanging foundation of the philosophically sound polis, then there could only be a single heir for each. In addition, given that recruitment into the polis' *phylai* was patrilineal—and the twelve *phylai* seem to correspond to the twelve divisions of the polis land[79]—a male head of household, a husband who would join the *epikleros* on her father's *kleros* and in his *phyle,* was essential. Only in this way would the distribution of the 5,040 lots among the twelve *phylai* remain unchanged. Thus Plato's rules on the heiress' marriage, unlike those of the historical Greek states, insist that the heiress' husband not already have a *kleros,* so that on the principle of one man/one indivisible *kleros* he could freely take up her father's position on the *kleros* and in tribe and polis. The claimants to the heiress were those paternal male relatives who would have been excluded by her own father from possessing a *kleros* plus a maternal uncle who is specifically said not to have a *kleros* himself. (See Figure 5.)

Plato's solution for a completely childless intestate estate is a logical extension of his rules on the heiress, but again a notable departure from contemporary Greek practice. In what seems a quite original move, Plato requires the two closest relatives on the paternal

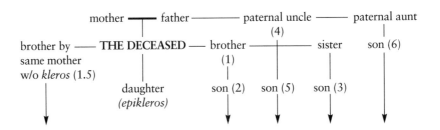

Numbers indicate sequence of claim; arrows indicate the claim continues through succeeding generations.

Figure 5. The order of claim to an *epikleros* (*Laws* 924–925)

side, male and female, to "go in harness" and take the property. Again, on the principle of indivisibility and a single heir for each *kleros,* this couple would have been previously without a *kleros.* Thus, the paternal side of a man's *anchisteia* (and, on the maternal side, the maternal half-brother without a *kleros*) continued to have a residual, custodial responsibility for the property even without being its owners.

In his prefatory remarks to the (deceased) father in the preamble to the law on the heiress,[80] Plato emphasizes the special circumstances of the heiress' marriage and the importance of family responsibility for that marriage. The husband of an heiress, he says, should be chosen on the basis of "only two out of three possible considerations: close kinship [*anchisteia tou genous*] and the security of the *kleros*" (11.924). The third consideration which a father normally took into account in betrothing a daughter, the man's character and habits, says Plato, will in this case have to be overlooked. Here as elsewhere in the *Laws* Plato has adapted the Athenian family structure and family law to fit more closely his philosophical goal of an unchanging, completely stable property system. In doing so he also implicitly casts a critical eye on the Spartan inattention to this issue, illuminates the concern for stable *pylai* that may be behind the Gortynian requirement of intra-*pyle* marriage, and also reinforces the interpretation of the Athenian *anchisteia* as the key to Athenian family law.

Conclusion

So it seems that a comparative analysis of the legal position of the heiress illustrates both the diversity and the commonality of experience in early Greek family history. Within a system of partible and diverging inheritance typical of the Greek world as a whole, the "brotherless daughter" presented a distinct problem. There could be no devolution of property if the heiress remained alone "holding" or "upon" the paternal estate. Failure to regulate who could (or could not) marry the heiress in a community of small property-owning citizens ran the risk of significant economic and political destabilization. The archaic lawgivers in Athens and Gortyn, and most likely in other *poleis* as well, prescribed criteria for claiming an heiress with her property that were based upon, rather than destructive of, kinship structures and networks peculiar to each polis and legally recognized by each polis. And Solon, if we can believe Plutarch, added interpersonal rules to further ensure the success of her marriage—in the public sense, by the production of children. Sparta, on the other hand, apparently allowed the father or guardian of the heiress considerable freedom of disposal without regard for the broader concerns of either her near kin or the stability of the polis as a whole. In none of the three *poleis*, however, can we see either a corporate clan, acting either in its own interest or in that of a lineage (neither *anchisteia* nor *epiballontes* qualify), or a simple pattern of polis expropriation of family authority or responsibility or of the family pushed into retirement and defeat.

Despite the notoriously fragmented character of our knowledge of early polis history, essentially a jigsaw puzzle with only a few pieces remaining, the importance of family law and the family in that history, and puzzle, is clear. The political institutions and organization of Sparta, Gortyn, and Athens were built upon and took for granted the essential relations of the household outlined by Aristotle in the *Politics:* husband and wife, parent and child, and master and slave. As the initial human bonds in the expanding series of human associations ending in the polis, as articulated by both Plato and Aristotle,[81] these private relationships had also a highly public significance. The internal histories of Sparta and Gortyn are for the most part inaccessible, but the specific ways in which the two *poleis* regulated or failed to regulate the relations of the household, persons, and property, allow us some glimpse of what made both distinctive. The internal history of Athens, on the other hand, is the best known of any Greek polis, and in the next two chapters I continue to follow the story of the creative partnership of Athenian family and Athenian state begun so notably by Solon.

—4—

MARRIAGE AND ADULTERY IN
DEMOCRATIC ATHENS

In one of his more memorable poetic moments, Solon had warned his fellow Athenians in the early sixth century that

> the public Ruin invades the house of each citizen,
>   and the courtyard doors no longer have strength to keep it
>   away,
> but it overleaps the lofty wall, and though a man runs in
>   and tries to hide in chamber or closet, it ferrets him out.[1]

These elegiac lines express with remarkable clarity both the recognition of the distinction between the public and private spheres and also their clear interconnection in the fortunes of the city as a whole. The *demosia kaka* ("public Ruin") are intruders into the private inner sanctum of the house (the *thalamos*), but their presence in the house—and their ability to leap over walls and enter closed doors to get there—reveal, as Solon goes on to make clear, that neither *dysnomia* ("Bad Government") nor *eunomia* ("Good Government") lives in the public sphere alone.

The moral interdependency of the public and private spheres so striking in Solon's poem and in his laws is an important and persistent feature of the development of democratic Athens. In the previous chapter I argued that the Greek polis did not rise by the unilateral defeat or "dismembering" of family or clan, but through a creative partnership—having better and worse results—with its households and their networks of supporting family or kindred. In this and the following chapter I consider the relatively abundant evidence for the distinctive stamp that classical and democratic Athens put upon the public meaning of private morality through its legislation on, and representation of, marriage and adultery.

Although the marital relationship, symbolized most often in Athenian literature by the marriage bed, belonged to the innermost and most private space of the house (Solon's *thalamos*), it also had a high public profile as the social relationship that legitimized an Athenian's status as a shareholder in both oikos and polis.[2] Likewise, the violation of the marriage bed, what for the moment we can call adultery, drew the public eye directly and dramatically to the private life of those citizens. Perhaps, as Pericles claimed, the Athenians were in fact tolerant of deviant lifestyles and did not "get into a state with our next-door neighbor if he enjoys himself in his own way"; but a violated marriage was more than a matter of private lifestyle.[3] The Athenian rules and categories of marriage and adultery, however, were neither systematic nor complete. Because Plato's discussion of these issues in the *Laws* gives a certain philosophic order to the issue and also brings into sharper focus some of the complexity of the Athenian public/private distinction, the chapter concludes with a brief look at Plato's philosophic legislation on marriage and adultery, which illuminates the public significance of these private relationships in ancient Athenian society.

Marriage: Social Process and Legal Rules

Despite the unquestioned importance, both practical and ideological, of marriage in Athenian society as the relationship that created and supported the citizen household, there was no formal legal recognition or legal definition of the state of matrimony in classical Athens. Marriage itself was not defined by Athenian law, nor were individual marriages legally certified or registered. But neither this situation nor the fact that, as Aristotle noted, there was no specific word for the "yoking together of man and woman" is reason to conclude that marriage was essentially a de facto arrangement and one not easily distinguishable from concubinage.[4] Although there were formal rules governing some aspects of the marital relationship, such as the laws on the heiress, marriage itself was recognized and validated not by a specific legal ceremony or piece of papyrus, but by the communally witnessed rituals and household events which over time established its legitimacy as an Athenian marriage. These included the formal betrothal and designation of the bride as the future mother of legitimate children *(engyan)*, the publicly witnessed wedding procession and feast preceding the wedding night itself *(gamein)*, the setting up of a new household *(synoikein)*, and the birth and recognition of children *(paidopoiein)*. Marriage thus should be understood as a social process rather than as a legal moment. These terms, though not in themselves the legal requirements for marriage, were the socially recognized signs of legitimate marriage. Marriage in Athens was not defined by a single legal rule. It was itself the essential "given" upon which laws on status and legitimacy, often termed "marriage laws," rested. I begin with the example of household or family legitimacy and then move to polis legitimacy or "citizenship."

In his speech "Against Leochares" Demosthenes cites a traditional, perhaps Solonian, law that defined legitimate children as those born from the woman whom "father or brother or grandfather betroths [*engyese*]."[5] This law identifies the *engye* (or betrothal) as the critical moment of acknowledgment between the groom and the bride's father that the prospective marriage will result in the "cultivation of legitimate children"[6]—children with an eventual claim to inherit from both the maternal and paternal side of the family. However, the law does not thereby define marriage as the legal equivalent to *engye*; rather, it assumes marriage as the larger process to which the *engye* contributes. The *engye* was a transaction at which the bride need not have been present and which might not in fact ever be fulfilled: by itself it produced neither children nor marriage. The social process of which the *engye* was but one part produced both. Legitimacy is legally defined; marriage is, in Athenian law, assumed rather than defined.

Similarly, when in the middle of the fifth century the Athenians voted to exclude from their increasingly self-conscious citizen family anyone who did not have two Athenian parents, marriage was also assumed but not formally defined.[7] In 451 Pericles proposed, and the Athenians approved by vote, that "anyone who has not been born from two *astoi* [native citizens] should not share in the polis."[8] The law's appropriation of household language is striking and important:

the polis belongs to its citizens as an inheritance in which each one shares as a legitimate heir. Reinforcing the point that citizenship was the legitimate Athenian's public inheritance, Plutarch refers to the Periclean legislation as the law "about *nothoi*"—those "bastard" children now excluded from both the responsibilities and privileges of membership in the public household (*Pericles* 37). The historicity of Plutarch's usage is confirmed by the following comic exchange between Peisthetairos and Heracles in Aristophanes' *Birds* (produced in 414):

> P: Watch your step, Herakles.
> You're being hoodwinked . . .
> You're a bastard [*nothos*].
> H: What's that: I'm a bastard?
> P: Of course you're a bastard—by Zeus. Your mother, you see, was an ordinary woman, not a goddess. In other words, she's a foreigner.[9]

The use of the language of legitimacy has led some to consider the Periclean law as essentially a law regulating marriage. In one book on Athenian law, for example, reference is made to the "other provision of Pericles' law," referring to an assumed prohibition on marriage between Athenian and non-Athenian.[10] A better alternative is to see that, just as in the law on the *engye*, marriage stands behind the legal delineation of status in Pericles' law.[11] The law as we have it makes no reference to marriage, but simply and straightforwardly notes the category of persons who, in this case, are not to be legitimate citizens because they do not have two Athenian parents. The law certainly would have consequences for the character of Athenian marriage, but it is not a marriage law. Analogously, although it had clear consequences in excluding some "illegitimates" from the citizen family, Pericles' law did not define citizenship. Athenian citizenship was not a simple legal right but rather a complex cluster of privileges and responsibilities belonging to the legitimate polis shareholder. Both marriage and citizenship can be considered part of the social matrix of customs and concepts which underlay Athenian law—but were not defined by it.

This point is further illustrated by the interesting set of so-called marriage laws which Apollodorus quotes in his prosecution of the over-fifty ex-prostitute Neaira, sometime in the 340s B.C.E. In this suit, the only extant case of *xenia* (a suit brought against a foreigner who acted as a citizen), Apollodorus argues that Neaira is guilty as charged because she has been living with an Athenian named Stephanos as his wife, and has passed off her children as the legitimate Athenian children of two Athenian parents.[12] In typical manner, Apollodorus lets the laws speak for themselves:

> If a foreigner shall live as husband with [*synoikei*] an Athenian woman in any way or manner whatsoever, he may be indicted before the *thesmothetai* by anyone who chooses to do so from among the Athenians having the right to bring charges. And if he is convicted, he shall be sold, himself and his property, and the third part shall belong to the one securing his conviction. The same principle shall hold also if a foreign woman shall live as wife with an Athenian man, and the Athenian who lives as husband with the foreign woman shall be fined one thousand drachmae.   (16)

Somewhat later he introduces another law:

> If anyone shall give a foreign woman in marriage to an Athenian man representing her as being related to himself, he shall suffer loss of citizen rights and his property shall be confiscated, and a third part of it shall belong to the one who secures his conviction. (52)[13]

These are, according to Apollodorus, just the things that Neaira and Stephanos have done, thus making Neaira, who is without question a foreigner, guilty of pretending to Athenian citizen status, and Stephanos guilty of knowingly contributing to the fraud. "For this is what *synoikein* is," says Apollodorus; it is "when someone produces children [*paidopoiein*] and introduces sons to phratry and deme and bestows daughters to husbands" (122). The argument may seem to a modern audience frustratingly indirect, but it reveals quite clearly the composite process of marriage which underlay Athenian laws on status and legitimacy. Such marriage was a central privilege of the citizen shareholder.

The law, as quoted by Apollodorus, specified who could marry whom, but it did not define marriage or the meaning of *synoikein*. That was left to the self-appointed legal expert, Apollodorus, to attempt himself. Understanding Athenian marriage in this way, as social process rather than as legal event, counters the widespread notion that as an institution marriage in Athens was both vague and difficult to distinguish from concubinage or just "living together." Without the existence of a legal certificate establishing the act of marriage, the judgment of whether or not two persons were married was certainly not a simple matter, nor one free of the possibility of error. Some litigants might appeal to the single recognizable act of the *engye* as "proof,"[14] while others, like Apollodorus, argued from the observation of behavior and relationships over time. The problem, of course, was that when a judgment was required quickly—in a court, in a matter of hours—allegations could be raised but less easily disproved. Marriage was difficult to prove in court just because it was the social basis, the "given," of Athenian rules of legitimacy and citizenship and was not defined by those rules.

Aeschylus' Apollo in the *Eumenides* also presents marriage as a not easily definable foundation for political society, asserting that marriage—literally, the marriage bed—was "bigger than oaths" and "guarded by the right of nature."[15] This is an extraordinary description of a relationship that was both natural and highly political. Another Athenian tragedy with significant bearing on the place of marriage in Athenian society is Sophocles' *Antigone*.

The central conflict of the *Antigone,* that between Antigone and Creon, can be read in many ways, as for example between individual conscience and public law, between the demands of the gods and decrees of the state, between female and male, or between family and state. Although each of these oppositions creates what may be a useful framework for the interpretation of the play, none is in itself an entirely satisfactory distillation of its characters and plot. One could note, for example, that as a female member of her brother's *anchisteia*, Antigone has a public (polis) responsibility to carry out burial rights for her nearest relative, and that the polis authorizes her ritual care of the dead even as it forbids it through Creon's decree.[16] Further, from the private or familial perspective, the conflicts of the play divide sister from sister, father from son, as well as niece from uncle. Acknowledging that there are many ways to read the *Antigone,* I focus here on the theme of marriage and the way it complicates the traditional view that this play sets family against state.[17]

It is not at all clear that Antigone by herself should be taken to represent the family and family interests, however that term may be employed. Not only are most of the members of the cast members of the same general family, but they are also connected in the stricter Athenian sense as members of the *anchisteia* of the dead brothers Eteocles and Polyneices—Antigone and Ismene as sisters, Creon as maternal uncle, and Haemon as maternal cousin. As Antigone's maternal uncle, Creon was also responsible for her marriage as an *epikleros.* Further, if the household is the moral center of Greek family relations, and marriage is recognized as the central formative relation of the household, then it is even clearer that this play does not set family against state, but instead depicts the tragedy of heroic opposition to and isolation from both oikos and polis. Creon and Antigone are members of the same *anchisteia* that should have protected the oikos in the interest of the larger polis, but in the *Antigone* they are instead set against each other as both take positions which increasingly isolate them from their own community and its well-being.

Though insisting on her responsibility to bury her brother, Antigone otherwise opposes the claims of household relationships, particularly that of marriage. This is evident both in her own chosen limitation of moral interest (906–912):

> Had I had children of their father dead,
> I'd let them moulder. I should not have chosen
>   in such a case to cross the state's decree.
> What is the law that lies behind these words?
> One husband gone, I might have found another,
> or a child from a new man in the first child's place,
> but with my parents hid away in death, no brother, ever, could
>   spring up for me;

and in her unchosen virgin death (917–918):

> No marriage bed, no marriage song for me,
> and since no wedding, so no child to rear.[18]

Thus Antigone stands as an isolated heroic figure, persevering in a courageous but limited vision of family and polis responsibility. Her isolation is in fact strikingly similar to that of Creon, who during the play becomes increasingly remote both from the citizens and from his own household, so prompting his son to say: "You'd rule a desert island beautifully alone" (739). And to Ismene's plea that he consider the welfare of his "own son's promised bride" (568), Creon can only say, "There are other furrows for his plough" (569), a comment which should probably be read as indicative of his hubristic disregard for traditional household relationships and not taken as representing the general Athenian view of marriage.[19]

In the end, both Creon and Antigone suffer alone, bereft of household and family in any sense: Antigone, bitter and unwed, in her "marriage-chamber of death"; and Creon, frantic with the knowledge that he is responsible for the suicides of his son and his wife, as well as for that of his niece who was his future daughter-in-law. In contrast to the destructive isolation of both Creon's and Antigone's positions in the play, marriage and the household it normally creates serve to legitimate the citizens' participation in the larger polis and to validate the responsibilities of family members both to one another and to the polis. Thus, in the *Antigone* Sophocles suggests in starkly tragic terms the public significance of marriage as a relationship tying together, through the oikos relationships it created, the private and public realms, and so underlying the well-being of both. Sophocles makes his point through the negative image of a "marriage to death," a marriage celebrated "in the halls of Hades" (1241).[20] Another negative image of marriage is the marriage violated by adultery, and to that issue of Athenian law I now turn.

What Was Adultery and Who Was Interested?

The subject of adultery in Athenian law and society takes us headlong into some of the more turbulent (some would say "muddied")[21] waters of Greek social history. Since the topic occupies a point of convergence of several cross-disciplinary currents—especially feminism, legal sociology, comparative anthropology—the recent discussion has been lively. In a book he describes as "an exercise in legal historical sociology," David Cohen has challenged both old and new scholarship on the character of "sexual offenses" in Athens, including adultery.[22]

Cohen's challenge to received opinion on Athenian adultery law consists essentially of two points: one on the nature of the crime and the other on the nature of public interest in the crime. Adopting the Greek word *moicheia* (defined by Liddell-Scott-Jones as "adultery") as the terminological basis of discussion, Cohen disputes the standard view that in Athens this was a broadly conceived offense and could refer to the sexual seduction of a mother, sister, or daughter, in addition to a wife. Relying both on a survey of classical Athenian usage and on the comparative principle that a failure to distinguish "the categories of intercourse with unmarried virgins from intercourse with married women" would "render Athens unique among ancient, medieval and modern Western legal systems," he insists that Athens was not in fact unique in this respect and that "Athenian linguistic usage, social norms, and legal culture reflect an understanding of *moikheia* as an offense against the marital relation." Then, as part of his larger thesis that classical Athenian democracy was concerned not with private sexual (mis)behavior itself, but only with the public consequences of that behavior, Cohen goes on to argue that adultery *(moicheia)* was prosecutable in Athens not as a sexual offense per se, but only insofar as it was conceived as a "source of public violence and disorder."[23] The vengeance and violence provoked by adultery, rather than the act itself, attracted the attention of Athenian public law.

Drawing extensively on comparative ethnographic data from contemporary Mediterranean societies, Cohen situates the act of adultery in the midst of an "honor-shame" culture in which a man's honor depends on the virtue of his wife, and in which the connection of masculinity with sexual prowess left men playing a "zero-sum game" of seduction in which the adulterer won, while the cuckold husband lost, the sum total of honor.[24] The explosive potential of adultery in such a society and the resulting public interest in regulating the methods and means of self-help and revenge are quite apparent. But the argument that the public interest in classical Athens lay only in the threat of such public violence turns on Cohen's further claim that Athens (or democratic Athenian ideology) articulated the principle of a "protected private sphere." According to Cohen, "Athenians who concerned themselves with such matters appear to have conceived of the notion of a protected private sphere as one of the constitutive characteristics of a democratic society." Cohen also argues that antidemocratic theorists were uniformly hostile to the sanctity of the private sphere, and "the ideology of Athenian radical democracy . . . points up the essentially anti-democratic nature of any legislative ideal which undermines the barriers between legitimate public interest and purely private concerns."[25]

The image of classical Athens presented by such statements features a distinctly classically liberal attitude toward private life, and Cohen's discussion of adultery thus appears rooted in an interestingly hybrid theoretical model (honor and shame with classical liberalism) of classical Athenian democracy. But although comparative evidence and paradigms are useful tools with which to interpret historical evidence, they sometimes run the risk of overwhelming that evidence. Indeed it is just this Athenian evidence which complicates, and in some instances disputes, Cohen's arguments on adultery and on Athenian public interest in sexual behavior.

In insisting that the term *moicheia* referred in Athens to the crime of adultery and had specific reference to sexual intercourse with a married woman, Cohen not only is led to dismiss some conflicting evidence;[26] he also, and more significantly to my mind, overlooks the ways in which the *moichos* himself was an ethically and socially marked character quite distinct from an honor-winning Don Juan, and considerably more (off-)colorful than the English "adulterer." The *moichos* was by himself a topos of the ancient Greek moral and social order. Further, the claim that the Athenians were not interested in the act of adultery per se, but only in the potential public disorder caused by that act, so marking off a "protected sphere" of private life, may be a difficult distinction to recognize in practice and is clearly a difficult one to reconcile with the specific ways in which the offense of *moicheia* and the *moichos* were publicly treated in Athenian law. The success of Cohen's challenge to received opinion depends in the end on its success in interpreting the full range of historical evidence on the meaning and legal consequences of adultery in Athens.

As is so often the case in discussions of Greek law and society, seemingly simple questions of definition have no simple answer. Is *moicheia* adultery? How did the Athenians identify and label the act of marital infidelity? To what extent was it a crime? The English word derives from the Latin *adulterium,* which in the discussions of the Roman jurists generally meant the sexual relationship between a married woman and a man other than her husband.[27] For classical Athens, we are left in the more difficult if creative situation of having to discover both the terminology and the substance of the law from quite disparate contexts and sources. Nonetheless, the standard modern formulation of what is called Athenian adultery law is provided with notable confidence by Kenneth Dover:

> It was *moikheia,* "adultery" to seduce the wife, widowed mother, unmarried daughter, sister or niece of a citizen; that much is clear from the law cited by Dem. xxiii 53–55 . . . The adulterer could be killed, if caught in the act, by the offended head of the household . . . or he could be held until he agreed to pay compensation . . . or he could be prosecuted or maltreated and injured; and, whatever else happened, he was shamed as having wronged a fellow citizen.[28]

In this formulation Dover implies that Athenian *moicheia* was a type or near relative of adultery, properly speaking, and that its public significance lay primarily in the wrong done to one male citizen by another. Both points bear further consideration. On the first, the law cited by Demosthenes does not at all establish "that much is clear." In his speech "Against Aristocrates" (23) Demosthenes quotes the law as follows: "If a man kills [another] unintentionally in an athletic contest, or overcoming him [in a fight] on the road, or unwittingly in battle, or [in intercourse] with [*epi*] his wife, or with his mother or with his sister or with his daughter or with the concubine he keeps for [procreation of] legitimate children, he shall not go into exile as a manslayer on that account."[29] Neither the term *moicheia* nor any related word appears in this passage, and the language does not specifically indicate seduction or corruption, as for example does the verb *diaphtherein* ("corrupt"), a general term which can include what seducers do to other men's wives; here there is only the notably uninformative preposition *epi.* As Cohen and others point out, the clause could refer just as easily to rape as to adultery, suggesting that the issue of the willingness or unwillingness of the woman was not a central concern of the lawgiver here.[30]

It is possible that adulterous intercourse could come under the umbrella of the general phrase *epi damarti* ("upon" or "against" the wife) which is used in the law. It is also true that Aristotle uses the term *moichos* when summarizing in the *Athenaion Politeia* the cases of justifiable homicide tried in the Delphinium. According to Aristotle (*Ath.Pol.* 57.3):

> If a person admits that he has killed someone but claims that he has a right to do so, as for instance, when he has surprised a *moichos* in the act, or if he has killed a fellow citizen in war, by mistake, or in a gymnastic contest, then the trial takes place in the Delphinium.

But this passage defines neither the *moichos* nor his act. Aristotle only provides examples of what might be justifiable homicide in his day, and one of these is the killing of a *moichos* caught in the act—both the character and the act apparently being well known to his audience. That this particular act of "self-help" within the oikos is linked with instances of clearly accidental or unintentional homicide is interesting. Perhaps the killing of the *moichos* was an example of intentional homicide that was nonetheless "justified" by the circumstances, or perhaps the law did not envision the killing of a man found *epi* a woman of the household as premeditated, since his finding someone in that position might have a definite element of "accident" to it and the resulting homicide could be considered an act of unplanned passion or anger. Looking to Plato's complex categories of homicide in the *Laws,* this would clearly be a case of unintentional homicide committed in a state of passion.[31]

So far what is at least clear from the law as quoted by Demosthenes is the type of act for which homicide is a justified response—the sexual violation of a woman within the household. It is still unclear that this is "what *moicheia* was" or even less "what adultery was" in Athens. An emphasis on the act rather than its label may be quite appropriate for a legal statute, since "criminal law ought to penalise people for having done something wrong, not for being something",[32] but it still leaves open the question of the relation of *moicheia* and *moichos* to our common understanding of "adultery" as defined in the *Oxford English Dictionary:* "the sexual relation of a married person with one who is not his or her lawful spouse."

A more significant source than Demosthenes or Aristotle for Dover's confident assertion of "what *moicheia* is" is apparently Lysias' well-known speech written in behalf of a certain Euphiletos who is on trial for murdering the man he found in bed with his wife.[33] In this speech Lysias uses the words *moichos* and *moicheuein* quite liberally in reference to Eratosthenes and to what Eratosthenes was caught doing—and indeed implicitly to what he claims Eratosthenes has also done, habitually or even professionally, with women of other Athenian households.[34] Lysias also calls upon the same venerable law on justifiable homicide quoted by Demosthenes, into which he inserts the term *moichos,* saying quite pointedly: "the court of the Areopagus . . . has expressly stated that whoever takes this vengeance on a *moichos* caught in the act with his wife shall not be convicted of murder."[35]

The connection made here between the homicide law and the murder/punishment of the *moichos* is crucial to Lysias' argument. Rather than simply resting his case on the principle of "justifiable homicide," Lysias has argued earlier that Euphiletos' act of homicide was indeed the legal penalty for "men who do such things."[36] It is not clear what specific law Lysias is appealing to here, and it is possible that this claim is simply a part of his rhetorical misreading of the homicide law as establishing the death penalty for the *moichos,* rather than simply allowing that a man caught in this situation could be killed by a husband or "head of household" with impunity.[37] But however many laws Lysias actually cited in this case, the rhetorical strategy of arguing the stronger case—not merely justified, but legally mandated homicide—and of painting the dead man as the type of man who customarily committed such acts is patent. With luck, and with the help of a judicial system lacking legal review or jury deliberation but certainly appreciating drama, Euphiletos perhaps will have managed to carry his audience with him and win an enthusiastic acquittal.

Although the speciousness of Euphiletos' claim to have acted as an agent of the law in committing homicide is generally recognized by modern scholars (who do at least have the benefit of review and de-

liberation), his (or Lysias') rhetorical use of the label *moichos* in
making his case, and his conflation of the punishment of this particular *moichos* with the act of justifiable homicide allowed by the old
homicide law, have continued to bedevil modern discussion of
Athenian adultery law. By linking so effectively Euphiletos' dramatic
story, in which the wife played a willing and active part, with the
homicide law, which showed no interest at all in the willingness or
unwillingness of the woman involved, Lysias has encouraged the
modern reader to suppose that the Athenians had an obtuse view of
adultery, which somehow refused to acknowledge the obvious role
of the female partner. So at least one could explain in that way the
often-heard comment that Athenians did not clearly distinguish assault from adultery and considered the woman equally passive in
both instances.[38]

Instead of immediately taking up these issues, I propose to take a
closer look at the *moichos* and his crime from a somewhat wider
perspective than that provided by Lysias in this speech. Neither
Lysias' rhetorical maneuvering nor Aristotle's more innocent usage
in the *Athenaion Politeia* establishes anything close to a law on
moicheia. But here again Apollodorus, that industrious student of
Athenian law, has something to contribute. In the course of describing an alleged scam carried out by Neaira and Stephanos, through
which a man was given access to Neaira's daughter and then charged
with *moicheia*, Apollodorus cites the following law:

> if someone unjustly imprisons another as being a *moichos*, the man
> in question can enter a public charge of "unjust imprisonment" be-
> fore the *thesmothetai*. And if he convicts the one who imprisoned
> him and seems to have been unjustly plotted against, then he shall
> be free from penalty and his sureties released. But if he appears to
> be a *moichos*, the law orders his sureties to give him over to the one
> who caught him[39] and in the courtroom the latter may treat him as
> he pleases, without a knife,[40] on the grounds that he is a *moichos*.
> (66)

Somewhat later he provides his audience with the legal consequences
of *moicheia* both for the woman involved and for her husband:

When he has caught the *moichos,* it is not lawful for the one who caught him to continue to live with [be married to] his wife. If he does continue to live with her, let him lose his citizen rights [be *atimos*]. And it is not lawful for the woman [wife] with whom a *moichos* is caught to enter into the public sanctuaries. And if she does so enter, let her suffer with impunity whatever she may suffer, except death.   (87)[41]

These quotations, and also the case to which they are applied, take us significantly closer to the issue of the public interest in marriage and adultery. They also usefully complicate some of the more simplistic views of Athenian adultery law noted earlier, particularly that the woman was considered a passive victim and so went unpunished, and that *moicheia* was a crime directed solely against male honor and property. But because Apollodorus' laws still assume, rather than define, the terms *moichos* and *moicheia,* I propose to cast the net wider still and to consider the general usage of these words, their connotations as well as specific denotations.

Who Is a *Moichos?*

The word *moicheia* is apparently a relatively late coinage and is known only from the later fifth century as a description of the act of the *moichos,* a term first appearing in the invective poetry of Hipponax in the sixth century. Homer uses the compound form *moichargia* ("*moichos* money") for the money that Ares was required to pay the cuckold Hephaestus, but does not actually call the god a *moichos.* In one very brief and otherwise unexceptionable fragment, though, Hipponax does use the word in connection with a certain Krites: "I do not think that Krites was justly taken as a *moichos . . .*"[42]

In deciding just how to translate *moichos* here it may be useful to consider the etymology of the term in the light of Hipponax's known penchant for vulgar or "obscene" language.[43] On the basis of what we have already gleaned from Lysias, Apollodorus, and Aristotle, it is reasonable to assume that the charge against Krites was that of entering another man's house and bed. But "adulterer" may be a somewhat elevated and unrevealing translation for the word *moichos* in an invective poem of this sort. According to Pierre Chantraine, "everyone" agrees that *moichos* is an agent noun derived from the verb *omeichein,* "to urinate," with the implication that originally the word was a vulgar form of slang based on a crude equation of urination and ejaculation.[44] A similar connection exists in Latin (*mingere* and *meiere* used in sexual context). In commenting on the Latin usage of such terms, J. N. Adams notes that "they seem to have been applied particularly to squalid or humiliating sexual acts."[45] If the analogy with Latin usage is justified, then it seems likely that in origin *moichos* was a highly pejorative and vulgar term of abuse for both the man in question and his activities. If so, then shame, not honor, was associated with *moicheia,* as in Xenophanes' complaint that Homer had attributed to the gods all the most shameful activities, including *moicheia.*[46] In the rest of his poem, Hipponax most likely continued in this abusive vein about Krites—or perhaps about the woman in question.

That *moichos* was not at all a word suited for polite society, but in fact a vulgar word of abuse, is supported by its complete absence from extant Athenian tragedy and by its prevalence in Aristophanes, whose vocabulary was often notably improper.[47] The *moichos* is a frequent butt of Aristophanic jokes, and from Aristophanes also comes the notice that when caught the *moichos* might be subjected to the particularly humiliating and painful penalty of being "radished"—or, as Dover explains, "a 'radish' was pushed up his anus and his pubic hair was pulled out with the help of hot ash."[48] It has been noted that such punishment "symbolically reduced [the *moichos*] to the status of a woman or slave."[49] And even if one discounts the reality of Aristophanes' "radishing," as it were, it remains true that the *moichos* is cast as a particularly base and essentially unmanly sort of sexual offender. This might also explain the unusual, and probably humiliating, punishment meted out to the *moichos* in the law cited by Apollodorus: the husband can do what he wants to him without the use of a knife. Finally, if *moichos* was such a word, and the *moichos* himself such a character, then the oath of the women in *Lysistrata* pledging to have intercourse with "neither *moichos* nor husband" (212) might have been just as "improper" and provocative as Lysistrata's earlier use of the graphic "we must abstain from the penis."[50]

From this perspective, we would have to suppose that Greek law and law courts were open to a broader range of language than scholars in their studies might tend to assume, and that words of abusive or vulgar origin could not only be heard in court and in the agora, but were written into law as well. In the Gortyn Code the Doric form of the participle, *moichion,* is used in a clause stipulating that "if a man is caught *moikion* a free woman in [the house] of her father or brother or husband, he should pay a hundred staters."[51] Perhaps such use in law and in the law courts dignified these terms to some extent; but that *moichos* remained a strongly abusive term is clear, for example, from the way in which Lysias in another speech adds the charge of corrupting free citizen women and being a *moichos* to his highly abusive attack on the (allegedly) servile and venal Agoratos.[52]

Whether or not this attempt to recover the contemporary connotations of the term is persuasive, the specific features of the word *moichos* that have been established should warn against taking *moicheia* as equivalent to the Athenian "concept" of adultery—and then remarking how "bizarre" that seems to be. Throughout the classical era the *moichos* remains essentially true to his origins. He is the nighttime sexual 'hief (a counterpart to other thieves and nighttime criminals)[53] who enters other men's houses and seduces the women within. He appears, in one of Aristotle's phrases, as "a dandy cruising at night." He is a topos not of manliness but of its opposite.

Similarly, the English word "adultery" does not adequately describe the specific character of *moicheia,* that is, what the *moichos* did. Most prominently, from a modern perspective, *moicheia* is a strikingly asymmetrical offense. It is committed by a man and not by a woman (until Plato evens the verbal field with the coining of *"moicheutria"* in the *Symposium*). The *moichos* commits the act of *moicheuein;* the woman who is his sexual partner is typically referred to either as the passive object of his action *(moicheumene)* or as the one "with whom" he committed his action (as in the law quoted above). The focus, verbal and otherwise, is on the figure and act of the *moichos. Moicheia* is a crime by a single actor in a single direction: one man enters the house and bed of another. No conclusion necessarily follows, however, about the sexual—as opposed to the semantic—passivity of the woman involved. As described above, *moicheia* refers quite specifically to what the man did. Although he has a partner, the act is his, not hers.

The gender asymmetry has a spatial and temporal component as well. *Moicheia* refers to the *moichos'* entry into another man's house and into his bed under cover of darkness. *Moicheia* is foreign both to open public spaces and to the light of day.[54] In addition, as the locus of *moicheia*, the house and household can also be seen as its victims, and against the *moichos* the head of household exercised the full force of "self-help" appropriate for such nocturnal entry, thievery, and seduction.

Finally, there will be a significant difference between *moicheia* and adultery in its modern sense (see the definition quoted earlier) if the former term applies to the illicit sexual intercourse with any female member of a household, not just with a wife. This is not stated in so many words by any Athenian source, although the Gortyn Code does offer comparative support for such a meaning with its establishment of a monetary fine for the man who is caught *moikion* (participle) a free woman in her father's, brother's, or husband's house.[55] Lacking Gortyn's clear codified statement, Dover and others have relied on the law on justifiable homicide quoted earlier and, like Lysias, have interpolated the word *moichos*. In contrast, Cohen disputes the validity of such interpolation, and on the basis of common Athenian usage argues instead that in Athens *moicheia* referred specifically to illicit intercourse with a married woman. What stands behind this argument?

Committed to the comparative principle that Athens, like other ancient societies, ought to have distinguished "the categories of intercourse with unmarried virgins from intercourse with married women,"[56] Cohen surveys the use of *moicheia* in classical Athenian sources and finds that the term was in fact commonly used of marital violation. So Cohen considers as standard the usage of the women in the *Lysistrata* who swear to have sex with "neither husband nor *moichos.*" Perhaps even more significant is Xenophon's comment in *Hiero* that the *moichos* destroys the *philia* between husband and wife (3.3), and Aristotle's depiction of the *moichos* in the *Eudemian Ethics* as one who has intercourse with a married woman (1221b).

These are indeed significant examples of common usage, but to establish that *moicheia* was typically or normally understood in classi-

cal Athens as "an offense against the marital relation" does not establish that it could be used only in this way or even that this was its
central meaning. In fact, in one of the very few surviving references
to a legal suit involving *moicheia* the woman involved is Phano, the
unmarried daughter of Neaira. Although Phano has been married
previously, there is no indication in Apollodorus' account of the en-
trapment of Epainetos (the poor man is said to have thought he was
visiting a brothel) that Phano "pretends to be married" in order to
carry off the charge of *moicheia*.[57]

I would suggest, then, that the common usage is significant in that
it provides one more indication of the conceptual centrality of marriage as the basis of the household (oikos) in classical Athens. The
highest-profile violation of the interior space of the household would
no doubt usually have been the "violation of marital *philia*."[58] But
given the focus of the term *moichos* on the male and his activity, it is
perhaps not surprising that his female partner could be a more
anonymous "woman of the household." Her semantic anonymity
and passivity do not, however, establish that the woman involved
bore no responsibility, for *moicheia* is not the equivalent of adultery,
but rather a particular activity, carried out by a man called a *moichos,* with women (and preeminently a wife) within the protected
household sphere. It covers an important part but not the whole of
the Athenian view of marital fidelity and infidelity, and thus of what
we call adultery, while on the other hand it can apply to the "corruption" of the entire female household and not just the wife. Thus, as a
legal or moral term its usage is both wider and narrower than the
English word "adultery."

The "Oriental Seclusion" of Athenian Women

The term "female household" just used raises another issue standing
somewhat further behind the modern discussion of Athenian adultery:
the "oriental seclusion" of Athenian women. As Beate Wagner-Hasel
has emphasized, this notion was a key part of the image of the "orient"
created by Europeans in the eighteenth century,[59] which by the nineteenth became a standard "fact" of ancient Greek social history and as
such occasioned expressions of moralizing disapproval from historians and comparisons, explicit or implicit, with the situation of Euro-

pean and American women. To a significant extent, however, modern belief in the seclusion of women, "locked within the squalid, dark, and damp confines of relatively primitive mud-brick houses,"[60] is a result of taking Greek moral and ideological ideas about the proper separation and separate functions of men and women as directly reflecting physical reality. Although there certainly were parts of the Greek (and Athenian) house which could be designated as particularly "female," these were the spaces in which women worked or cared for family members, not in which they were routinely locked. Furthermore, the term *gynaikeion* (or *gynaikonitis*) should not necessarily be taken to refer to one specific room; in practical terms, like the family hearth itself the *gynaikeion* was clearly movable.[61] The women's quarters were, in essence, those places in which the women of the household were working; and it is hardly true that Greek women worked or socialized only in those places. On this subject Cohen draws a useful distinction between separation (men and women have separate public and private spaces and roles in society) and seclusion (women are kept indoors as much as possible):

> Separation of spheres of activity does not imply physical sequestration, and consequently utter subjection, as does seclusion. While it is undeniable that women did not operate in the public and political spheres in the way that men did, it does not necessarily follow that they did not have public, social, and economic spheres of their own, nor that these categories were not fluid and manipulable as opposed to rigid and eternally fixed.[62]

The dominant paradigm of Greek family history not only takes such seclusion or sequestering as given, but also posits an inverse relationship between the development of Athenian democracy and the status of Athenian women, who were sent more emphatically into their houses just as Athenian men took up opportunities for active political participation outside those houses. Furthermore, as Engels in particular developed the paradigm, this democratic order was rooted economically in the system of private property. Athenian women, in an echo of their sex's earlier "world historic defeat," were themselves the subordinate property of the household rather than property owners in their own right. In the context of these assumptions which despite challenges from Cohen and others are still routinely made, the standard view of *moicheia,* as referring generally to the violation of any female member of a man's household and constituting an assault on his male property-owning citizen status as well as his property, has seemed virtually self-evident. The view also has a powerful rhetorical and ideological appeal, in the twentieth as in the eighteenth and nineteenth centuries, resulting in its frequent repetition both within and outside the field of ancient social history. Yet a more nuanced view of the status of Athenian women supports the claim that the celebrated freedom of Athenian democracy belonged in a number of important ways to women as well as to men.

It is probably not necessary to argue at length here against the extreme view that Athenian women and wives were chattel. Evidence for their status as privileged insiders—protected by law, invested with religious responsibility, and included in the inheritance network—is available in any book on Athenian law.[63] The arguments which seem to underlie the more extreme position, "if not property owners with full rights of disposal, then not property owners at all" and "if not property owners, then property," are obviously fallacious. In addition, they fail to appreciate the peculiar character of the Athenian household, which was itself both persons and property.[64] It still may be useful, however, to consider the significance of the "protected" female household envisioned by the law on justifiable homicide, since it is frequently taken as central to the reconstruction of the classical Athenian view on women, their nature, and their position in the polis. The clause ("with wife or mother or sister or daughter or concubine") epitomizes for some critics the Athenian male's fear of the sexuality of the women of his family, whether free or slave, married or virgin, and his resulting anxiety that they be kept under close control ("in seclusion") for the sake of the community—and his own public honor.

An initial problem with this approach is one of historical context. By all accounts the law on justifiable homicide which defines the protected female household has its origins in the predemocratic era of Athenian history. It is not a democratic law and, even if quoted by "democratic" speakers such as Demosthenes, cannot unreflectively be taken as revealing either democratic or classical Athenian attitudes toward the relative place of women and men in the polis and the household, or the democratic Athenian construction of gender.[65] This law belongs to the developing polis institutions of the later seventh century, and seems to reflect the early concern of the polis with establishing and defining the sphere of public action—where, and in what contexts, does the killer come under the authority of the public law?—as well as the preeminent citizen right to the protection of person and property even in circumstances or situations outside the polis' control. In the interior space of the household, as on the battlefield or on the open road, a man could protect himself and those dependent on him, including the *pallake*, or slave concubine, with the use of force without being liable to a charge of murder. The law, and specifically this portion of it, draws a figurative line around the household, similar to that drawn around the polis itself, to clarify the proper spheres of self-help. As it stands, the law makes clear the valid response to an act of aggression in that private household sphere.

Thus, the grouping together of potential female members of the household, both free and slave, reveals not so much a concern about the dangerous promiscuity of all women as the composite character of the household itself, which included both persons and property, free and slave. Not surprisingly, the male head of household was considered the appropriate wielder of force in the defense of that household. Further, although the law as quoted by Demosthenes envisions only action taken against a man for having sexual relations with female members of the household, Athenian (Solonian) law also protected male members of the household, and particularly underaged sons, from physical or sexual assault.[66] The law on justifiable homicide strongly suggests that within the walls of the house—a space as distinct from the public communal space of the polis as was the battlefield or the highway—a man could use force justifiably to protect both that house and its household. It therefore speaks more to the interests of the archaic polis in establishing a public sphere, while at the same time protecting the private sphere, than to a democratic view of women as household property in constant need of control.

When we look more carefully at the evidence of women's activities from the democratic era itself, the picture becomes more complex. Women can be seen to have had economic, social, and religious interests which regularly took them outside the confines of their houses. Women did work outside the home in classical Athens, as is

clear both from the orators and from a number of comic references—even if Aristotle did not directly say as much when he asked
rhetorically and critically, "in a democracy who could prevent the
wives of the poor [citizens] from going out?" (*Politics* 1300a4).
Moreover, as managers of household property women could hardly
remain unaware of the world outside their doors. So, in accounts of
family disputes that found their way into court, we hear of women
standing up for their own economic interests and for those of their
households.[67] Finally, although the undisputable involvement of
Athenian women in public religion is often represented as the exception to their general exclusion from public life, and although for
some modern critics religion is not quite properly part of the public
sphere in any case, the breadth and significance of women's participation in religious rituals and festivals, ranging from serving as
priestess of a major deity to participating in the funeral of a relative,
make the exception outweigh in significance the supposed rule. Classical and democratic Athens was famous for its plenitude of public
festivals, and here it would seem that women as well as men enjoyed
the privileges and prerogatives of membership in this radical and
prosperous democracy. Plato, for one, connects democracy with excessive freedom for both slaves and women (*Republic* 563d), and it
would seem reasonable to take the voicing of concerns by some male
citizens (playwrights, philosophers, or politicians) about women's
proper place as evidence of not a static but a dynamic state of affairs
in gender relations. Democratic Athens, I would suggest, could be a
lively place for both men and women. Recent specialized studies of
women in Athenian society lend support to this idea, but have not
dislodged that general principle of an inverse relation between the
development of Athenian democracy and the status of Athenian
women. This disjunction of specialized study and general paradigm
produces such odd statements as Sue Blundell's conclusion that "for
Athenian women 'citizenship' meant only that they had a share in
the religious, legal and economic order of the Athenian community."[68] The nature of her participation was determined by her sex,
but the Athenian woman was nonetheless a privileged "shareholder"
in the Athenian polis. She was a member of a legally defined and
protected elite, and that membership had real consequences if and
when she should be a party to *moicheia*.

Adultery and the Public Interest

What does Athenian law on *moicheia* suggest about the larger public interest in the *moichos* and his crime—and in the woman *moicheumene* or the household so corrupted? What public danger was there in such behavior? Can it be shown that democratic Athens was interested only in the public consequences of private sexual behavior and not with the behavior itself—that there were in fact no "sexual offenses" in classical Athens?[69]

In arguing this position, Cohen lays great weight upon the well-known words of Pericles in his funeral oration: "we do not get into a state with our next-door neighbor if he enjoys himself in his own way" (Thucydides 2.37)—words which he interprets as including the enjoyment of adultery. Such tolerance is also evident, on Cohen's view, in the construction of laws on *moicheia,* which attempt to control not the act itself but the public violence which is likely to stem from the act of adultery. Thus he goes to some length to argue that there was no Athenian *graphe moicheias*—that is, there was no public suit on the charge of the act of adultery itself, but only suits that had to do with the consequences of adultery or of the apprehension of an adulterer.[70]

The argument about whether adultery itself presented a public threat in democratic Athens cannot rest, however, on the simple existence or nonexistence of a *graphe*. The nature of that threat emerges in both rhetorical and dramatic discussions of *moicheia* and adultery, which are the focus of the next chapter. But the legally prescribed punishment for the woman caught with a *moichos* makes the point quite clearly as well. Such a woman could not continue to live with her husband and could no longer enter the public sanctuaries. If she continued her public religious activities, then she should "suffer with impunity whatever she may suffer, except death."[71] Cohen considers this punishment as essentially private, since it did not mandate public corporal punishment as in other ancient Mediterranean codes, and since, he suggests, she could just marry someone else without loss of status.[72] This inference overlooks both the important factor of the woman's citizen status in protecting her from corporal punishment and the genuinely public character of the punishment she did receive.

First, except in some extreme circumstances, no Athenian citizen, male or female, could be physically tortured or sold into slavery.[73] This protection of the person was a legacy from Solon, and in this respect Athenian women were within the privileged circle of the citizen elite. Thus I suggest that it is this protected citizen status and not the protected private sphere that initially prevented the adulteress from being, for example, publicly whipped or stoned for her offense. From this perspective, both the old "Draconian" condoning of the killing of a man, citizen or not, caught *epi* a female member of the household, and also the "Solonian" rule allowing the sale of a promiscuous daughter, may reflect an earlier traditional social ethic more consonant with that of the rest of the ancient Mediterranean world. The articulation of citizenship and its privileges was a progressively significant feature of classical Athenian democracy, with clear consequences for the punishment of citizen crime, sexual or otherwise. A citizen was a privileged person and a protected body, even if he was charged with being a *moichos* or she with being caught with one.[74] The task undertaken by Lysias in defending Euphiletos, the murderer of a citizen, was not a trivial one.

Second, the punishment of the woman caught with a *moichos*—exclusion from sacred places, expulsion from the oikos, and mandatory divorce—are very public forms of censure. This is essentially the female equivalent of *atimia,* the stripping away of a woman's citizen responsibilities and privileges, based on household and on religion. There is in fact no clear evidence that such a woman could expect to remarry, and if she was so brazen as to continue to participate in religious activities, then she was further stripped of her citizenship by being subject to whatever physical treatment any citizen wanted to inflict upon her except death. If her husband did not divorce her, he too suffered *atimia.*[75] Rather than a lack of interest in private sexual behavior, these punishments suggest a quite vital public interest in household behavior and integrity.

Although marriage and adultery were a part of the classical Athenian social, political, and moral "order of things," neither the institution of marriage nor its violation is defined in formal law alone. Marriage should be understood as the composite process that resulted in the establishment of a legitimate household and underlay the legitimate participation of the Athenian in his or her polis. Marriage is a relationship that is assumed, not defined, in prescriptive law on both familial and political legitimacy, and one that is central to the public image of a well-run or healthy polis. Both the *Antigone* and Apollodorus' speech "Against Neaira" make this last point. Adultery, the betrayal or violation of marriage, on the other hand, finds a very specific legal focus in the figure of the *moichos*, a particular kind of adulterous criminal and sexual thief whose legal identity, however, is considerably less substantial than his rhetorical and dramatic persona. For both Athenian marriage and Athenian adultery, it is especially true that the law needs to be read against the larger social background. The corollary follows that public interest cannot be limited to the sanction of the law alone, but is evident in other pervasive means of social control such as the shame that attends the public charge or reputation as a *moichos* or the isolation that the *moicheumene* will experience even if she is not legally prohibited from remarrying.

Further, the question of to what extent public law and other kinds of social control extended, or transgressed, into the private realm by the noting and marking of those who were properly married and those who were improperly adulterous is complicated by the fact that the oikos had both a public and a private face. It was the focus of the most private and intimate relationships, but also the basis of an individual Athenian's public identity and of the polis' well-being. In addition, as will become clear in the next chapter, private sexual behavior like that of the *moichos* could be taken to reveal important features of public character. Could a *moichos* be a real man and a good soldier? To speak of the public interest's transgressing or not transgressing into the private sphere implies the existence of fixed and defined boundaries. In classical Athens, however, those boundaries were considerably more fluid than is allowed in contemporary modern arguments on the sanctity of the private realm. When the interests of the larger polis family seemed to require certain private behavior, as in the case of the heiress, or to prohibit it, as in the case of the *moichos,* even the most intimate family relationships were subject to public scrutiny. In sum, the household had both a public and a private face, and household roles and responsibilities had both public and private significance.

Plato on Marriage and Adultery

Just as Plato's regulation of the marriage of the heiress, where the personal suitability of a groom is secondary to the larger interests of the community, provides a valuable commentary on the inheritance law of his society, so also his legislation on marriage and adultery further illuminates, as well as complicates, the nature of public interest in private behavior in his native polis. Plato has more of interest to say on this subject, particularly in his last dialogue, the *Laws*, than is generally recognized; and his acknowledgment that law is only one, and not necessarily the most effective, way of ensuring proper behavior is an effective antidote to the narrow focus on the *graphe moicheias* in modern discussions. Similarly, Plato's view of adultery is significantly broader than the term *moicheia* (which he avoids), as his view of marriage is broader than *gamos* or *engye*, and in this respect as well his perspective is a useful one.

As in the *Republic,* marriage in the *Laws* is a citizen's duty, a service to both gods and the city (773e). Unlike the system envisioned in the *Republic,* however, where couples are paired in public marriage festivals on the basis of eugenics (459a–e), in the *Laws* the young male citizen, though advised how best to choose a spouse, makes his own choice of "a congenial and suitable match for the common procreation of children" (772e). Following traditional Athenian practice, the woman is betrothed (through *engye*) by her father or, in his absence, by her paternal or, if those are also lacking, her maternal male relatives. Next Plato turns to the ceremonies of marriage and the "rites it may be proper to fulfill before, during, or after the nuptials," for which he says the "exponents of religious law" should be consulted. The specific reference to these rites, which are particularly important to Plato in his emphasis on the sacred character of human marriage, is a useful reminder that Athenian marriage was a social process with many components, including ritual, not all of which were legally or formally regulated. Finally, like Solon, Plato also regulated the economic transactions and household festivities surrounding marriage, prohibiting dowries and limiting expense (774c–d, 775a–b).

Where Plato most notably parted company from the rules of his own society was in the legal requirement that his citizens enter into such marriages, in his formal surveillance of their behavior by female officials during a ten-year period devoted to the production of children, and in his recognition of adultery as a symmetrical offense in its modern sense—as the infidelity of either partner within a marriage. The punishments Plato outlines for failure to marry and for adultery are remarkably complex and reveal an interesting recognition of the uses and the limits of both traditional penalties and also of honor and shame as controls for citizens' private behavior.

Failure to marry presents the simpler case, but shows clearly Plato's two-part strategy. If a man refuses to marry, and comes to the age of thirty-five unmarried,

> he shall pay a yearly fine of a hundred drachmas if he belongs to the wealthiest class, of seventy if to the second, of sixty for the third and thirty for the fourth, and this fine shall be dedicated to Hera. He that defaults in his yearly payment shall be indebted ten times the amount. Payment shall be enforced by the treasurer of that goddess, who shall be liable himself to the debt in case of nonexaction, and all shall be bound to render account of such matters at the audits. This shall be the pecuniary penalty of refusal to marry.

And then, Plato continues:

> As to marks of honor from his juniors, the offender shall receive none, and no junior, if he can help it, shall show him any deference whatsoever. If he presume to chastise any of them, all shall come to the support and defense of the injured party, and any citizen present who fails in this shall be legally proclaimed a coward and a bad [kakos] man.[76]

There is no question but that Plato knew the strength of public honor and shame in his own society, and also that he wanted to put it to use in the support of his marriage laws. His laws on adultery are particularly interesting both in this respect and for the way in which they articulate the relative spheres of public and private interest and behavior. Plato actually legislates on adultery twice in the *Laws*, in book 6, following the marriage rules discussed above, and again in book 8, in the context of a discussion on the control of natural passions. It is immediately striking that he does not use the terms or labels *moichos* or *moicheia* at all in these passages but rather describes the offense itself, for example at 784: "if a husband has intercourse with another woman or a wife with another man . . . ," and the penalty follows. The language is both general and symmetrical. Plato was certainly familiar with the terms *moichos* and *moicheia* and their connotations, as is evident, for example, in his telling of the story of Gyges' *moicheia* in the *Republic,* or in Aristophanes' myth of the origin of the sexes and of *moichoi* and *moicheutriai* in the *Symposium.* In the *Laws* as well he uses the phrase "all kinds of *moicheiai*" when discussing the dangers of sexual passions of all sorts, but in regulating marriage it is clear that he has in mind not simply *moicheia* but adultery in a broader sense, as committed by either husband or wife with any sexual partner other than his or her spouse. For the husband, this explicitly includes homosexual or slave partners. Certainly, says the Athenian to his elderly companions, humans ought to be no worse than birds and other animals who, after choosing a spouse, "live in a pious and law-abiding way, firmly faithful to the promises they made when they first fell in love."[77]

Plato's discussion of adultery (and not *moicheia*) in book 6 begins somewhat indirectly with the role of the female supervisors of marriage, who are supposed to report on any "wife or husband of childbearing age . . . who is concerned with anything but the duties imposed by him or her at the time of the sacrifices and rites of their marriage" (784a). Somewhat later he notes that "if some dispute arises about the duties and interest of the parties," they should find arbitrators and abide by their decision, while the supervisors of marriage should "enter their houses" and "by a combination of admonition and threats try to make them give up their ignorant and sinful ways." If these efforts are unsuccessful, *then* the case should become public and the names of the offending parties posted. Unless the accused can prove that the charge is unfounded, by convicting in court the one who posted his or her name, then he or she is excluded from weddings and parties celebrating the birth of children. If he continues to attend, he can be beaten by anyone who wishes to do so. The female offender is likewise excluded from female processions and distinctions, as well as weddings and birthday parties, and can be beaten if she continues to attend.

All of that has been said without direct reference to what the parties have actually done. When Plato turns next to what should be done if one of the parties is beyond the official childbearing years, he refers more explicitly to adultery:

> When children have been produced as demanded by law, if a husband has intercourse with another woman, or a wife with another man, and the other party is still of an age to bear children, they must suffer the same penalty as was specified for those who are still having children.[78]

And finally:

> After the period of childbearing, the chaste [*sophron*] man or woman should be highly respected and the promiscuous should be held in the opposite kind of "repute" (though disrepute would be a better word). When the majority of people conduct themselves with moderation in sexual matters, no such regulations should be mentioned or enacted; but if there is misbehavior, regulations should be made and enforced after the pattern of the laws just laid down.[79]

Thus in book 6 Plato gives prime importance to sexual fidelity during the childbearing years of marriage, certainly with an eye to the legitimacy of children. But since the husband is also limited to one partner during his procreative years, there is also an implicit suggestion (made explicit in book 8) that the partnership of procreative marriage benefits from a certain amount of *philia* and loyalty. But after the required years of procreation, Plato seems to suggest that discreet or "moderate" adultery can be tolerated though not approved. But if matters get out of hand, the law or its agent will step in. Again there is here a clear criterion for establishing public interest in sexual behavior.

When Plato returns to the subject of adultery in book 8 it is in connection with the larger class of illicit sexual behaviors which do not have the purpose of producing legitimate children, including homosexual relations as well as relations with female prostitutes or concubines (838e, 841e). He now divides his analysis somewhat differently, but on recognizably similar principles. The best solution, he argues, would be for the same "unwritten law" that keeps people from committing incest to apply to these behaviors as well. People would thus be brought to believe that adultery, as well as homosexuality and recourse to prostitutes, was "absolutely unholy and an abomination in the sight of the gods." The next-best solution relies not on religious awe but on shame—such behavior should carry a sense of shame that would ensure that it would remain within the private realm (841). "If a man does have intercourse with any woman (hired or procured in some other way) except the wife he wed in holy marriage with the blessing of the gods, he must do so without any other man or woman getting to know about it." Then, as a last resort, "if he fails to keep the affair secret" Plato declares such a man *atimos*—he strips him of his citizenship—"on the grounds that he is no better than an alien" (841e).

So Plato attempts to find a way to reconcile the public interest of his polis in productive households, legitimate children, and in general a self-controlled and pious citizenry, with what he recognizes as the most unruly and necessary of human passions. There is, in fact, a protected private sphere in Plato's polis, but one protected by the citizens' sense of respect and shame, not by the laws themselves. In Plato's *Laws,* as in Plato's Athens, formal laws with formal penalties are only part of the way in which, to quote Solon, *Eunomia* ("good order" and "good law")

> levels rough places, stops Glut and Greed, takes the force from
>   Violence
>   . . . dries up the growing flowers of Despair as they grow
> . . . straightens out crooked judgments given, gentles the swollen
>   ambitions, and puts an end to acts of divisional strife.[80]

Another recourse lay, as Plato saw, in the common education the community received through its religious festivals and political institutions. In the next chapter I will consider what Athenians learned about the public significance of adultery in dramas on stage and oratory in court and what this theme suggests for understanding the place of the household in the democratic polis.

ADULTERY ONSTAGE
AND IN COURT

Two of the most distinctive features of democratic Athens were its public theater and its popular courts, both of which gathered together a large proportion of the population for open reflection on questions and cases of interest to the community as a whole. The close connection between the two institutions is apparent in the interconnections of their genre: Athenian drama is notable for the rhetorical character of its dialogue, and Athenian oratory for its sense of high drama. Following the treatment of adultery in the theater and the law courts should enlarge our understanding of the public significance of private morality and behavior within the oikos.

The Fifth-Century Drama of Adultery

That adultery is a significant theme in Athenian drama is neither surprising nor unrecognized. With its triangular plot and inevitable intrigue, adultery is an inherently dramatic story. It is also a theme deeply embedded in the common Greek literary and mythic tradition of which the Athenians partook.[1] There are few if any cultural traditions in which this theme is not significant, but adultery is hardly a culturally monotonous or uniform literary motif. Rather, the story of adultery displays in the many varieties of its telling and retelling the differing, and at times contradictory, interests of the audiences to which it is told. The adultery triangle is the structural constant to which each storyteller and each society add their variables, thereby making the story or drama of adultery a signally important historical key for the social history of marriage and the family.[2] And just as the stories of the adultery of Guinevere, Hester Prynne, Emma Bovary, or Mrs. Johnson in Madison County, Iowa, reveal both their authors and their audiences,[3] so also the Athenian popular theater, and especially the drama of Clytemnestra and her family, can help reveal the moral values and tensions surrounding the theme of marriage and its violation in fifth-century Athens.

The ancient Greek "drama of adultery" begins with Homer, who provides the archetype or archetypes for later Athenian dramatic variations. Of the two Homeric epics, the *Iliad* is motivated directly by a very famous act of adultery and its consequences.[4] But the *Odyssey* is actually richer in stories of adultery, real and potential, and none more celebrated than the elegant story of divine adultery sung by Demodokos at the Phaeacian court. The rhapsode sings of the love of Ares and Aphrodite and "of how first they lay together in the house of Hephaestus secretly; and Ares gave her many gifts, and shamed the bed of the lord Hephaestus."[5] But, as it happens, Hephaestus is alerted to this deception by ever-watchful Helios and sets a snare to bring the adultery to the attention of all the Olympians. Ares and Aphrodite are caught in Hephaestus' bonds, "fine as spider webs" (290); and, answering Hephaestus' call, the gods gather to observe the culprits and oversee a settlement. Despite some laughter and wishful thinking from the brothers Hermes and Apollo, the matter requires formal settlement, and only when assured by Poseidon that Ares' *moichagria* (*moichos* money) will be paid does Hephaestus loose the two gods from their bonds, allowing them to go their merry separate ways (359–365).

In this brief and essentially lighthearted story, we have a distinctly comic representation of Ares as a divine *moichos*, although Homer does not use the term. Caught in Hephaestus' bed with Hephaestus' spouse, even the warrior god must submit both to public shame and to the fine named especially for his crime. But as *moichos*, Ares represents only one element of what might be called the "adultery plot" as it appears in later Athenian literature. In addition to the handsome adulterer who brings gifts to his quite willing partner, there is the aggrieved husband who is determined to catch the adulterers "in the act" even at the price of public ridicule, the public witnesses (friends or relatives) who assemble to verify the crime, and of course the wife herself. The story ends with a publicly sanctioned penalty, and the case is closed. Still, as an archetype for mortal adultery, this story is obviously incomplete. For whereas mortal adultery could at times be a source of laughter like the story of Ares and Aphrodite, and Aristophanes later gave his distinctive comic stamp to the theme, this offense was also the source of violence and tragedy. Mortality and its corollary, the need for children to reproduce the family and household, complicated the story in the human realm and added the element of tragedy.

The Human Tragedy: The Oresteia

Looking again to the *Odyssey,* and now to its mortal heroes, it is clear that from the opening lines (1.23–41) the dark story of adulterous Clytemnestra and murdered Agamemnon shadows the romantic adventures of Odysseus and the steadfast faithfulness of Penelope. Helen's infidelity was perhaps more celebrated, but as developed and amplified on the Athenian stage, Clytemnestra's was more tragic. In Aeschylus' *Oresteia* the image and memory of Helen haunt the chorus (*Agamemnon* 681 ff.), but the tragic action of the trilogy begins with Clytemnestra. As the story is told and retold by successive poets, Clytemnestra, her husband, Agamemnon, her paramour, Aegisthus, and indeed the entire household repeatedly act out the drama of adultery on the Athenian stage, so revealing in powerful ways the nature and significance of adultery in the public realm. In the *Oresteia* (produced in 458) and again in the Electra plays of Sophocles and Euripides (420–410 and 413) we observe the crime of Clytemnestra and Aegisthus as dramatized for a popular audience at either end of an extraordinarily creative and turbulent half-century of Athenian history which saw the rise and fall of Athens' empire and her democracy.

From the opening of Aeschylus' trilogy, it is clear that adultery is rooted in and also productive of violence; it is an integral part of the perversion of the natural order of things afflicting the royal house of Atreus.[6] Violence is not simply provoked by Clytemnestra's adultery; it is the expression of it.[7] The words of the watchman, sitting "dog-like" on the roof of the house, are full of shameful reticence about what has happened and foreboding about what is about to happen within that house ruled by a queen who "maneuvers like a man" (11). Of what has gone on within the walls of the house, he will say nothing:

> The ox is on my tongue,
> Aye, but the *oikos* and these old stones,
> give them a voice and what a tale they'd tell.
> And so would I, gladly . . .
> I speak to those who know; to those who don't
> my mind's a blank. I never say a word.[8]

Long before Agamemnon returned from Troy, we learn, his oikos has been shamed and corrupted by Clytemnestra's and Aegisthus' adultery, and as the drama proceeds the crimes of adultery and murder are shown to be inextricable. Clytemnestra's single-handed murder of Agamemnon is the culmination of her earlier betrayal and the end of the complex "tale" that the watchman refuses to tell. This murder is Clytemnestra's alone, but violence has pervaded and perverted the household even before Agamemnon's departure. In justifying her act to the chorus, Clytemnestra asserts that the murder she committed "by this right hand" is a "masterpiece of justice," a rightful act of vengeance for Agamemnon's sacrifice of their daughter Iphigenia, the "wealth of the household" and the offspring of their love.[9] But in the midst of this entangled family love and family violence, the chorus and Cassandra see only an act of horrifying pride and daring—not justice but rather a perversion of the right order of the household. So Cassandra has cried out earlier in her prophetic frenzy: "what outrage—the woman kills the man."[10]

Listening to Clytemnestra and seeing the dead body of their king, the chorus is inspired to widen the circle of corruption and violence, conjuring up the image of a wild, demonic Helen—"out-of-her-mind [*paranous*] Helen" (1455)—who destroyed so many Greek men at Troy. By linking the crime of adultery with public death and violence in this way, and by insisting on the active agency of Clytemnestra in both adultery and murder, Aeschylus unmistakably highlights the female role in adultery and suggests that neither its effects nor its causes can be contained within the walls of the house. Since the corruption will come one way or another into the public realm, it must be forcibly avenged and brought before the light of day.

That task of public vengeance belongs to Agamemnon's son, Orestes, who returns from exile in the second play of the trilogy, *The Libation Bearers,* in order to restore the order of the house by killing first his mother and then her partner Aegisthus. Just as Aeschylus insisted before on Clytemnestra's agency, so here the deeds are Orestes' alone. His sister Electra, for all her devotion to her father and hatred of her mother's crime, cannot herself act as either judge or avenger.[11] Those properly masculine roles which Clytemnestra usurped, even if with right, Electra leaves to her brother Orestes. Orestes' vengeance, however, becomes problematic as soon as it is accomplished. It is right and justifiable for a son to kill his mother's partner in adultery (the intrusive *moichos,* although the word is not used here) in order to protect the interests of the house. Is it also right to kill his mother?

Standing over the two dead bodies, as Clytemnestra stood over those of Agamemnon and Cassandra, Orestes makes clear his judgment that the crime of both was the violation of marriage. Displaying the very robes in which Agamemnon was trapped and killed, he calls upon Helios (still, as in the *Odyssey,* "the one who watches over all") to look upon the "shameless deeds of his mother" and make them publicly known. Taking the easier case first, however, Orestes claims that Aegisthus' death is simply the carrying out of the letter of the law, a matter of *nomos.* "Aegisthus, why mention him? The one who shames dies. An old custom, justice."[12] But for Clytemnestra he has words that are more fierce by far:

> But she who plotted this horror against her husband,
> she carried his children, growing in her womb
> and she—I loved her once
> and now I loathe, I have to loathe—what is she
> Some moray eel, some viper born to rot her mate
> with a single touch, no fang to strike him,
> just the wrong, the reckless fury in her heart.[13]

The crime Orestes describes is not simply murder or *moicheia* but the murderous betrayal of marriage and husband and, as becomes clear in this second play of the trilogy, the household as well. Adultery is a crime of corruption rather than of simple aggression, and Clytemnestra has destroyed and corrupted what she should have preserved. So Cassandra had prophesied: the bedmate became the deathmate.

In the *Agamemnon* Aeschylus reveals Agamemnon's deadly betrayal of his own child, the "wealth" of his own household, as a possible motivating factor in his death at the hands of his wife. In the second play of the trilogy Clytemnestra also dies as a traitor to those she should have nurtured and supported, her children Electra and Orestes. At the grave of Agamemnon, Electra complains: "Mother has pawned us for a man, Aegisthus, her partner in her murdering. I go like a slave, Orestes driven from his estates while they, they roll in the fruits of all your labors, magnificent and sleek."[14] The perversion of Clytemnestra's maternal role is revealed in her terrifying dream in which she bore, swaddled, and nursed not a human child, but a snake—a snake which, as she recognizes too late, grows up not to support its mother but to destroy her.

In emphasizing the betrayal of both husband and children inherent in Clytemnestra's adultery, Aeschylus makes it clear that her crime is against the household as a whole and not simply against Agamemnon or, even less, his patriline. It is a crime against the living household, as was Agamemnon's murder of Iphigenia. In contrast with the usual modern emphasis on adultery on endangering the family lineage, Orestes does not charge his mother with polluting the paternal line with bastard children, but with plotting against the man whose children she had already borne (992) and thereby depriving those children of their rightful place in the household.[15] The mother who was once *philos* is now *echthros* (hostile, an enemy; 993), a clear sign of the perverted state of this household. Orestes' interest in revenge is rooted in a present and pressing need for an inheritance. He wants to avenge his father by killing his murderers, but beyond that filial duty—for which he needs a lot of encouragement from Apollo—stands practical self-interest: "Besides, the lack of patrimony presses hard" (301). Despite some modern assumptions to the contrary, it is not the dead ancestors who are offended by Clytemnestra's adultery, but the living members of her now ruined household. "Up from nothing," Orestes prays to Zeus, "rear a *domos* [house] to greatness."[16]

The troubles of this household of course extend back to previous generations, and repeatedly feature the murder of children and adultery of husband and wife.[17] But the fact that the violence is recurrent and passed down from one generation to the next does not in any way undercut the position taken here that in this trilogy adultery is essentially represented as a complex crime of corruption directed against a household rather than a lineage. Indeed, insofar as the acts of violence against children, infidelity toward spouses, corruption of oikos, and the destruction of a polis are all inextricably connected, the story of the *Oresteia* reinforces the image of adultery as the destruction of the many-stranded web of household relationships rather than simply the adulteration of a single paternal line. By taking as her lover Aegisthus, who is her husband's own paternal cousin and the one surviving child of Thyestes, Clytemnestra significantly intensifies the crime of adultery.[18]

The complex interweaving of violence and adultery in this tragedy makes it difficult to find only one guilty party. In the *Agamemnon* Aeschylus allows Clytemnestra the defense, effectively supported by the chorus' haunting memory, that Agamemnon himself had betrayed his own house and household by killing Iphigenia, the wealth of the house and product of their love. If the oikos, persons and property, demands loyalty and protection, then both Agamemnon and Clytemnestra were guilty of its betrayal. The question lingers: killing the adulterer Aegisthus was a simple, straightforward, and traditional act; but could it really be just for a son to kill a mother?

This difficult question requires the change of venue to Athens and the establishment of a public court of law under the guidance of Athena herself. The arguments used in this court by Apollo and the Furies raise interesting questions about Athenian attitudes toward kinship and reproduction, and about the extent to which a single character should be taken to represent either Aeschylus' own view or the *communis opinio*. Here, however, it may be enough to note that Athena does not accept *either* litigant's extreme position, but says— as she casts the final, deciding vote in favor of Orestes:

> I cannot set more store by the wife's death,
> she who killed her husband, guardian of their house [*episkopon domaton*].[19]

So the new public court brings an end to the violence within the royal house of Argos. In no manner, however, is Agamemnon's act of violence against his household condoned; rather, his proper role and responsibility as "guardian" is made explicit and emphasized. Both he and Clytemnestra were properly, in her words, the "watch-dogs" of their house (607, 896), but both betrayed that role. Athena's persuasive words to the Furies,

> Here in our homeland never cast the stones
>   that whet our bloodlust. Never waste our youth,
> inflaming them with the burning wine of strife.
> Never pluck the heart of the battle cock
>   and plant it in our people—intestine war
> seething against themselves. Let our wars
>   rage on abroad [*thyraios*], with all their force, to satisfy
> our powerful lust for fame. But as for the bird
>   that fights at home [*ornithos enoikiou*]—my curse on civil
>   war,[20]

make unmistakably clear the connection between what is inside the house *(enoikios)* and what is outside *(thyraios),* and between the well-being of the household and polis *eunomia.*

"Give joy in return for joy,/one common will for love,/and hate with one strong heart," say the Furies,[21] who are now the public defenders of marriage and marital fertility—and therefore also the avengers of adultery, a corruption of that common love and a form of civil war. By transforming the character and domain of the Furies in this way Aeschylus' *Oresteia* makes a powerful case for the public significance of adultery, that is, the betrayal of marriage and the marital relationship, not simply as an offense against the patrilineal line or patriarchal authority,[22] but as an offense against the oikos/household itself, which is itself the microcosm of the polis. Clytemnestra is guilty because she betrayed and killed her partner, her fellow watchdog, and took inside instead a "wolf" who was hardly a man. Certainly the oikos is corrupted and "sick" not because of any adulteration of the patriline but because of the violation of responsibility, perversion of male/female roles, and the exclusion of existing children from rightful inheritance.

In the *Oresteia* adultery is indeed that "bird that fights at home," analogous to civil war and having deadly effects for the whole community. It seems therefore quite difficult to separate the sexual from the economic or political elements of this crime, or to make a clear demarcation between a public interest in potential violence and a lack of public interest in sexual behavior. The violence against persons and property engendered by adultery would seem to be not an accidental but an essential element of the tragic vision of the violated marriage.

The *Oresteia* premiered in Athens in 458, just four years after a major democratic reform of the Athenian "constitution." The details of this reform are not entirely clear, and the actual reformers are somewhat mysterious,[23] but one of its main results seems to have been the encouragement of popular participation in Athenian public life and decision-making by the entrusting of public business to three large public bodies: the full citizen assembly; the popular courts, with a total of 6,000 daily jurors at work; and the council *(boule)* of 500 citizens. The last group, which served as the closest thing in the classical Athenian democracy to a representative executive council, was selected by lot each year from previously selected candidates who were allowed to have served only once before.[24] To the extent that classical Athens was a fully participatory democracy, it was the assembly, the courts, and the council that made her so.

The democratic reforms of 462 were made possible and perhaps even necessary by the rise of Athens to a position of military and economic dominance in the Aegean, propelled by her role in the Persian wars of 480–479. In the heady decades of the 460s and 450s, Athens was becoming an imperial power, and the empire generated public business for all three of the main democratic bodies. Empires, however, produce enemies as well, and in the year the *Oresteia* was first performed the Athenians were in the third year of a war with the Spartans and their allies, bogged down in a disastrous campaign in Egypt, and also aggressively pursuing their interests in the northern Aegean.[25] There were also, perhaps inevitably, enemies within. Thucydides reports for the year immediately following the production of the *Oresteia* that "there was a party in Athens who were secretly negotiating with [the Spartans] in the hope of putting an end to democratic government."[26]

This was the political climate in which Aeschylus presented to the Athenian public, now gathered as theater audience, the story of the household of Agamemnon and Clytemnestra, a story which ends with Orestes' pledge of eternal Argive military alliance and the Furies' blessing of Athens, including a prayer to "give joy in return for joy, one common will for love, and hate with one strong heart." A tale of domestic strife ends with a call for communal and political solidarity. Although Aeschylus' personal political views, specifically his view of radical democratic reform, are a vexed issue which may be in the end unresolvable, the way in which the *Oresteia* represents the household as both a political community in itself and also a building block of the larger political community of the polis reflects the increasing politicization of Athenian life attendant on the growing involvement of Athenians in the public realm. Aeschylus is relatively uninterested in Aegisthus, a straightforward villain, a *moichos* in fact if not in tragic diction, with a straightforward crime. His new focus on Clytemnestra results in an image of adultery as essentially a political crime, insofar as it corrupts the relationships of the household necessary for active participation of both men and women in that household and in the community at large. *Philoi* become *echthroi,* and civil war comes indoors.

Similarly, when the conflict moves to the level of the polis, the public justice that is dispensed with Athena's help restores order to the community as a whole. As the Furies are convinced to become the guardians of household relations and well-being, so also the participation of men and women in the now rightly ordered community is made clear. The "best of the Athenians" (men; 487) are established as a court of public law, while the "bright eye of the land of Theseus" (women; 1025–26) publicly escort the Furies to their new home. Aeschylus thus emphasizes and celebrates community participation as rooted in family and household relationships, and suggests that the greatest threat to the political community of Athens lies in corruption and betrayal from within rather than simple aggression from without. It was Clytemnestra's crime and its punishment, not Aegisthus', that necessitated the move from the Argive royal palace to the public court of Athens.

So Aeschylus told the story in 458 when Athens was still in the early years of her adventure with participatory democracy and aggressive imperialism. When Sophocles and Euripides undertook to tell the same story roughly a half-century later, the empire was in its last hours, and democracy itself was headed for a dramatic if temporary collapse. What significance could adultery have now? What public interest did it provoke?

Adultery in the Two Electras

In both Sophocles' and Euripides' plays titled *Electra* the adultery of Aegisthus and Clytemnestra is seen through the eyes of the next generation, children of the household whose lives it has corrupted. In these two plays, as in Plato's *Laws*, adultery is indeed "impious marriage" *(anosios gamos)*, whose consequences, like those of the impious union in the tragedy of Oedipus, are played out in the following generation. The grimness of the story's ending in both plays is striking. Both end with acts of murder. Unlike the *Oresteia*, in which Orestes is in the end restored to his rightful position in Argos and the Furies are established in a place rightfully theirs in Athens, these dramas offer little or no hope that the public world can restore order to the private or that the moral order can be restored. The end of the *Oresteia* envisions a harmony between household and polis order, with civil war kept out of both, and looks specifically to a beneficial alliance between the newly righted Argive royal household and the polis of Athens. The endings of the two *Electras*, even if not necessarily their authors' final word, are notably pessimistic—Sophocles' cryptically so and Euripides' more openly. By the end of Euripides' *Electra*, not only is the family of Agamemnon and Clytemnestra essentially "dismembered" rather than restored, but the representation of adultery itself comes from a mind already sick with its corruption and violence.

Despite its title, the action of Sophocles' *Electra* is primarily the return and revenge of Orestes. As in the *Oresteia*, Electra presents a distinct contrast to Clytemnestra, that unwomanly "man-hearted" active agent of revenge. Orestes takes revenge both for himself and for Electra, first upon his mother and then upon her partner in adultery. As he takes Aegisthus indoors to his death, Orestes offers the rather hollow rationalization:

> Justice shall be taken
> directly on all who act above the law—
> justice by killing. So we would have fewer villains.[27]

The lines seem appropriate to Aegisthus, who as in the *Oresteia* presents a quite unambiguous case. The *nomos* is clear, so Orestes claimed in the earlier play, that "the one who shames [the marriage bed] dies." By taking Aegisthus indoors to the scene of his crimes, Sophocles' Orestes might be seen as retroactively carrying out the justified homicide of a *moichos* taken "in the act." Aegisthus is a villain pure and simple, and the punishment follows accordingly. Apparently taken in by the confidence of Orestes' statement, and forgetting the morally complicated and complicating earlier murder of his mother, the chorus joins in with words of blind congratulation:

> O race of Atreus, how many sufferings
> were yours before you came at last so hardly
> to freedom, perfected by this day's deed.[28]

If indeed it were simply a matter of punishing the single villain, the chorus' words might be justified; but as has been argued here, adultery is a complex crime whose effects implicate the entire household and especially its children and heirs. Sophocles' ending is in fact belied by all that precedes, and in particular by Electra's bitter feuding words with members of her own family.

Any hope Orestes might have had at the opening of the play that his was the relatively simple task of taking "revenge for my father's murder on those that did the murder"[29] is undercut by Electra's colloquies with the chorus of women and with her sister, which illuminate the impious crime of adultery as inseparable from Agamemnon's murder. It was, says Electra, Clytemnestra *and* Aegisthus "the bed-partner" who together "split his head with a murderous ax." She prays for vengeance to the Furies, "who look upon both men who die unjustly and also marriage-beds which are stolen away." The chorus agrees that this was a crime rooted in illicit passion, saying, "craft was the contriver, passion the killer," and later calls again on the "bronze-footed" Fury to light upon such "unhallowed, unwedded struggles of a murder stained and unlawful love."[30] It is clear to both Electra and the chorus that this impious love has perverted and "made sick" (e.g., 1070) the entire household. Clytemnestra has been seduced and drawn away from her proper role by the *kakos* (evil) man with whom she now cohabits and breeds children: the use of the descriptive language of marriage—live with, have children with—emphasizes the way in which Clytemnestra's adultery is the perversion of the marital relationship. She has driven out her legitimate children (589) and destroys what is rightfully their inheritance by turning it over to Aegisthus, who, as Orestes later charges, "drains my father's wealth by luxury or waste" (1289). Clytemnestra is just barely allowed to justify herself with the claim that there is no hubris in her actions, rather only justice taken against Agamemnon, who dared to kill their child Iphigenia. But her position is undercut by Electra and Orestes, who bitterly accuse her not simply for her role in murdering their father, but even more for her lack of self-control over the passion which seduced her and for her failure to protect her children and preserve their rightful patrimony. Killing Aegisthus may indeed have rid the world of one villain, but could it restore a household now corrupted from within, first by adultery and now by matricide? Sophocles definitely leaves the question open.

In Euripides' *Electra* the sickness of adultery has even more pointedly infected the next generation. With a typically interesting twist, Euripides presents the crime of adultery largely through the hate-ridden eyes of the daughter. He also further complicates the moral perspective of the drama by undermining the piety and justice of the punishment meted out to both Aegisthus and Clytemnestra. Orestes kills Aegisthus out-of-doors, while a guest at the sacrifice and feast in honor of the nymphs. He thus kills Aegisthus not "in the act" of adultery but rather in an act of piety and hospitality. Can this be just? Similarly, Electra lures Clytemnestra to her death with a deceptive request for a mother's help in the traditional rituals following childbirth, and only after the deed is done is it clear that she, who might be seen as actually living Clytemnestra's punishment for adultery in her exclusion from both a real marriage and religious rituals, is as guilty as her mother. She, like Clytemnestra, claims responsibility ("I touched the sword beside your hand"; 1225), and she has also killed one who is "both *philos* and not *philos*" (1230).

Electra's entanglement in the complex corruption of her own household is revealed by the way in which she imagines and reconstructs the adultery of Aegisthus and her mother, and insists, against her brother's doubts, on the necessity of matricide. From the outset, completely absorbed in her own suffering, Electra emphasizes the way in which her mother's murderous and unholy adultery with Aegisthus has pushed her from her rightful place. Their illicit sexual union has denied her both a place in the household and a respectable marriage of her own. In her opening soliloquy she complains:

> . . . she, Tyndareus' deadly daughter
> has thrown me out like dirt from the house, to her husband's
>   joy,
> and while she breeds new children in Aegisthus' bed
> has made me and Orestes aliens to her love.[31]

Later, in conversation with the chorus of Mycenaean women, she says:

> And I! I in a peasant's hut
> waste my life like wax in the sun,
> thrust and barred from my father's home
> to a scarred mountain exile
> while my mother rolls in her bloody bed
> and plays at love with a stranger.[32]

The resentful contrast between her view of her mother's sexual promiscuity and her own self-imposed chastity is clear.

For Orestes, on the other hand, the preeminent issues are requital for his father's murder and regaining his inheritance. And in this undertaking, he is entirely on his own. When first recognized by his *paedagogus* (tutor) and then by his sister, Orestes asks how, when, and with whom he should act. To these questions the *paedagogus* responds that vengeance will not be by plot or nighttime attack, but

> In your own hand and the grace of god you hold all poised
> to capture back your city, place, and patrimony.[33]

And so it happens. With Aegisthus killed off first, however, it becomes possible for Orestes to have second thoughts: "hold off a little, we might find another plan." Electra rebukes him for his pity and warns him not to fall into "unmanliness."[34] The charge gains force from her earlier attack on the dead Aegisthus, spat out over his dead body. If Electra could have spoken the word *moichos,* she would have done so in this bitter attack on her mother's lover, for the image she draws of Aegisthus is precisely that. Aegisthus, on Electra's view, was a man who got what he wanted with money and good looks—not a "real man" but a nighttime seducer weaker than and subordinate to the woman he seduced. And, she says knowingly, he would no doubt in turn have been cuckolded himself. For herself, Electra wants none of this girlish-faced man but rather someone of "manly ways," a man who would father warlike sons and not one whose "good looks were ornamental only at the dance."[35] Her fantasy of even the possibility of an affair with Aegisthus is a clear sign of her own emotional and sexual instability. Continuing to reveal herself further in her confrontation with her mother, Electra creates a caricature of the wanton and promiscuous wife that distances her from the real woman she is about to kill.

Electra brushes aside Clytemnestra's frank admission that in addition to Agamemnon's sacrifice of their daughter Iphigenia, her act was especially driven by the fact that the sacrifice was made "for the sake of Helen's lust and for the man / who took a wife and could not punish her seducer."[36] Furthermore, Agamemnon's return with Cassandra as a second "bride" for his own house had added fuel to her anger. Electra does not hear. Instead of allowing her mother to present herself as a wife trying to uphold the privilege of her position in the face of unequal social rules, and driven to desperate measures only by the treatment she has received, Electra concocts an image of a totally promiscuous woman, disloyal to her husband the day he walked out the door, or even before:

> you, long before your daughter came near sacrifice,
> the very hour your husband marched away from home,
> you were setting your brown curls by the bronze mirror's light.
> Now any woman who works on her beauty when her man
> is gone from home indicts herself as being a whore.[37]

In her own absorption with what she has lost through Clytemnestra's adultery, and perhaps in her jealousy of her mother's independence and sexuality, Electra adopts the extreme view of woman as sexual temptress and "the enemy within." This, together with the similarly typecast figure of Aegisthus, essentially the unmanly and weak *moichos,* lends Electra's version of events the air of embittered comic parody. And indeed, the adultery drama as she creates it bears some resemblance to the representations of *moicheia* in comedy.

Thus Euripides presents the crime of adultery from the particular and often peculiar perspective of the children who are its victims. Orestes returns to exact a revenge that Electra is incompetent to achieve on her own—both to punish the "godless defilers" (*anosious miastoras;* 683) and to reclaim his rightful place in polis and oikos. Clytemnestra's adultery has alienated both children from their own household and so prevented them from coming of age as full members of their community and polis. Electra cannot or will not marry or take part in religious festivals with other women. Orestes' *atimia*—loss of honor and status in his own community—is even more apparent. So we see that the corruption of adultery has settled on the next generation, affecting their lives and, especially for Electra, the very perception of those lives.

The moral significance and public danger of adultery are further revealed in Euripides' repeated use in *Electra* of the word *anosios* in reference to both the adulterers and their act.[38] As noted in the previous chapter, Plato used the same language. Such usage reflects but also intensifies the clear ideological commitment to Athenian marriage as the cornerstone of Athenian public order that had been signaled fifty years earlier in the *Oresteia.* Under the long-term pressure on household persons and property inflicted by the years of constant war, the Athenian sense of urgency about oikos integrity and stability seems to have intensified. But the ability of the polis and of public law to ensure that stability was no longer confidently upheld. At the end of Euripides' *Electra,* to be sure, the god Castor enters to marry off Electra to Pylades. She now has "husband and home," says Castor; but this marriage neither preserves nor restores the corrupted household of her parents.

The impiety of adultery and its deadly effects on both family and society are also prominent themes in the *Hippolytus,* a play Euripides wrote in 428, somewhat earlier in his career and earlier in the war. The unholiness of desired, suspected, or potential adultery in the *Hippolytus* is made all the more vivid by the additional sugges- tion of incest.[39] Victimized by Aphrodite, Phaedra has fallen in love with her husband's son, Hippolytus, and even though this is not a blood relation, the horror and shame of her love are repeatedly em- phasized by both sympathetic and unsympathetic bystanders. What brings this desire into the category of incest is not blood relationship but marriage, another indication of the strong emotional investment in household relationships, rather than simply lineage, as the opera- tive form of "family" in classical Athens.

Amidst strong choral disapproval, however, Phaedra's nurse offers some words of practical advice. For the health of its victim and the peace of society, she says, adulterous love should be indulged in se- cretly and under cover of darkness. The contrast here with the horri- fied response of the chorus, and with Phaedra's own horror of her passion, is striking, but still shows very clearly that from either per- spective, ethical or pragmatic, adultery represented the very antithe- sis of the publicly recognized and honored marriage relationship. It has no place in the open, public, and enlightened world of the Athenian polis—but yet belongs quite decidedly to the "other" Athens where citizen virtues of *sophrosyne* ("self-control") and fam- ily loyalty might give way before basic "laws" of sexual and selfish appetite.[40]

Moicheia *in Aristophanic Comedy*

Because the satisfaction of inherently unpolitical appetites of self- indulgence, in what was a highly public and political setting, is a prominent feature of the comedies of Aristophanes, it is hardly sur- prising to find the poet making pointed and frequent use of bits and pieces of adultery plots in several of his comedies. The comedy in which the theme is given most play is the *Thesmophoriazousai*. Here the chorus of Athenian women in their opening hymn curses the "cheaters" in the adultery game—the *moichos* who fails to produce what he promises, the old woman who buys herself a *moichos*,[41] the hetaira who receives but then betrays her lover. They then go on to try Euripides on the charge of libel—of so damaging their reputations that they have lost all freedom of action in conducting their affairs. The husband comes home from the theater, and from Euripides' plays in particular, certain that a *moichos* is hidden in the house (397).

For better or worse, Athenian drama generally presents its female characters as active agents, and any doubt that Aristophanes' women were running their own sexual affairs and relations with *moichoi* is decisively and comically eliminated as Mnesilochos, Euripides' father-in-law, disguised as a woman and acting as defense attorney, offers the argument that the truth about women's behavior is in fact much worse, and so Euripides is not libeling them at all. Mnesilochos cites a few examples from "her" own repertoire. On only the third night of her marriage, for example, hearing her lover at the door,

> I slip out of bed, just as easy as easy, and all of a sudden up pops my husband's head. "Where you going?" he says. "Where?" says I, all innocence, "Why, you know where. I got a cramp. Something I ate." "Go ahead," he says, and damned if he doesn't get up too and start boiling up a juniper-and-anise recipe for that cramp! Well, I get down to the door, pour some water on the hinge to kill the squeaking, and sure enough there's the boy friend [*moichos*] out in the street.[42]

Or there is the case of the wife who managed to smuggle a *moichos* out of the house, hidden behind her own shawl, as she pretended to show that garment off in front of her husband (499–501). To the women's indignant protest that such stories dishonor them all exceedingly, Mnesilochos responds with tales of even worse crimes supposedly unreported by Euripides, such as the woman who killed her husband with an ax, or the one who drove hers mad with drugs (560–591). Mnesilochos' strategy has clearly backfired, and the counsel for the defense is soon denounced, stripped of his disguise, and barely escapes with his life.

Further evidence for the characteristic *topoi* of the adultery plot comes in the *Clouds*, where "Worse Argument" describes the *moichos* as that one who is "weaker than love and also women" (1081–82), a representation that fits well with the quite unmanly figure of the *moichos* hiding behind a woman's garment, and with his generally passive role by comparison with the more active manipulative wife. Despite his typical wealth and physical charm, the *moichos*' fate is not in his own hands but in those of the women into whose plans and houses he enters. Grammatically *moicheia* may describe an active male act, but dramatically such a man was notably less than manly: comedy shows the wife herself as actively planning and protecting the sexual affair.

Even with its farcical plots and typecasting of both the *moichos* and his partners, Aristophanes' comedy has some serious words of advice for his public audience. Just after uncovering Mnesilochos' disguise, the chorus pauses to rebuke all those who commit impious acts (*anosia; 668*) and to warn that retribution follows all unjust behavior. The fact that this Hesiodic message is inspired by the disrobing of Mnesilochos and accompanies the rabid search for any other male spies who might be present does not diminish the impression, made clearly by the chorus' language, that they, and perhaps Aristophanes, are quite serious about the punishment of unholy acts of hubris committed against and within the household, including adultery.

Thus Athenian drama presents both the comic and tragic faces of adultery. Both emphasize the central violence that adultery and *moicheia* commit against household relations—husband and wife, parent and child, persons and property. To the question "Why is adultery a public offense?" drama suggests a complex answer rooted in the importance of household relations and responsibilities for both the moral and material well-being of the city. It is clear that adultery is an insult to a husband's honor and may also cause real anxiety about the paternity of his children. But he is hardly the only victim. The crime corrupts the entire household into which it enters, producing, as Aeschylus sees it, a kind of household civil war in which all members and all relationships, of persons and property alike, suffer. Both Clytemnestra and Agamemnon bring "foreigners" into the house and destroy and dishonor a household they should have preserved and honored.

The adultery within the house of Atreus also brought violence into the community as a whole. Despite the inherently ambiguous character of Helen's departure from Sparta, its deadly effects for both Greeks and Trojans is clear. The *Agamemnon* makes clear an essen-

tial and even necessary connection between adultery and such violence. Rather than creating barriers between the public and private
spheres, protecting the latter from the intrusion of the former, the
Oresteia as a whole stresses the interconnectedness of public and private morality and well-being. The dramas considered above make
quite clear a public interest in marital behavior and in the internal
well-being of the household. The household in Athenian drama and
in Athenian life was both the microcosm of the polis and the human
association which legitimized participation in the polis. In 458,
Aeschylus as *didaskalos* (teacher) instructed his audience that the violence and corruption of adultery could be ended by the intervention
of public justice and the protection of marriage, by both law and the
now kindly Furies. At the end of the century, Euripides seems less
confident that the Argive royal household—and perhaps the Athenians as well—could survive its own internal violence. Both poets illuminate the household as the moral center of the polis and adultery as
its violation.

Adultery and Adulterers in the Fourth-Century Courts

Athenian drama significantly expands our understanding of the public significance of adultery beyond the scope of the limited legal evidence. The kinship between Plato and the tragedians on this issue
should also be clear. As represented in the tragic story of Clytemnestra and Agamemnon, adultery is a complex crime of marital betrayal
and household corruption described best not by the word *moicheia*
but by *anosios gamos* ("unholy marriage"). As such, it disrupts the
public order which is rooted both metaphorically and literally in
the stability of household and family relations. The Athenians of the
fifth century had built their democracy as an elite family community,
in which membership was an inherited privilege of legitimate Athenian birth. As the family was "politicized," so also was adultery. Public and private were not entirely discrete spheres in the democracy of
Aeschylus, Sophocles, and Euripides. Rather, the public world ap-
propriated the language of private life as it also claimed a higher loyalty and purpose. "You should fix your eyes every day on the greatness of Athens as she really is and should fall in love with her," said
Pericles to the Athenians.[43] As a higher form of family the polis

ought not to be the competitor, but rather the completion *(telos)* of family loyalty and love.

The twenty-seven-year Peloponnesian War severely tested Athenian confidence in the Periclean model of political unity and self-sufficiency and strained the Periclean ideal of a polis so dedicated to its public identity that the private man (the *idios*) was of no use *(achreios)*. As has often been noted, private (that is, nonpolitical) life enjoys a positive reevaluation in postwar fourth-century Athens, and "opting out" is now a respectable choice for Athenian citizens. Already in the last years of the fifth century, grave reliefs show a prizing of intimate family relationships, and public drama, while not at all abandoning the world of politics, has a new domestic tone.[44] This was a new chapter, however, not a new book in Athenian history. Democracy and democratic institutions, restored in the last years of the fifth century, thrived in the fourth. The public world continued to be a sphere of intense competition and political activity, and, while private life was prized, it was not by any means closed to public scrutiny. In many respects fourth-century Athens represents the culmination of Athenian political development, particularly as seen in the active life of the large public courts. Not unreasonably, the speeches delivered before these courts are frequently taken as a revealing guide to Athenian political ideology.[45] How then did the adulterer fare in this forum, which was as distinctive of fourth-century Athens as the theater was of the fifth? What kind of crime was adultery in these courts, and why was the public interested?

In trying to answer these questions we will not be considering actual cases of either prosecution or defense on the charge of *moicheia*. Just as there is no surviving legal definition of what constituted adultery in Athens, or even more specifically of what constituted *moicheia*, there are also no surviving speeches from a formally charged case of adultery. This is hardly, however, an argument against the existence of a *graphe moicheias* (the public suit against *moicheia*) and of a public interest in the act of adultery per se, since this was clearly a difficult and hazardous suit to introduce and prove in the public courts.[46] Formal or informal mediation and arbitration would have been safer for all concerned, and indeed there are indications that this was a preferred course of action.[47] The public significance of a specific charge is not necessarily measured by the number of suits. Certainly the charge of *xenia* (false claim to being an Athenian citizen) was of great public interest and significance even though only one speech prosecuting it survives.[48] As with *xenia*, implications and innuendos of the charge of adultery or *moicheia* are often effectively employed in cases ostensibly or formally concerned with something else altogether. For present purposes this oblique or rhetorical presence is sufficient; the character of the *moichos* and the nature of fourth-century public interest in that character become quite clear.

In contrast to drama, where the female partner of adultery is the focus of active interest, oratory highlights the figure of the adulterer, the Aegisthus-figure and the *moichos,* leaving the women of the household, including those implicated in adultery, as much "in private" as possible. But this notable protection of the privacy of family life and relationships does not extend to the private sexual life of the *moichos,* whose activities and habits are fair targets in public oratory. Indeed, the *moichos,* whose behavior repeatedly reveals him to be unsuited for public trust and citizen responsibilities, emerges in Athenian oratory as a kind of negative model of the citizen. The law also judged the woman who was his partner to be unsuited to her citizen responsibilities, but we know of none so judged by an Athenian jury. While drama looks into the interior corruption of the household produced by adultery, oratory maintains a more reserved pose toward the private sphere and emphasizes the public danger posed by the male but unmanly *moichos.* Courtroom stories of three such *moichoi* will serve as an introduction to the two court cases in which *moicheia* is directly confronted.

Three (Alleged) Moichoi

The first of these *moichoi* is one of Athens' most famous or infamous citizens, Alcibiades son of Cleinias. The charge that he is a *moichos* is made in an oration of unknown authorship with a dramatic date of 417 B.C.E. This was the year in which the Athenians held their last ostracism, an "election" for which Alcibiades had been a leading candidate.[49] The speech itself, however, seems to have been written later in the fourth century, when Alcibiades' career had already come to its disastrous end in the Hellespont, amidst fire and Phrygian arrows, with his concubine at his side. For present purposes the question of authorship or specific date makes little difference. What is relevant is the way in which the author connects Alcibiades' moral and sexual vices to his political ones.

The speaker identifies himself as a prominent politician who, like Alcibiades, is at risk for ostracism but, unlike Alcibiades, does not deserve it. After a brief introduction, he launches into an all-out attack on Alcibiades, saying that "on account of the multitude of his crimes [*hamartemata*] I am at a loss where to begin" (10). Time is too short, the speaker complains, to describe in detail all his "*moicheia* and *harpage* [plundering] of other men's wives and his other violent and lawless behavior." So the speaker focuses on specific deeds committed against the polis, against his relatives, and against various others, citizens and foreigners, who were unfortunate enough to have "crossed his path." In fact, however, he has very little to say about any crimes committed by Alcibiades in an official capacity. After a rather weak attack on Alcibiades' role in raising the tribute paid by the Athenian allies, and a suggestion of personal gain in the process (11–12), the speaker enters into a broad attack on his character as revealed by his private life. "I am amazed," he says, "at those who are persuaded that Alcibiades is a lover of Democracy" (13). Such people, he asserts, are not looking at him from the perspective of his private life, which shows him to be the sort of person who insults his wife by bringing mistresses into the house and plots to murder his own brother-in-law. Alcibiades has even produced a son with the Melian woman he bought as a slave after the brutal destruction of her city.[50] The birth of that child is "more unlawful and unnatural" *(paranomoteros)* than that of Aegisthus,[51] and it is time, the speaker advises, for the Athenians to recognize Alcibiades' outrages for what they are and ostracize him.

Alcibiades' *moicheia*, which the speaker puts off at the beginning as too long a story (and also one which might hurt too many citizens by making public their sufferings), is then but one piece of the larger picture of personal, sexual, and moral misbehavior which is indeed worthy of the house of Atreus. But the speaker's concern lies not so much with what this behavior has done to its private victims and their households as with its implications for Alcibiades' public worth. Such a man can be neither a good citizen nor a good democrat and is definitely not a man of manly virtue. The speaker, on the other hand, has always been a worthy public servant, has fulfilled his liturgies, and gained public victories, even one in manliness *(euandria)*! There should be no question here for the ancient audience about who is the better citizen or, for a modern audience, about the significance of private behavior for the public evaluation of character. Would you, the speaker essentially says to his court, elect an "Aegisthus" to public office? We do not have to agree with the sentiment to appreciate its force in classical Athens.[52]

The second reputed *moichos*, a certain Agoratos, is a man with a very different social background than the blue-blooded Alcibiades. As presented by Lysias in a speech written for an unknown client sometime in the early fourth century, Agoratos is a man of servile birth who acted as an informer and agent for the Thirty Tyrants in the era of oligarchic revolution (404–403 B.C.E). In that capacity, the speaker charges, Agoratos had been responsible for the deaths of many good Athenian citizens, including the speaker's own brother-in-law and cousin, Dionysodoros. The charge then is murder or political assassination. In addition to his detailed account of Agoratos' role in the political violence and intrigue that plagued Athens at the end of the Peloponnesian War, Lysias adds a character sketch of his family. Agoratos had three brothers, he says. The first was caught giving signals to the enemy in Sicily and executed for treason; the second was caught in Corinth abducting the *paidiske* (young female slave) of a citizen woman and was imprisoned and killed; the third is a "clothes thief" *(lopodytes)* who was caught, tried, and also condemned to death in Athens.[53] And Agoratos himself, says Lysias, is another sort of traitor and thief who trumps his brothers' crimes with his own. He is a *moichos* who enters into other men's beds and corrupts their wives. Indeed, he has already been "caught in the act" for which, claims the speaker, the penalty is death. Just why Agoratos is still around is left unclear.[54] Such a man, the implication is clear, could very reasonably be expected to be "caught in the act" of political assassination. Once again, public character is taken as an extrapolation of private character, and the character of this *moichos*, the composite household thief and public traitor, is well known.

Finally, our third *moichos* is none other than Timarchos, the object of the most celebrated morals case in classical Athens, heard by the popular court in the spring of 345 B.C.E. Aeschines' speech

"Against Timarchos" is best known, and most discussed in recent years, for its charge that by prostituting his body Timarchos has thereby disqualified himself from the privileges of Athenian citizenship. Not surprisingly, this speech has figured largely in recent debates over Greek (and Athenian) attitudes toward homosexuality.[55] The case, however, has even broader implications for Athenian popular morality, for Timarchos' vices are considerably more wideranging than prostitution.[56] The speech is in fact a veritable textbook of Athenian popular morality as well as a testament to the importance of reputation in Athenian public life. Aeschines demonstrates for his audience in no uncertain terms the public danger of male citizen prostitution. The basis for that danger, however, is a corruption of character whose effects are hardly limited to the sale of sexual favors. Most significantly, Timarchos' behavior reveals a lack of self-control in the face of physical desire, money, or both. It is not the sexual act itself that disqualifies him for citizenship but the circumstances in which he commits it. A man who lives a shameful life "enslaved" to money and desire cannot possibly lead a truly "free" citizen life. Like the *kinaidos* (a generally lewd or debauched person), the *moichos* cannot be a trustworthy citizen. He lacks the requisite manly self-control. As Jack Winkler puts it, "Athenian ideology did not employ our more careful distinction of sex from politics; instead it assumed that good men were those who in the cause of social solidarity exercised control over all their various personal impulses to acquisitiveness."[57]

Furthermore, Aeschines makes it clear that Timarchos' crime is rooted in a general abuse of the basic relationships of family and household. Not only has he corrupted young men; he has also treated the "wives of free men" with a licentiousness not before known. He has squandered his patrimony, sold his mother's burial plot, and allowed his uncle to fall into the ranks of disabled paupers (97–104). His crimes, like those of all "clothes thieves, *moichoi*, and murderers" (91), may be carried out secretly, but their effects are highly public. Similarly Timarchos' reputation is public, and Aeschines advises the Athenians that "by his reputation you shall know him and convict him." The goddess Reputation *(Pheme)* is Aeschines' best witness (130). Upon examination, the only family resources Timarchos has left are his family of vices: "lewdness, calumny, impudence, wantonness, cowardice, effrontery, a face that knows not the blush of shame," from which is produced the worst and most useless of citizens (105). His abuse of his own body is but one part of the larger picture of sexual and familial abuse which makes him a most undesirable and unworthy citizen. He was a *moichos* and much more. Thus, insofar as the evidence permits a general conclusion, this and the two previous cases suggest that there was no separation of private vice from the sphere of public interest in classical Athens.

Two Courtroom Stories of Moicheia

None of these three men, however, was on trial specifically for *moicheia*. This was an offense especially suited to out-of-court settlement or, as in the three cases discussed above, to the larger project of character assassination. The closest we come to actual cases of adultery heard in the public courts are three speeches covering two cases: "On the Murder of Eratosthenes," written by Lysias (most likely early in the fourth century) for his client Euphiletos, who claimed to have justifiably killed Eratosthenes when he caught him in bed with his wife; and the fragmentary and less familiar pair of speeches, written by Hypereides and perhaps another orator later in the century, in behalf of a certain Lycophron who in 333 was brought before the people by formal impeachment *(eisangelia)* and charged with betraying the state—and the source of this treason is said to be *moicheia*. Although in neither case is adultery or *moicheia* the official charge— Euphiletos is on trial for murder and Lycophron for betraying the state[58]—both are of interest here and present their own peculiar puzzles. I begin with the later case and with Lycophron.

Lycophron was a wealthy Athenian, a breeder of horses and a cavalry commander. In 333, at roughly the age of fifty, he was recalled from the island of Lemnos where he had served for three years to stand trial for "undermining the democracy by breaking the law." At least one part of his offense was the act (or acts) of *moicheia*. The case, obscure though it now is, was apparently significant enough for the prominent politician Lycurgus personally to have delivered two speeches against Lycophron and also to have amplified the formal public impeachment with secondhand gossip about Lycophron's nighttime activities.[59]

Unfortunately, there survive only three sentences from Lycurgus' speeches for the prosecution, including the following general charge preserved in the Suda under the entry *mochtheria:* "It is not right to let a man go unpunished who is breaking the laws through which democracy is preserved and who is the initiator and 'legislator' of other bad habits." That violation of marriage and of the household relations was counted among his "wicked habits" is consistent with the other two fragments: "I am amazed that if we punish with death the slave-dealers who rob us of our slaves . . . [we would let the *moichos* off?]"; and "When a woman [wife] loses understanding [like-mindedness] with her husband, life henceforth is unlivable."[60] The case for the prosecution, however, remains a puzzle.

On the other hand, the defense, as written by the orator Hypereides, seems relatively straightforward. Lycophron argues first that the whole procedure is improper, that an impeachment is inappropriate to the charge,[61] which properly should have been taken through a public indictment *(graphe)* to judicial magistrates (the *thesmothetai*) and a jury, rather than to the assembly as a whole. He claims that an impeachment carried less risk for the prosecutors and, more interesting for present purposes, that it gave them more scope—and a larger audience—for the "tragedies" they would write into their case, as in their charge that "I am making many women grow old unmarried within their houses and many marry against the laws those whom it is not fitting [to marry]."[62]

Procedural issues aside, Lycophron clearly needs to confront the substance of the "tragic" charge against his loyalty to the democracy, and he does this essentially by saying not that the charges are in any way irrelevant but that they are absurd, improbable, and totally without foundation. He could not possibly have said the compromising things to the widow at her remarriage that Lycurgus said he did, since her brother Dioxippos the famous wrestler—indeed "the strongest man in Greece"—would have strangled him on the spot (6). In general, he just was not that sort of man, nor had he been so in the past. Since being a *moichos* is not a habit a man takes up after fifty, the uprightness of his previous life should be proof against the charge (15). Finally, his manly virtue or courage *(andragathia)* in military service was recognized and honored with a crown by all his fellow cavalrymen (16). Such a man could be no *moichos*.

The author of the second speech in Lycophron's behalf also seems to have used the "argument from improbability." He objects in the first fragment that "as for his digging through the wall to have intercourse with the woman: that is quite incredible"—especially, he goes on to assert, since he had free and easy access to her house anyway.[63] In addition to mocking the false theatricality of an entrance via a tunnel, the author may also have implied that the status of the woman in question was not above suspicion. He does not call her *gyne,* meaning "woman" or "wife," but rather "that female," a term which may throw some doubt on either her free status or her occupation. Obviously another way to get off a charge of *moicheia* was to claim that the woman in question was "no lady."

Perhaps in fact there was more than one woman implicated in this case. The sister of Dioxippos the wrestler had been respectfully called *gyne* by Hypereides in the first speech and is also mentioned in the same properly periphrastic way in another fragment of this second speech. It may be that Lycophron was accused of being a *moichos* not once but many times, and that the charges were made with an abundance of dramatic or "tragic" detail. The prosecution may have claimed that *moicheia* had been his habit for some time, so provoking Lycophron to protest that this was not a habit of his at all. The element of repeated and habitual behavior is also a key part of Lysias' representation of *moicheia* in "On the Murder of Eratosthenes." And in his own defense, Lycophron appealed to evidence of his character that challenged the *moichos* image—his military record, his manly virtue, and ultimately the claim that he is just not "that kind of guy."

The case came to trial in 333 amidst considerable anxiety and turmoil over the future of Athenian democracy and autonomy.[64] Philip was dead, and Demosthenes was still leading resistance to Macedon; but Alexander had shown that he was as tough as his father, and the Athenians were hardly of one mind in their deliberations over how to respond to the Macedonian hegemony. In these tense moments, how safe were Athens' "walls, ships, and dockyards"? Who was a friend of Athens and a good citizen, and who was not? Thus, even though the circumstances behind Lycophron's case are obscure, the fact that it entered the courts at all betrays the lines of tension in Athenian society at the time. It also reveals just as clearly that private morals were considered a reliable guide to public worth. The outcome of the trial is unknown, as is the extent to which Lycophron was or was not miscast in the role of *moichos*. Most likely the prosecution emphasized his wealth and advanced bachelor "playboy" status.[65] But that the Athenian assembly could have been treated to such a show, directed by one of its leading public figures, suggests that there was significantly more to the public interest in adultery or *moicheia* than the simple controlling of violent revenge on the part of wronged and shamed husbands or fathers. Dioxippos, the proper defender of his sister's honor, does not seem to have taken any action against Lycophron.[66] Although the speakers may have trod lightly, with what might be called fourth-century tact, regarding the part played by any of Lycophron's free Athenian partners, and so obscured the full picture of household corruption so vivid in drama, they do insist strongly that Lycophron's behavior in the bedroom undermined his ability to perform his male citizen roles in the public realm. However foreign the idea may be to a modern audience, it is necessary to take seriously the charge by Lycurgus that Lycophron was guilty of subverting the democracy by cultivating in himself the habit of corrupting citizen women and their households.

Lycophron speaks of the "tragedies" his opponents spout, and the image of women growing old unmarried does indeed recall the plight of Electra, but there are touches of comedy in the case as well. Similarly, despite the utmost seriousness of the charge against Lysias' client Euphiletos—he is on trial for murdering a fellow citizen—the household melodrama he narrates for the jury contains some moments that might come straight out of comedy. "I was simple-minded enough," he says, "to suppose that my wife was the most self-controlled [*sophron*] of all the women in the polis" (10). But it was not so. Like Aristophanes' cuckold husband in the *Thesmophoriazousai,* Euphiletos is tricked by his clever young wife, who manages to entertain a lover *(moichos)* within the house without his knowledge over a considerable period. The story is well known and entertaining, but its various elements, such as the crying child who gives the wife an excuse to go downstairs to her lover, the locked and squeaking doors, and her suspiciously powdered face, must have been pieced together retrospectively after Euphiletos' enlightenment about his wife's activities. There would have been ample opportunity for a dramatic shaping of the facts. Similarly, his very careful account of how he rounded up his friends as witnesses, and how he (as previously arranged with the slave-girl) confronted and slew the adulterer, saying, "It is not I who am about to kill you, but the law of the city," definitely has a staged character. Perhaps an audience might have recalled the scene in Euripides' *Electra* when Orestes, intent on revenge, asks the *paedagogus* when and with whom he should take his revenge. An even older paradigm is the carefully staged revenge of Hephaestus.

From the dramatic perspective, the missing piece of Euphiletos' story is the motivation and fate of his adulterous wife. Perhaps her motivation is not totally missing, since in contrast to the completely silent sister of Dioxippos, the wife of Euphiletos[67] is allowed one small, suggestive moment of protest. According to her husband, when he urged her to go down and take care of the crying baby, she replied: "so that you can have a try with the slave-girl; even as once before, when you were drunk, you dragged her around" (12). Otherwise, however, in Euphiletos' retelling of the events she remains a silent participant in the drama. The reasons for Euphiletos' reticence on this matter seem quite as obvious as the difficulty he was in. By exposing Eratosthenes, he also exposed his wife. Yet did he really want to convict, punish, or divorce her (as was required by the law Apollodorus cites)? Although he is careful to note that his first child was born before his wife became unfaithful, he now seems to have at least two children. Does he really want to invite public scrutiny of the legitimacy of his household? As much as possible, Euphiletos seems to want to keep his household from the fate of the house of Atreus. He does not emphasize his wife's bad character so much as place her in the role of Eratosthenes' victim, and he cites no comparable punishment meted out for her by "The Law." If he wanted to remain married, it was in his interest to present his wife, along with himself, as a simple victim of Eratosthenes' villainy. Therefore, in the circumstances, the less said about her the better. Better to focus, like the word *moicheia* itself, on the character of the nighttime seducer and his activities. Likewise, it was good rhetorical strategy to call upon the "justifiable" homicide law, not only for the justification of his homicide, but also for its focus on the more simple act of aggression *epi* (upon) his wife. Any discussion of his wife's role in the more

complex triangulated plot of adultery would have made the story
more dramatic, but also more dangerous for Euphiletos and his
household. Perhaps it is this absence of a dramatic role for the wife
that gives the story its air of comic parody. Note that Euphiletos' response to his wife's protest was "I laughed" (12).

However one views the relation of art and reality in Euphiletos'
speech, it is certainly part of Lysias' plan to present Eratosthenes as a
dramatic and ethical *type*, the habitual and slippery-footed adulterer
who enters another man's bed, in other words, the *moichos*. Not
without purpose does Euphiletos report that a certain old woman
approached him with the information that Eratosthenes was violently outraging *(hybrizon)* both him and his wife—and that this was
in fact the man's "craft": "Eratosthenes of Oe is doing these things,
who not only has corrupted your wife but also many others; he has it
as his *techne*."[68] The emphasis on the habitual character of Eratosthenes' adultery, as also in the case against Lycophron, suggests that
it may have been important to the successful argument of *moicheia*
to establish that the transgression was not a single, onetime occur-
rence or the result perhaps of a temporary drunken loss of self-
control, but a completely intentional and "professional" act of
hubris against a household—husband and wife, children and property. A man might be "caught" with a wife only once, but the presumption of *moicheia* is that of habitual, regular, and clandestine
nighttime seduction. Thus, although it is the specific moment of sexual intercourse in which Euphiletos claimed to have found Eratosthenes that makes the law on justifiable homicide legally relevant, it
is the larger rhetorical picture of repeated behavior and moral character which Lysias hopes will justify Euphiletos' application of that
law in this case. There is perhaps no better example of the highly
rhetorical character of the Athenian courts and the strangeness of
Athenian justice to modern notions of due process.

In addition to creating a highly rhetorical image of Eratosthenes
the *moichos,* for whose death the city ought rather to thank Euphiletos than convict him, Lysias provides his audience with an analysis
of Eratosthenes' crime intended to incite their indignation and sense
of public outrage. It has also, if for somewhat different reasons, in-
cited the outrage of some modern critics, particularly on the question
of which is the "worse" crime: rape or adultery?

Before turning to that question, we need to consider Lysias' presentation of Eratosthenes' crime as having more than one victim. Although it is typically said that Lysias represents Eratosthenes as having wronged Euphiletos alone, that view seems based on a too hasty reading of Euphiletos' charge that "Eratosthenes was committing *moicheia* with my wife and corrupting her and shaming my children and outraging [*hybrizen*] me" (4). Of this interesting set of charges, including the actions of *moicheuein, diaphtherein* (corruption), *aischynein* (shaming), and *hybrizein* (outrage), particular attention has been given to the last—"he outrages me." The conclusion follows that Eratosthenes' offense was essentially an actionable act of *hybris* (violent outrage or abuse) against Euphiletos, the husband.

That the husband is said to be wronged or outraged is hardly a surprise—this was a major blow to his public reputation and status. What is remarkable is the way in which Euphiletos' words implicate the whole household in this crime and, even more, the way in which by virtue of her relation to that household the wife is in fact conceived of as both a party to and the victim of the crime. As the old woman warned Euphiletos, Eratosthenes was "outraging [*hybrizon*] both you and your wife" (16). This was a complex crime if there ever was one, and one which left the husband and father, who was the agent of public justice, in a very awkward situation. His own "dishonor" was inseparable from that of his wife and his whole oikos. However much Euphiletos would have also preferred his jury to see the case as a simple one of rightful exercise of self-defense by a male head of household—so the appeal to the old law on justifiable homicide—his own words and story have already significantly complicated his case.

Yet he continues to try to put the onus upon Eratosthenes, and to incite the jury with the following argument on the seriousness of Eratosthenes' crime:

> You hear, sirs, how [the law] directs that if anyone forcibly rapes a free adult or child, he shall be liable to double damages; while if he so rapes a woman, in one of the cases where it is permitted to kill him, he is subject to the same rule. Thus the lawgiver, sirs, considered that those who use force deserve a lesser penalty than those who use persuasion, for the latter he condemned to death, whereas

for the former he doubled the damages, considering that those who achieve their ends by force are hated by the persons forced; while those who used persuasion corrupted thereby their victims' souls, thus making the wives of others more closely attached to themselves than to their husbands, and got the whole house into their hands, and caused uncertainty as to whose the children really were, the husband's or the adulterer's.[69]

The reliability of Euphiletos' reading of the law here is sometimes thought to be supported by a passage in Plutarch's *Solon:*

> He made it legal to kill any adulterer who was caught in the act, but the offence of rape against a free woman was punished by a fine of no more than 100 drachmae. If the man seduced her, he would be fined twenty drachmae, except in the case of women who openly sell their bodies . . . But it is surely quite absurd that the same offence should be treated in the one case with the most remorseless severity and in the other with the most genial tolerance, by the imposition of nothing more than a nominal fine.[70]

In fact Plutarch is puzzled by the conflicting evidence he apparently has on these issues, which may well have included Lysias 1, and by the discrepancy between killing a man and fining him twenty drachmas for what seems to be the same act of seduction. Some modern critics, however, have not paused to be puzzled but have immediately expressed shock that the Athenians could have considered adultery a greater crime than rape. After all, adultery now is virtually decriminalized in the public sphere and not necessarily morally condemned even in private, while rape is a felony. That the Athenians thought otherwise only reinforces for many the well-entrenched image of classical Athens as a misogynistic utopia (or dystopia) in which women were legally passive pieces of male property. In the Athenian "phallocracy," we are told, it was worse if the property was corrupted as well as damaged.[71] But before jumping to that conclusion, we need perhaps to admit with Plutarch that there is a puzzle here and that in order to solve it, it may be necessary to look more carefully at Lysias' rhetorical argument, particularly in the context of the previous discussion about *moicheia* and adultery.

First, it is quite clear that Lysias has misrepresented the relevance of the law on justifiable homicide in two specific ways:

The law does not set death as the punishment for a *moichos,* but simply allows the killing of a man caught "*epi* wife, sister, mother, etc." to go unpunished.

The language of the law does not specify whether the woman has been seduced or assaulted or whether the woman in question is a wife.[72]

Lysias' rhetorical contrast is therefore suspect from the start. That is, finding a man *epi* wife, mother, sister, or daughter could include finding him in the act of rape, so making death a justifiable but not legally mandated response to rape as well as to adultery. Again, this point should not be taken to imply that the Athenians could not distinguish the two acts, but rather that this particular law was concerned not with the woman's state of mind, but with the more specific and perhaps archaic issue of the criminal intrusion into private household space.

In citing this law, Lysias focuses on the particular figure of the *moichos* as the criminal in question. Indeed, he inserts the word into his quotation of the law: "whoever takes vengeance on a *moichos* caught in the act" (30). Carefully portrayed as a *moichos,* Eratosthenes can now be judged to have been caught and killed in complete accordance with the law. There could not be a better illustration of Aristotle's advice in the *Rhetoric* (1375a–b) on how to use the law itself as a witness.

Athenian law, however, cannot be pressed so far as to "testify" for Euphiletos' claim about the comparative value of the two offenses, rape and adultery. An important feature of Athenian law of which Lysias has taken advantage here, and which puzzles Plutarch, is that it allowed several different kinds of legal action for what we might consider a single legal offense.[73] Thus for both rape and adultery there seem to have been several possible legal routes that an injured party or his/her advocates might take. Euphiletos took an extreme and perhaps somewhat archaic route which, despite his claim to the contrary, was most likely applicable to both offenses.

Any physical assault, including sexual assault, on an Athenian man, woman, or child was a serious crime in Athens, reflecting the great importance Athenians ascribed to the physical protection of the person as a central privilege of citizenship. The inclusion of the murder of a man caught *epi* a woman of the household in the category of "justifiable homicide" is also a reflection of the invasive nature of the crime and the seriousness with which early Athenian society viewed such intrusions. It reveals, however, nothing about the relative status of rape and adultery. Also important is the fact that the law on rape cited by Lysias refers to "shaming by force" a free adult or child, thus clearly implying a commensurability of the crime against free men, women, and children. In sum, it should be evident that in making his rhetorical comparison, Lysias has compared apples and oranges—several different laws with different circumstances, different procedures, and perhaps different dates. But still, he seems to have thought that the argument and the comparison were worth making. Even if the Athenian laws were not "guilty as charged," was the Athenian audience susceptible to this argument? We still need to confront the persuasive basis of Lysias' argument.

How can adultery be seen as a worse crime, in the public sense, than rape? Perhaps we would do better in understanding the Athenian jury's response to such a claim if we focused on the complex character of adultery and the way in which the household as a whole was implicated as both participant and victim. His wife was shamed both as a part of Euphiletos' violated oikos and as a contributing party to that shame. The point is not that adultery is worse from any individual's point of view, but that it is worse from the point of view of the household as a whole, whose stability in turn underlay the stability of the polis. Adultery (or, in this case, more specifically *moicheia*, with a focus on Eratosthenes) could be a greater public crime than rape in that its consequences were more complex and of greater duration. As such it might be distinguished from single or isolated acts of either moral weakness or sexual violence, which might not have any larger social, political, or familial repercussions. So at least Xenophon implies when in the *Hiero* he follows his comment on the death penalty for *moichoi* with the comment "When a wife 'has sexual intercourse by accident' [*aphrodisi-asthe kata symphoran*] husbands do not honor them the less on this account, if the wives' *philia* seems to remain unaffected."[74] Whether one takes the odd expression "sexual intercourse by accident" as a euphemistic reference to rape or to a temporary seduction (once again there is notable reticence about the woman's state of mind), it clearly alludes to a distinction between an act which occurs once and repeated acts which corrupt the basic bond of household *philia*. The latter, not the former, is the Athenian public crime of adultery. As Lysias makes clear, *moicheia* is a habitual activity, and, as the history of Agamemnon and Clytemnestra illustrates through the dramatic paradigm, the effects of adultery on all members of the household can be long-term.

This is a point on which Eratosthenes does not and cannot dwell. His reticence about his wife's role and the actual duration of the affair,[75] and his need to protect his household by presenting her as a passive object of Eratosthenes' *moicheia* produce a kind of flattening of the image of adultery and its effects.[76] When read against a dramatic background, the two-dimensional character of the story of "On the Murder of Eratosthenes" is even more marked. Eratosthenes is the *moichos* familiar from the theater. He is a cowardly man who steals into the women's quarters, recalling both the "woman-hearted" Aegisthus and also some of the more fortunate *moichoi* of comedy who are hidden, for example, in chests or in the woman's shawl. He offers to pay his way out of trouble, but is killed ignominiously within the house. Just as Aegisthus' death is a simple matter of law and justice,[77] so Euphiletos confidently claims that he himself is only the instrument of the city's laws. Although the dramatists go on to demonstrate in no uncertain terms that killing the *moichos* (or tragic equivalent) does not put all pieces of the household back together, Lysias/Euphiletos tells his audience no more.

In portraying the effects of adultery upon the tragic house of Atreus, the dramatists represent the household and its members as suffering from what might be called the loss of public honor, or *atimia*. When Aegisthus has taken their father's place and excluded them from what is properly their own, Orestes and Electra cannot grow up to take on their proper citizen roles. Orestes is an exile, and in Euripides' version Electra is caught in a marriage that is not a marriage and is also unwilling to participate in any of the women's religious activities which marked the active citizen life of Athenian women. The property, too, like the children, is being wasted; the integrity and very identity of the household are in question. While I do not suggest that Euphiletos' household necessarily suffered the same fate, it remains true that he has not solved all his problems by the murder of Eratosthenes.

If his wife has been shown to have been caught with a *moichos,* she will suffer a kind of female loss of citizen rights or *atimia,* divorced from her husband and oikos and excluded from the religious sanctuaries of the city.[78] For her Athenian husband as well, defying those public penalties for adultery is a hazardous course. If he continues to live with a wife "with whom the *moichos* is caught," he himself will suffer the loss of his citizen privileges. This is a strikingly severe punishment typically meted out in Athens to such public offenders as public debtors or sycophants. This is of course law, not "reality," and we know of no such convicted husbands and wives. The very extremity of the punishment may be a good argument for considering these laws, so assiduously collected by Apollodorus, as better evidence of Athenian family ideology than family reality. In a cumulative sense, law, drama, and rhetoric all contribute to our understanding of the public ideology of the family that underlay classical Athenian democracy.

Aristotle's Perspective on *Moicheia*

Plato's philosophical and legislative analysis of adultery law illuminates important principles of the intersection of public and private interests distinctive of classical Athens, the community in which he lived and had deep roots. In contrast, Aristotle, always a resident alien and never a member of the Athenian polis "family," was decidedly less concerned with the communal and tragic character of adultery, but more interested in the figure of the *moichos* as a rhetorical and ethical topos. Although Aristotle dutifully follows Plato in prohibiting adultery in his ideal polis, and does so in completely symmetrical terms, without using the word *moicheia* (*Politics* 1335b38), he shows considerably less interest in its public consequences. His prohibition lacks the moral fervor so striking in Plato, and one does not get the impression from the *Politics* that he envisions an active role for "superintendents of marriage" in the households of his ideal polis.[79] Despite the important principle of expanding human associations articulated in book 1 of the *Politics,* Aristotle's household is considerably more private than either Plato's or those of contemporary Athenians.

In both the *Rhetoric* and *Ethics* Aristotle treats the *moichos* as a publicly recognizable figure, but he classifies his crime as private rather than public. With what might strike some as a quite modern separation of the two spheres, Aristotle comments in the *Rhetoric* that when someone *moicheuon* or when he beats (someone) up *(typton)*, he does wrong against a specific person, but when he does not serve in the army he wrongs the community *(to koinon;* 1373b23). Of course private wrongs can have repercussions in the public sphere, and in the *Politics* Aristotle cites *moicheia* as one of the category of "private" issues that may give rise to public strife (1306a38). Though still acknowledging the potential public importance of private behavior, Aristotle seems to draw the line much more unambiguously between the private life of the household, that within the courtyard walls, and the public world of political decision-making and military action.[80] As was seen earlier, Plato reveals a deeper sympathy with the perspective of Athenian tragedy, both in avoiding the term *moicheia* and in emphasizing the impiety or unholiness of marital infidelity. Aristotle in contrast narrows his focus to just the figure of the *moichos* (a term which he shows no compunction about using) and in so doing reveals his interest in the rhetorical and ethical *topoi* suggested by the man and his act.

"A poor and ugly man," says Aristotle, "is not likely to be suspected of being a *moichos*." He also notes the useful argument that "if another person who is fastidious about appearance is to be judged a *moichos*, then so must this man." Similarly, Aristotle types the *moichos* as "a dandy who cruises at night."[81] In scattered comments in both the *Nicomachean* and *Eudemian Ethics*, Aristotle paints a very clear picture of the *moichos* as a man of profligate character and habits *(akolastes),* and of *moicheia* as a close relative of such furtive crimes as theft and poisoning.[82] In a portrait that matches well the one already observed in comedy and rhetoric, Aristotle's *moichos* distinguishes himself from other nighttime criminals by his handsome face and ready money. In Aristotle's view, moreover, the behavior of the *moichos* is not the result of "weakness of the will" *(akrasia)* in the face of strong sexual desire, but rather of a vicious character. The *moichos* is not one of those men whose principles cannot constrain his desire but rather a man of no principles at all. His actions are an expression of his character. For Aristotle, it is not the act of sexual intercourse itself with the "wrong woman" that makes a man a *moichos,* but the vicious character which leads him to that act. (So according to Aristotle, one could commit *moicheia* without being a *moichos.*) Thus, Aristotle's analysis of the character of the *moichos* lends support to the position that *moicheia* was envisioned in Athens as an act committed by a certain kind of person. It was a matter of habit and character rather than one of simple passion or sexual desire.

From Aristotle's analysis on this point, and also from much of the preceding discussion, it can be seen that the criteria for public approval or disapproval of sexual behavior in Athens were rooted in the ethical and at times political character of the relationship. Was it mercenary? Was it corrupting? Was it in the city's best interests? Just as there could be "bad" heterosexual behavior (epitomized by the *moichos* himself) as well as "good" (that which produces children for the city), so also there were same-sex relationships which were beneficial to the city and those that were not. Aristotle (along with Plato and many others) can both praise the friendship *(philia)* between men, including that which is sexual in nature, and also consider *aphrodisia tois arresin* a form of pathological vice *(Nicomachean Ethics* 1148b29). The pathological is determined neither by the sex of the partner nor by the position or manner of the sexual act, but by the social context in which and for which the sexual act occurs. If the act is a mercenary one, then it undermines the citizen's integrity (he can be bought); if it is an adulterous one, it undermines a household, upon which the welfare of the city rests. The key element in distinguishing "good" from "bad" sexual relations in classical Athens is evidently the extent to which the relationship is beneficial or harmful to the larger polis community and to the households that make up that community. Public interest in sexual behavior would then seem undeniable in a society which uses the criteria of social context and consequence, rather than simply "same" or "different," in making moral judgments about sexual acts.

Marriage, Adultery, and the Politics of the Family

The Athenian polis developed in the archaic era as the guardian of its individual households. The responsibility of family members to one another and to the polis as a whole was articulated through the *anchisteia,* the web of kin focused on each male Athenian extending bilaterally to the "children of cousins."[83] The public authority of the *anchisteia* served to guarantee the welfare and integrity of the oikos. This relationship between the public and private spheres essential to Solon's reforms developed further in the fifth century, as the Athenians built a distinctive participatory democratic society which was itself envisioned as a communal household or family. If democratic Athens was a "family of families," as is suggested by the homonymity between the language of civic membership and that of household membership,[84] then the issue of public and private interests becomes increasingly both more problematic and more interesting. Public interest, when understood as the interest of a collective public household, should not then be set against or seen as conflicting with private interest; rather, the interests of the polis ought to be the true completion, the telos, of those of the oikos. From this perspective, the category distinctions "public" and "private" might seem to collapse, with only that of scale remaining; and Pericles could urge his fellow citizens to "fall in love" with their polis (literally "become her lover") and to invest their hopes for happiness and honor in the success and well-being of Athens herself.[85]

The reverberations of this radical democratic perspective (justifiably associated with the name of Pericles but revised for philosophical purposes by the anti-Periclean and antidemocratic Plato) are signally apparent in contemporary Athenian drama. The privatization of the public or publicization of the private represented in Pericles' strongly worded exhortation becomes a favorite source of humor for Aristophanes.[86] The fervent protestations of love for Demos (the people) put forth by the Paphlagonian (= Cleon) in the *Knights* (732) are perhaps a parody of Pericles' words.[87] The idea that the polis might function as one large household, for which a marriage celebration at the end of the play is the essential "happy ending," is a recurrent Aristophanic fantasy. Athenian tragedy likewise articulates and complicates the tension between public and private interests, often highlighting that tension through stories of gender conflict and vio-lence.[88] Sophocles' *Antigone*, for example, tells a story of conflict be-tween (private) family and (public) state, or between (private) indi-vidual and (public) state, but from another perspective the quarrel between Antigone and Creon can also be seen as a dramatic discus-sion of the Periclean position of the state as a higher form of family. In a discussion of the play through a study of the words *philos* and *echthros*, Simon Goldhill writes: "Creon adapts the vocabulary of generation and the household to the order of the city in a single hier-archical model (which itself marks the impossible separation of the vocabularies of civic and household organization), but this system-atization is split and challenged by the disasters in his own complex household." Likewise, Antigone's insistence on one single bond of *philia*—that owed to her brother alone—is called into question by her own tragic "marriage" to death and consequent failure to enter into productive household *philia*. So Goldhill speaks of the "para-doxical nature of her attitude to *philia*" after noting that "the very household which Antigone claims and is claimed to support is also the source and transmission of the curse which she consummates in death. Her backward-looking support is for the house of the dead, the ancestors whom she places above the possibilities of procreation, marriage, and a future home, a future of the home."[89] As in the *Oresteia*, marriage plays a pivotal role here as the essential (missing) link between household and polis *philia*. Without marriage and mar-ital *philia*, or with only Antigone's perverted "marriage to death," both household and polis seem doomed. Marriage creates the house-hold in which the intimate bonds of *philia* prized by Antigone are born and bred and from which citizens go forth to take part in the public world of the polis.

The democratic conception of the polis as a household thus has both a metaphorical and a more literal significance. On the one hand the polis is like one large household to which all Athenians are legiti-mate heirs and of which they are custodians. On the other, it is through the mediation of the household that the Athenians establish those positions of heir and custodian. In this context, adultery carries an analogously double threat to the public well-being. Metaphorically, it is a treacherous attack on the household-community involving collusion from a traitor within; literally, it is an offense severely threatening the citizen capabilities of the members of household. Rather than articulating the separation of the public and private spheres and the protection of private sexual behavior from public control, the political character of adultery reveals in negative relief the significance of marriage as connecting, and, in extreme terms, as equating, the two worlds of public and private.

This radical view of family and state was not unchallenged. Sophocles seems at least to raise serious questions about a conception of *philia* which insists either on an exclusively public or an exclusively private meaning. In answer to those who find in Sophocles' play a simple conservative message, Goldhill argues that "it is precisely through the limitations and contradictions of the conventional and conservative morality surrounding the terms of *philos and echthros* in juxtaposition to the values of the city that the tragedy of *Antigone* develops." The same point can of course be made against any who would see Sophocles as in fact supporting Creon's extreme position of polis priority. "The questioning of the morality and obligations surrounding the terms of relations and relationships remains unresolved."[90]

Still, a substantial number of Athenians undoubtedly agreed with Pericles that the public business was the only true business and that the polis was the true object of familial loyalty and love, especially in the later fifth century as they continued energetically to fight the war into which he had led them for a full quarter-century after his death. The Peloponnesian War ended in Athens' decisive military defeat, followed by the fall of her democracy in the year 404—but within months of its overthrow, democracy was restored; within ten years after their destruction Athens' walls had been rebuilt; and within thirty years democratic Athens had reconstituted for itself a new maritime empire, politely called a "league." Although many Athenians in the fourth century were no longer so eager or willing to venture their all for the public cause and looked increasingly to the attractions of private life and private wealth, the democratic principle that polis and household were conceptually and morally akin remained clear. More simply, and more eloquently than anything said in court, the famous statue of Eirene with her infant child Ploutos (Peace and Wealth) erected in the Athenian agora supports this last point and reveals fourth-century Athens' particular concern for prosperity within, as well as prestige and power beyond, its "household" doors.

―6―

PUBLIC AND PRIVATE IN EARLY
HELLENISTIC ATHENS

Although Plato and Aristotle are often spoken of almost in one breath as the primary creators and expounders of classical political theory, such yoking of the two should not obscure their profound differences in political perspective and theory. Certainly it was not only on issues of metaphysics that Plato and Aristotle parted company; they also disagreed on the "best *politeia*" and in particular on the way in which the private world of family and household ought to relate to the public world of officeholding and decision-making in the ideal polis society. The traditional linking of the two philosophers as proponents of the "primacy of politics" masks these important philosophical differences;[1] it also ignores the different historical and personal perspectives from which each reflected upon the relative claims of public and private life—the one, an Athenian citizen with strong ties to the fifth-century political elite; the other, a resident alien with strong ties to the Macedonian royal family. Before examining Menander's distinctive reorientation of the public and private spheres in his comedies, produced in the early years of the Hellenistic era, it will be helpful to consider briefly the particular way in which these two philosophers define and relate the public and private spheres. Plato's view of the polis as ideally an organic unity may be seen as a radical philosophical extension of a position taken by radical democrats in the late fifth century. In contrast, Aristotle's separation of household life and relationships from the more strictly defined political world of public assemblies and officeholding reflects the changing political and social climate of early Hellenistic Athens and provides an important context for the historical interpretation of Menander's comedies.

Plato lived his life as a member of the citizen elite in a democratic society; and despite his profound disagreement with the principle of equality underlying democratic rule, his view of the ideal city as a family "writ large" *(Republic)* and of the "second-best" city as a community of self-perpetuating households *(Laws)* directly reflects the centrality, both ideological and practical, of the family in democratic Athens.[2] Indeed Plato's image of the ideal polis as one single organic family, in which "our people will think of the same things as their own, aim at the same goal, and, as far as possible, feel pleasure and pain in unison," can be seen as a characteristic, and for some readers characteristically perverse, Platonic reinterpretation of the values and ideology of his own society.[3] The Athenians employed the language of family membership (for example, "having a share") in creating their rules of community membership. In the *Republic* Plato goes further and insists on taking such family language quite literally, for "it would be absurd if they only mouthed kinship names without doing the things that go along with them" (463e). For Plato the polis should be one single family, not simply be like one.

From this perspective, it is hard to agree with Hannah Arendt that Plato's "political plans foresaw . . . an extension of the public sphere to the point of annihilation of private life altogether."[4] Perhaps Arendt herself saw this as the effect of Plato's political theory, but unless his use of the language of family membership in the *Republic,* and of the laws of family membership in the *Laws,* is consciously empty, it would seem more appropriate to say that Plato privileges the family rather than that he annihilates it and that he "familiarizes" the polis as much as he "politicizes" the family. Marriage and adultery are issues of public and political significance in Plato's ideal cities, just as they were in democratic Athens. On the question of public and private, in contrast to that of equality, Plato's political theory may be seen as radically extending, and not rejecting, the prevailing language and ideology of his own society. Further, in Plato's polis, as in Periclean Athens, the isolated and self-absorbed *idiotes* (the private man)—not the household or family per se—stood as the ethical and structural private antithesis to the public polis community.[5] The individual desire and identity of such an *idiotes* might be said to suffer "annihilation" in the *Republic* (as also perhaps in Pericles' vision of the community as recorded by Thucydides), while the family as such experiences a sort of apotheosis.

Nor, on the other hand, was Aristotle's construction of the public/private dichotomy quite as obvious or as simple as Arendt implies in her explication of the famous statement "man is by nature a *zoon politikon*" (*Politics* 1253a):

> To be political, to live in a polis, meant that everything was decided through words and persuasion and not through force and violence. In Greek self-understanding, to force people by violence, to command rather than persuade, were prepolitical ways to deal with people characteristic of life outside the polis, of home and family life, where the household head ruled with uncontested, despotic powers, or of life in the barbarian empires of Asia, whose despotism was frequently likened to the organization of the household.[6]

On this reading, Aristotle saw the household (oikos or *oikia*) as the antithesis of the polis (as in fact essentially barbarian); its function was the provision of the necessities of life, while the polis and politics provided the "good life." However, although Aristotle clearly privileges certain "political" activities of public life in his discussion of citizenship and "constitutions" *(politeiai),* he does not by any stretch of the imagination collapse all household relationships into that of despotism. Rather, in his analysis of the household in book 1 of the *Politics,* Aristotle carefully distinguishes household relationships one from another, using analogies taken from the public sphere:

> There are . . . three parts of household management, corresponding to three types of rule, one as of a master, despotic . . . next the rule of a father, and a third which arises out of the marriage relationship . . . Over wife, rule is as of a statesman, political; over children, as of a king, royal . . . It is true that in the majority of those states in which government is truly political there is an interchange of the role of ruler and ruled, which aims at equality and non-differentiation; but so long as one is ruling and the other is being ruled, there is a strong tendency to mark distinctions in outward

dignity, in style of address, and in honours paid . . . As between male and female this kind of relationship is permanent. Rule over children is royal, for the begetter is ruler by virtue both of affection and of age; and this is the prototype of royal rule.[7]

Further, the character of the household has a direct and non-metaphorical connection to the character of the state, since for Aristotle the "economics," or the methods of production, of the citizen household play an important part in shaping the character of the public sphere and its constitution (or *politeia*).[8] Among democracies—that is, those *poleis* in which the *demos* rules in its own interest—the best according to Aristotle is that in which the great majority of the population is engaged in agriculture ("yeoman" democracy) at some distance from the center of power—so allowing the better sort to rule (1328b6). On the other hand, the worst democracy has a citizen population consisting largely of craftsmen, laborers, and the like; and these baser sorts of citizens promote their "oikos/economic" interests through the institutions of radical democracy. So, better and worse economic interests and activities will produce better and worse citizens, and also better and worse *politeiai*.

Still, although Aristotle posits in this way an essential connection between the nature of private "economy" and the character of public *politeia,* he also sharply separates the properly political activities of citizens from the economic activities of households. "Economics" might be the basis of political action, but it is not itself a political activity; and Aristotle is clear in his view that being a citizen (a *polites*) is something different from being a member of a family and a household. The point is central to Aristotle's well-known criticism of Plato's *Republic*.[9] The polis, argues Aristotle, is not simply the household writ large, but rather a different kind (as well as different size) of social entity (see 1.1.1252a). Plato errs, in Aristotle's view, in attempting to create household unity in his ideal polis, because a polis is necessarily plural (1263b). Thus, even though Aristotle himself uses the analogy of political rule in his analysis of the household in book 1, he insists in book 2 in criticizing Plato's *Republic* on the principle that political relationships should not be understood or constructed as in fact equivalent to household relationships, a move which he claims weakens the latter while at the same time eliminating the former altogether: "There comes a point where the state, if it does not cease to be a state altogether, will certainly come to be a very much worse one; it is as if one were to reduce concord to unison or rhythm to a single beat."[10]

The activity of the householder is distinct from that of the citizen (polites), defined succinctly by Aristotle as one who holds deliberative and judicial office. This conceptual separation or "uncoupling" of strictly political forms of participation from the larger sphere of economic and social life distinguished Aristotle from Plato and also from the public ideology of classical Athens. This separation is an integral part of the way in which Aristotle privileges the public sphere of citizen participation in law and public decision-making over other kinds of participation. It is a key element of the "primacy of politics" in Aristotle's political theory.

But just how representative is Aristotle's emphasis in the Politics on the narrowly political aspects of Greek public life as the defining elements of both polis and polites? What is its larger historical significance? It might be argued, in fact, that Aristotle privileged office-holding and separated the strictly "political" activities of the citizen from other important kinds of polis participation (most prominently religious participation) just because these were the facets of Athenian polis life that he as a resident alien was always explicitly denied,[11] and that his definitions should not be broadly generalized as a reflection of the Athenian or Greek political perspective. But even if—as seems reasonable—we grant the philosopher a larger perspective than his own immediate circumstances, it still seems necessary to ground his discussion of the polis in the realities of society and politics in his own day (the late fourth century); and from that perspective it seems clear, as Josiah Ober has argued, that Aristotle was a "prescient observer" of a changing political world. "Aristotle foresaw," says Ober, "a radical rupture between political and socioeconomic roles, between polity and society." As a friend of the Macedonian royal house and also a longtime resident observer of Athenian politics, Aristotle was in a good position to see, as Ober puts it, "the wave of the future . . . the divorce of the social from the overtly political: the end of the classical polis."[12] Politics, we might say, became a more narrowly defined sphere of activity just as the source and center of political power and decision-making was no longer found within the community itself, and the "primacy" with which Aristotle endowed such politics expresses not their equation with society but a separation of one part of the public from the larger polis whole.

Thus, Aristotle's academic privileging of the politics of the assembly and courtroom is quite different in character from the "primacy" of Plato's politics in the *Republic*—and also that of democratic politics in classical Athens; rather than separating the social, religious, and familial life of households from the sphere of politics proper, Plato and democratic Athenian ideology brought all together within a polis which was itself imagined or constructed as a single metaphorical family. So although both Aristotle and Plato may be said to have given "primacy" to "politics," their conception of the meaning of that term and of the public/private distinction is significantly different.

Menander's comedies, on the other hand, construct a public/private relationship which acknowledges the Aristotelian separation of state (the polis as a collection of active officeholding *politai*) and society, as well as the classical opposition of *idiotes* and society (polis in its larger sense); his plays end, however, by privileging neither state nor *idiotes* but a third alternative: a private community of families/households.

The Politics of Menander's Athens

We do not learn about historical events from Menander himself. Indeed, for readers of Greek drama perhaps the most immediately striking feature of Menander's drama is the absence of contemporary political issues and commentary. So Peter Green calls Menander's drama the "private comedy of manners" and observes that Menander's characters, "rustic or urban, are concerned with their own rather than the state's affairs, with money and marriage, not with politics."[13] What then can such apolitical drama tell us about the society for which it was written—or indeed about the politics that are so markedly absent from its plots? What was happening in Menander's Athens?

One possible answer might be "nothing much," and indeed in their commentary on Menander A. W. Gomme and F. H. Sandbach argue against this suggestion (not attributed to any specific author) with their own emphatic claim that politics were far from dead in Menander's Athens. Politics were not dead, they insist, but deadly— and "far too grim and frustrated to make a suitable subject for an audience that wished to be entertained on a public holiday."[14] Since, however, some 100 years earlier the very grim and frustrating twenty-seven-year war with the Spartans and their allies did not keep Aristophanes (or Euripides) from bringing contemporary politics into the theater, the explanation is unconvincing. To understand the different and distinctive character of politics in the late fourth and early third centuries when Menander was writing his comedies, we need to begin with Macedon.

The Macedonian victory at Chaeronea in 338 B.C.E. did not immediately bring about the end of Athenian democracy, but rather marked the beginning of its Indian summer of independent action and radical, open participation. Both Philip and his son Alexander preferred to be seen as friends of Athens and her democracy rather than as barbarian tyrants, and both treated the city with remarkable restraint. From 338 to the death of Alexander in 323, the same years in which Aristotle most likely wrote his *Politics*,[15] Athenian popular democratic institutions of public assembly and courts, so important to Aristotle's discussion of citizen life and governmental form, continued to operate and to exemplify Athenian public life. Demosthenes' oration "On the Crown," a public defense of his public career (and private life) delivered in 330, is as much a monument to Athenian democracy as is the sculptured stele on which Demokratia herself crowns Demos and celebrates the decree of 336 B.C.E. inscribed beneath, a decree prescribing the penalties for any attempt to overthrow the democracy.[16] And it was also in 330 that the wealthy horsebreeding bachelor Lycophron defended his public career and private life when charged with subverting the democracy through *moicheia*. Politics and political prosecutions, and the public examination of private lives, went on seemingly undaunted by the Macedonian presence and power.

The death of Alexander in 323, however, was followed by an Athenian-led rebellion against Macedonian rule and eventually by an

Athenian defeat. The illusion that a popular participatory democracy could operate under foreign military domination was now quickly dispelled. Antipater, the victorious Macedonian general, insisted that "the constitution be changed from democracy, and a constitution on the basis of property be established" in which those who had more than 2,000 drachmas would be "masters [*kyrioi*] of the state and the vote." He insisted also that Athens receive a Macedonian garrison.[17] It is clear that the garrison was Antipater's main concern; the impetus and language of constitutional change came from within the political circles of Athens itself and represent the victory of a long-suppressed minority voice.

The terms of the new order were hardly new; they belong to the political debates extending back to at least the late fifth century and specifically to the short-lived Athenian experiment with oligarchic rule in the latter years of the Peloponnesian War, when the city was put in the hands of those "best qualified in person and property to serve the state."[18] Turning the city over to those Athenians able to serve, those with enough money to serve, those meeting a specified census requirement, or those who were hoplites were solutions that had been suggested and tried before in times of tension or defeat.[19] The defeat of the Sicilian expedition in 413 was followed in 411 by the overthrow of the democracy and installation of an oligarchic council of 400 (chosen through a system of co-optation) who ruled in behalf of a now oligarchic citizen body of 5,000 citizens best able to serve.[20] The fifth-century Athenians, however, did not long tolerate this limitation of political privilege and separation of political responsibility from the broader sphere of social and communal participation: the democracy—open participation based on parentage; that is, on membership in an Athenian family—was restored in a matter of months. Likewise, even after Athens' complete defeat in 405 and unconditional surrender in 404, the Spartan-backed oligarchic regime lasted less than a year before falling to a resurgent democracy—a democracy which even came close to adopting into its citizen-family those slaves and foreigners who had contributed to the cause.[21]

Although the Macedonian-enforced oligarchy of 322 was also short-lived, it was considerably more ominous for the future character of Athenian politics. Taking advantage of the power struggle between rival Macedonian generals after the death of Antipater in 319, anti-Macedonian Athenians engineered a democratic restoration which abolished the property qualifications for active citizenship. Virtually the first act of the restored democracy was the condemnation of the most prominent pro-Macedonian Athenian leader, Phocion. The old general, thoroughly compromised by his cooperation with the Macedonian military rulers, was returned by those rulers to the Athenian demos and to public trial in the theater, which according to Plutarch was filled with slaves, foreigners, and women.[22] Phocion was convicted by that public assembly and ordered to drink hemlock. The trial is instructive not only as an example of the excesses of Athenian popular justice (and of the philosophical oligarch's worst nightmare of democratic rule), but also as an indication of the extent to which Athenian politics were now driven by the issues and alliances created by the Macedonian domination, and by powers outside the Athenian community.

The hollowness of the late fourth-century democratic restoration in comparison to that of the fifth century, and indeed of any Athenian hopes of reviving an independent and active democratic community in an occupied city, was almost immediately evident. In the following autumn (of 318) the Macedonian general Cassander emerged the winner over the supposed supporter of Greek "freedom," Polyperchon, and immediately turned the city over to Demetrius of Phaleron, a student of Theophrastus (Aristotle's nephew and successor as head of the Lyceum), friend of Macedon, and now would-be "philosopher king." Real political independence of action, however, was no longer possible, even for one backed up by both Aristotelian theory and a Macedonian garrison. The center of power lay outside Athens, and Demetrius' laws are conspicuously limited in scope and ambition. It was at just about this time that the young Menander began his dramatic career, and it seems clear that the disappearance of politics from his comedies reflects not so much the inherent grimness of events themselves as the removal of political authority from its traditional classical locus in the community of Athenian citizens, and the resulting sense of disengagement on the part of many citizens.

The laws that Demetrius set down for the Athenians at this time, like those of Solon much earlier, are known by later quotation rather than by documentary record. But from what survives in such sources as Athenaeus or Diogenes Laertius, it seems that Demetrius, unlike Solon, restricted his legislative interest largely to the public life and citizen participation of the propertied members of the community. Reflecting his Aristotelian education and principles, Demetrius restricted citizenship and political rights to persons of substance (now, however, those with 1,000 drachmas rather than the earlier figure of 2,000).[23] Similarly, his new social and economic code was squarely directed at those wealthy enough to indulge in conspicuous consumption and display. In the *Politics* Aristotle makes the interesting comment that real control of female citizens' behavior—under the authority of officials he calls *gynaikonomoi*—is possible only in oligarchies (or aristocracies), because in democracies citizen women (that is, "poor" women) must go out to work (1300a4). In his own newly established oligarchy, Demetrius followed Aristotle in giving reality to the office of *gynaikonomoi,* men who were apparently entrusted with overseeing the public display of wealthy Athenians at funerals and weddings, where women were traditionally present, and in general with preventing extravagant female display with clothes, ornaments, or means of transportation. Like Aristotle, Demetrius seems to have ignored the behavior of "working-class" men and women.

In addition to the fact that Demetrius' *gynaikonomoi* have a limited concern in activities which only the rich could afford, his laws as a whole have also a distinctly circumscribed interest in the visible public behavior of the female members of that elite. They do not address what should or should not happen in the interior and more intimate part of the house. In contrast to Solon's legislation, which was directed to the polis as a whole and also assumed a legitimate public interest in household relations and behavior (such as frequency of sexual intercourse between the heiress and her husband, or the mutual responsibilities of fathers and sons), there is no indication that Demetrius' officials or their "justice" were expected to look over—let alone leap over—the courtyard wall.

Such a distinction of sphere between female or family behavior in public and in private is not usually a feature of discussions of Demetrius' laws. Nonetheless, it seems significant for present purposes that certain kinds of private or family behavior which were of concern to Solon in the early sixth century, to the dramatists in the fifth, and still to Plato in the fourth—such as the punishment of adultery, the marriage of the heiress, and the behavior and relationship of parents and children—seem from the admittedly fragmentary evidence not to have been addressed. Demetrius' legislation then is "Solonian" in character only to the limited extent that it set up constitutional rules and regulated conspicuous public display. Relationships and behavior within the oikos were not in themselves his concern. In this way, Demetrius' interest as lawgiver in his citizens' public identity and attributes—their eligibility for public office and their public use of wealth—rather than their "private" relationships or household economy reflects, on the one hand, his Aristotelian perspective and, on the other, the real emerging disjunction between polis institutions and private life in late fourth-century Athens which, I shall argue, is mirrored in the comedies of Menander.[24]

Demetrius of Phaleron's regime ended as it had begun, caught up in the larger struggle for power between the Macedonian successors. Proclaiming the restoration of Athenian freedom, Demetrius Poliorcetes, the son of Antigonos, drove the resident Macedonian garrison out of the city in 307 B.C.E. and was rewarded by the Athenians with extravagant honors, including not only the establishment of new games—the Antigonia and Demetria—but also the addition of two new civic tribes (Antigonis and Demetrias). In the following years Athens frequently found itself a pawn in the larger battle for control of the eastern Mediterranean, and its political institutions as frequently overturned and then restored. But if in 292, the year Menander died, Athens was ostensibly a democracy, if only in the limited Aristotelian sense that citizenship was not formally limited on the basis of property, it was a democracy under the thumb of one Macedonian potentate (Demetrius Poliorcetes, now king of Macedon) and looking desperately for "liberation" once again from another (Ptolemy Soter in Egypt). By this time, as J. K. Davies notes, "rare exceptions apart, most Hellenistic cities had a government described as 'democratic'"[25]—although most political decisions were hardly being made by any demos. The situation is not unknown in the modern world.

In the world of Menander's comedies, the public sphere of activity in which citizen privileges were traditionally exercised is background, not foreground, to the dramatic action. Here the public sphere of Aristotle's polis—of citizen action and decision-making—is present but overshadowed by the dramatic focus on the fortunes and relationships of families and households, and also by the broadened "cosmopolitan" perspective of a society now part of a Macedonian empire. This was a world in which it was often more important to be an *anthropos* than a *polites*. Again, the absence of politics in Menander's drama reflects neither a real dearth of political activity nor its unprecedented "grimness," but rather the distancing of politics from the sphere of those activities over which either Menander or any other Athenian citizen had influence or control. In this context, his entertaining yet instructive illumination of the private lives of families within a community of citizen households makes Menander's drama a distinctive and valuable source for social history.

Menander and Social History

In 1896, when Menander was known almost entirely through fragmentary quotation by other ancient authors and by adaptation for the Roman stage, the eminently quotable J. P. Mahaffy had this to say about his value for the historian: "But when all has been said that ought to be, or can be, in praise of Menander's style, and when we come to inquire from him and from the New Comedy what they have to tell us about their age, the outcome is miserably small. They appear carefully to avoid all the great events of the day, all large political interests, all serious philosophy, and merely to reflect the idlest, the most trivial, and the most decayed gentility of Athens." And as for the hope of future finds: "It is usual to lament the irreparable loss of the plays of Menander, but it may be doubted whether, apart from style, history would gain from a further knowledge of him."[26] The discovery in the twentieth century of considerable and substantial portions of Menander's plays surviving on Egyptian papyrus has not necessarily changed this judgment. Peter Green, clearly no admirer of Menander, seems to concur completely with Mahaffy, as he pointedly contrasts the "private comedy of manners" which he calls "escapist" with the politically engaged fifth-century drama "fueled" by "high-voltage civic and tribal conflicts." Menander's characters, says Green, "are concerned with their own rather than the state's affairs, with money and marriage, not with politics."[27] The reluctance to take Menander seriously as a historical source is not limited, however, to those who see an essential connection between politics and (serious) history. In *The Harvest of Hellenism,* a cultural, intellectual, and political history, F. E. Peters also finds in Menander little intellectual content or interest; rather, Menander's plays are mere "reflections of the life of a prosperous but politically inane bourgeoisie in the Athens that had to reckon with Antipater, Cassander, Antigonus, and Demetrius Poliorcetes." Furthermore, although "one can perhaps read between his lines the failing morale of political impotence . . . there is no hint there of the intellectual energies that were at work in the Lyceum or of the serious moral issues being debated in the Stoa and the school of Epicurus."[28] And even in the area of social history, where "marriage and money" are central issues, Menander has been more often mined for specific details of private life (for example, the size of dowries) than analyzed as a significant source on the character and structures of social life. In a less direct but no less clear manner, Davies' careful warning about the dangers of using literature as "the mirror of reality" and his almost complete exclusion of Menander from his chapter "Cultural, Social and Economic Features of the Hellenistic World" for the new edition of *The Cambridge Ancient History* suggest an implicit judgment on the historical value of Menander once again not so very far from Mahaffy's.

Literary discussions of Menander, on the other hand, often include comments on his depiction of society and social relations; and in particular topics of "sex and gender" have recently received considerable attention.[29] But despite the interest of such discussions there is usually little attempt to place these issues in a larger historical, political or social, context—leading at times to the historically naive, even if unintended, implication that such figures as the "goodhearted concubine" or such ideas as "romantic love" were distinctive novelties of Menander's world.[30]

In part, the neglect of Menander as a serious source for social history may stem from an apparent historical marginality. Just how significant was the Athens of the late fourth and early third centuries, the city in which Menander lived and worked? Was Menander's Athens a part of the newly emerging Hellenistic world or merely a provincial Hellenic backwater? For whom and to whom does Menander speak? It is notable that the conventional division of Greek history into Hellenic and Hellenistic eras has often left Menander and his comedies awkwardly appended to the former (so Ferguson: "New Comedy belongs, as a whole, to the Hellenic and not to the Hellenistic"),[31] with the result that their larger historical significance has been underappreciated—all this despite the fact that Menander's plays were extremely popular throughout the Hellenistic world.

By contrast, I argue that Menander's dramas are a significant source, not so much for the details of private life per se as for the re-orientation of the spheres of public and private life, of politics and society, in Athens under Macedonian control. And rather than mar-ginalizing these plays, I suggest that Menander's specific Athenian identity actually enhances their historical significance, since his rep-resentation of the public interest in private household issues such as marriage, heiresses, adultery, and rape stands in a clear Athenian tra-dition of both legal and dramatic discussion of these essential points of intersection of the public and private spheres.

Menander's late Hellenic and early Hellenistic Athenian identity is not the most significant obstacle to his recognition as a legitimate historical source. Much more problematic, and perhaps ironically so, is the notion that Menander's drama functions as a "mirror" of soci-ety. The idea, of course, has a certain authority, since Aristophanes of Byzantium is supposed to have exclaimed on reading Menander: "O Menander and Life, which of you imitates the other?" Taken at face value, this sentiment might suggest that Menander's comedies present an unmediated image of daily life and so are essentially "documents" of social history. But this is both a simplistic under-standing of mimesis and also an unlikely reading of the comedies as comic drama. If the value of Menander to the social historian is in fact limited to finding in the plays a record of daily life, of what peo-ple spent their days doing, then the conclusion of Mahaffy quoted above seems inevitable: this is the social record of an absurdly frivo-lous and inconsequential leisured elite—and real history must be found elsewhere.

In 1911 W. S. Ferguson responded to what he called Mahaffy's "diatribe on Attic society at the time of the New Comedy" with the observation that Menander was "still a comedian by profession," and that the fact that he created characters "lacking in ideals" or "without more than ludicrous enthusiasms" does not necessarily reflect upon the general character of contemporary Athenian society. The defense, however well intentioned, falls far short, since by arguing that Menander offers the modern reader something in between a true "mirror of life" and total comic distortion, Ferguson leaves him once again in limbo as a historical source. And with the summary comment that "taken as a whole, the New Comedy and the *Characters* of Theophrastus probably admit us only to what was least worthy in the life of Athens at the end of the fourth and the beginning of the third century B.C.—the relaxation of the rich youth of Athens on being freed at length from the intolerable financial and military burdens of imperialism"[32]—he himself relapses into reading Menander's plays as social record rather than as social comedy produced for the public festival of Dionysus.

Just because Menander's comic plots seem so much more "ordinary" than those of Aristophanes (of Athens)—household confusions and crises rather than imperial ventures in the sky or dramatic rescue operations in the underworld—a strong temptation exists to take them as detailing "ordinary" everyday Athenian life and as mimesis in this limited sense.[33] But the temptation should be resisted. This is still festival comedy, even if performed in costumes that were considerably closer to ordinary Athenian dress than those of Old Comedy.[34] Menander's comedies are still wish-fulfillment public drama, and there is no reason to consider as historically "real" an Athenian society consumed entirely with sorting out family relationships and squabbles, and eventually celebrating happy endings with elaborate dinner parties. We would not unwarily assume that "situation comedies" and "soap operas" on television directly correspond to ordinary realities of American life; even less should we assume that the plot lines of comedy produced at the festival of Dionysus in Athens reveal the daily routines of any segment of the citizen community. As in the case of the fifth-century comedies of Aristophanes, political and historical realism is not a necessary condition of political and historical relevance.[35]

For present purposes, the significance of Menander's plays lies not in the details of "daily life" but in the nature of the social relationships he chooses to depict. "Daily life" is not the only way to understand *bios,* nor is mimesis necessarily a documentary or photographic record. What Menander offers us through his comic lens is an image (mimesis) of the life *(bios)* of the society as a whole and its central human relationships. And when attention is focused on the distinctive features of that society, on the structure of the households which constitute Menander's society and on their interaction with the world of traditional politics, then Menander becomes a much more interesting and more convincing source for social history. His plays become in fact a legitimate, and even essential, source for the historical experience of the family within Greek history. And rather than marginalizing his dramas as "neither fish nor fowl"—neither full-bloodedly Hellenistic nor healthily Hellenic—Menander's identity and age, an Athenian of the first post-Alexander generation, establish him as a key historical witness in the investigation of the historical evolution of private and public interests in ancient Greece. The Athenian context of his drama in fact makes available to us a much enriched historical perspective, since the social, familial, legal, and political relationships dramatized in his plays have a historical context and stand in a historical tradition of public drama. And while Athens may not be in any sense "typical," here again it stands as the model against which the experience of other, less well-known and less literate societies can be gauged.

Family and Household in Menander

In the Introduction I argued that despite—indeed even because of—its plethora of possible meanings, "family" is a useful word for the discussion of the historical construction and interaction of public and private spheres in ancient Greece. The single English word "family" covers a semantic field which in Greek includes numerous terms (*genos, oikos, anchisteis, kedestes,* and so forth), but it is in fact what we, from our more singularly focused modern perspective, are interested in investigating in ancient Greece. What role did the many personal relationships which come under the umbrella term "family" play in the historical experience of the Greek polis? In previous chapters I have argued that the household (oikos or *oikia*) was the key to understanding the historical experience of the family in both early Greece and classical Athens, and that the dynamic character of Greek family history lies in the interaction and interrelation of household and polis. In contrast, "clans," "lineages," and "blood-lines," so prominent in modern discussions of ancient Greek society, are noticeably absent. It is hardly surprising then that in Menander's drama the household is once again, and perhaps even more promi-nently, the premiere form of family organization. It is also the fea-tured building block of a newly emphasized nonpolitical commu-nity.[36]

With near-Aristotelian clarity, Menander builds his households, and their comic dramas, on the relations of husband and wife, par-ent and child, and master and slave (see *Politics* 1.1252a–b). Like Aristotle, Menander prefers *oikia* over *oikos* (the standard term of modern discussion) to denote both "house" and "household," and once again, the close connection of persons and property is clear. Menander, however, expands the Aristotelian model by the addition of sibling relationships, as well as the often ambiguous figure of the courtesan or concubine who plays a central role in resolving her family's crisis. And when adult siblings are involved (as in the *Aspis,* in which two brothers are at odds over the marriage of a third brother's daughter) the drama moves beyond the single household to the interconnected stories of several households. Then, moving a step further, the *Samia* and *Dyskolos* show completely unrelated and eco-nomically disparate households becoming related and connected through marriage, the standard "happy ending." Menander's plays feature the lives and crises of not one but several interconnected households that constitute a household community. These are not truly private comedies at all, but social comedies articulating the so-cial truth that a narrowly familial and private life is not the only al-ternative to the narrowly political public realm.

A prominent feature of Menander's household community is its emphasis on connections brought about through the oikos—on the relationship of *oikeiotes* (kindred/family) or the quality of being *oikeios.* Like the *anchisteia* (those "nearest" family members), *oikeiotes* does not connect its members in a narrowly lineal fashion, but embraces those connected to, and having interests in, a house-hold. And even more than the *anchisteia, oikeioi* are a living net-work of mutually dependent household members. Lineal ancestors

have no discernible significance in Menander's drama. Three generations—grandfather, son/daughter, and grandchild—are the typical
focus of the plot. Lineal descendants, that is, children and heirs, are
of course highly significant for the creation of plots as well as highly
desirable for the households involved, but there is little emphasis on
"blood" connection or lineage. Adoption is also an accepted practice
(for example, *Samia, Dyskolos*).

A particularly revealing glimpse of this web of familial household
connection, rooted in *oikia* rather than in *genos,* is provided by the
Dyskolos. In that play the double marriage of brother and sister
from one family with the sister and half-brother from another results
in a new family connection or relation of *oikeiotes* for the two
households. But the rustic Gorgias is reluctant to join a party which
includes women from his new fiancée's family, protesting: "I'm shy
with women in the same room" (871). To this, his new brother-in-
law, the urbane Sostratos, replies: "Nonsense—you have to remember that everything is *oikeia* now" (872–873). Somewhat later the
sentiment is strikingly echoed by the household slave Getas. When
considering possible avenues of revenge against the cantankerous
title character, Getas says to the cook, a fellow slave: "It's our duty
to make him a civilized man [*anthropos hemeroteos*]. For he is
oikeios with us now" (903–904).[37]

The relationship of *oikeiotes* thus draws together even those at the
extreme opposite ends of the oikos hierarchy, free and slave. The
web of relationships within the oikos is as unmistakably hierarchical
in Menander's drama as it is in Aristotle's *Politics.* It is worth emphasizing, however, that in itself *genos*—"birth" or "blood"—did
not determine whether one was free or slave. If the abandoned child
of the *Epitrepontes,* for example, is reared by the slave Habrotonon
as her own, he will be brought up a slave; if recognized by his father,
Charisios, the child might enjoy the somewhat preferable free status
of a *nothos,* or bastard; but when identified as the child of the married couple, Charisios and Pamphile, he will have a better status still.
He is now a citizen and an heir, a status that is made possible when
household members themselves recognize not only that he is free, but
that he is one of their own. Status and identity in the household are
then essentially relational: they are rooted in the central and mutually defined relationships of the household: a slave is a slave of a

master, a child is a child of a parent, and a wife is the wife of a husband. Again, the structure of the household in Menander's drama is unmistakably Aristotelian; but what gives his drama life are the creative characters and plot motifs he weaves around this structure. One character and one motif in particular merit further discussion here: the "good-hearted concubine" and "romantic love." Both of these are favorites of Menander but are completely neglected by Aristotle. They are also topics of current interest in Menandrian studies, and central to assumptions about historical progress or change in Greek family relations.

The free or slave concubine or courtesan is a household character whom Aristotle notably neglects and in whom Menander shows a special interest.[38] In her study of courtesans in Menander, Madeleine Henry has called attention to his distinctive use of the "good-hearted courtesan" who plays a positive and enabling role in bringing his comedies to their happy conclusion.[39] The best example is the character Habrotonon of the *Epitrepontes,* a slave musician who sympathetically and single-handedly orchestrates the reunion of the young married but estranged couple, Charisios and Pamphile, and also the recognition of their son. With remarkable care and good sense, Habrotonon reveals to Charisios that he himself is the father of his own wife's illegitimate child—that it was he who raped Pamphile when as a young unmarried virgin she was participating in a nocturnal festival. Ashamed at his own double standard—he blamed his wife for something he had done himself[40]—Charisios now returns happily to his loyal wife. Also interesting for Henry's analysis and for the present discussion is the figure of Chrysis in the *Samia,* a free concubine who protects, to her own cost, the child born as a result of the seduction of the "girl next door," during another nocturnal festival, by her partner's young son.[41]

Henry notes the irony of the scenario of both plays, in which women with at best a marginal place in the household are committed to, and in the end responsible for, the restoration of household stability and harmony. The irony is a real one, but also one with a long history in Athenian drama. In Sophocles' *Ajax,* it is the concubine Tecmessa who undertakes the familial responsibility of burying the dead Ajax; and in Euripides' *Andromache,* it is the Trojan slave and concubine Andromache who proves the true "wife" in her loyalty to the household and especially in her production of a son for Neoptolemos. Again, it is clear that in its ancient Greek construction, family loyalty extends beyond the nuclear, or parent-child, bond and that family identity is a matter of active relationships, not simple genetic relation. Another marginal family member who sometimes plays an oikos-supporting role in drama is the *nothos*. In Sophocles' *Ajax*, the bastard brother of Ajax, Teucros, proves himself at least the moral equal of Agamemnon; and in the tragic conclusion of Euripides' *Hippolytos*, Theseus recognizes his *nothos* son as fully "wellborn" *(gnesios)* when he realizes that Hippolytos has not in fact betrayed him by seducing his wife Phaedra.[42] Interesting comic variations of this latter theme appear in Menander's *Dyskolos* and *Samia;* in the one case a previously neglected stepson rescues his stepfather from drowning and so is rewarded with adoption, and in the other an adopted and quite dutiful son is wrongly thought by his father to have seduced the latter's concubine. The practical realities of fragmented or "broken" families reinforce the practical benefits of an inclusive construction of family relations.

But although Menander's drama may allow the stepson to become an adopted son and a bastard to be recognized as at least morally legitimate, the courtesan's good services will not result in improvement in her status. Chrysis does not become a wife, nor is it even certain that Habrotonon becomes free. Such a conclusion would contradict the clear rules of social alliance and household hierarchy in Menander's drama—even though a modern audience might think that such rules should certainly be broken in these cases. But if Chrysis is a Samian woman whom Demeas has taken in as his concubine, then she cannot become an Athenian wife. Rather the comedy's "happy ending" implies that she is restored to her role as Demeas' mistress by the end of the play and as such participates in the marriage of Moschion and Plangon. Chrysis' behavior shows that she properly belongs to, and promotes the interests of, the household of Demeas and his son Moschion, but she belongs (that is, she shares in the relationship of *oikeiotes*) not as a wife but as a concubine (hetaira).

Habrotonon's fate is less clear in what survives of the text of the *Epitrepontes*. Again, one would like to imagine that she was in fact rewarded as she had hoped for her services with her freedom (line 547), but it is not clear that Menander allowed that to happen. If she had been able to establish her membership in a free household, for example by bringing forward free parents (or simply a free father), she would have been recognized as free and perhaps even as a citizen, as are the concubines of the *Perikeiromene* and the *Sicyonios*. But apparently she cannot do so, and her good services to the household of Charisios cannot change the hierarchical nature of both the household and society at large as Menander constructs them. Perhaps she became at the end of the play the concubine of Charisios' friend Chaerestratos—and so at least earned a place in an oikos and a position superior to that in which she began the play, that is, independent hired musician and prostitute.

Henry explicitly declines to draw historical conclusions from her interesting observations on the role played by Menander's courtesans. If, however, Menander's comedies are pressed on the currently popular question of whether or not the "status" of women improved in the Hellenistic era, they would seem to answer in the negative.[43] Understanding "status" to include above all formal and informal authority and responsibility, we can see the women, including the concubine, in Menander's plays only as highly traditional figures. The devoted concubine is a familiar character in Greek literature, and the wives and daughters who populate Menander's plays are also overwhelmingly traditional, whether in their behind-the-scenes nagging *(Samia)*, their devotion to religious rituals *(Dyskolos, Samia)*, or their central role as pawns or players in the game of marriage alliance. Even a case which might at first be seen as evidence of a new assertiveness is in fact the espousal of a very traditional idea. Arguing with her father in behalf of her own marriage (to which she is loyal despite her husband's bad behavior), the young wife Pamphile says: "If you force me you are a *despotes* not a father," clearly illustrating Aristotle's classic distinction in the *Politics* between the different kinds of household rule: a daughter should be ruled as a royal subject not a slave. But if her father chose to coerce her, she apparently had no legal right to resist.

Rather than anything novel or progressive, Menander's plays assume a highly traditional hierarchy of female roles, with a firm line drawn between the modest and protected citizen woman and the unprotected and certainly less modest female slave and courtesan. The apparent public "freedom" of the unattached independent woman—

in contrast to the dependency of the wife or daughter—is a traditional irony of Greek literature. That the courtesan is such a prominent and significant figure in Menander's comedies may in fact have
a different kind of historical significance; it may suggest that the
playwright and his audience were particularly interested in the social
justification of such women in a family- or oikos-based society.[44]
However, just as in the fifth century, concubines are not appropriate
members of an oikos that contains a wife. The point is starkly made
by Deianeira in Sophocles' *Trachiniai* when she speaks angrily of
having to share a bed with the war captive Iole, and is also of course
an issue for Clytemnestra in the *Agamemnon*. In general, Athenian
men do not seem to have had both a resident concubine and a wife—
Alcibiades' extravagant flouting of this rule was a significant part of
his "un-Athenian" behavior—although they might visit or even support courtesans in separate establishments. Menander's male characters generally act in accord with conventional propriety; e.g., in
Samia, it is the bachelor Demeas who lives with a concubine while
his married neighbor does not; and in *Epitrepontes* Charios leaves
his wife before he takes up with a hetaira.

David Konstan has recently called attention to another of these
free and independent concubines who stands up for her own interests in the face of violent mistreatment at the hands of her partner.[45]
In the play called the *Perikeiromene* (translated by G. B. Shaw as
"The Rape of the Locks"),[46] a professional soldier named Polemon is
desperately in love with his concubine, Glykera, and considers her
"like a wife" (488). In that emotional state and also in ignorance of
the fact that the man whom Glykera has been seen to have publicly
embraced is in fact her own brother, Polemon angrily seizes his mistress and cuts off her hair (so the title). And in response, she quite
forthrightly leaves him. The situation is now difficult for Polemon,
for as the old man Pataikos comments, Glykera is her own mistress
(kyria heautes) and cannot be forced to return. Defending her own
actions to Pataikos, she says: "Let him insult [*hybrizeto*] [someone
else] in the future!" (723). Her forthrightness and insistence that she
knows what is best for herself is quite striking. Indeed, as Konstan
notes, her speech here is even more remarkable in contrast with her
silence at the end of the play, where, after the revelation that she is in
fact not only free but Athenian, she is formally given back in mar-

riage to the very man (now also discovered to be an Athenian) who has treated her so insultingly. Konstan comments: "Her deferential silence, if indeed she maintained it throughout the final act of the play, appears as the sign of her new citizen status, and the marriage that it brings . . . Glycera's change in status, imposing as it does a silence that is the sign of dutiful obedience, cancels the independence she had enjoyed as a [*pallake*]."[47]

Before, however, assuming that the *Perikeiromene* should be read (in feminist terms) as a tragedy rather than a comedy, it is advisable to take a second look at Glykera's likely fate if she had not been recognized and returned, now as proper wife, to Polemon. Essentially she would have been out in the street and looking for another position as concubine or whatever other employment was available to a free and independent woman. The possibilities are quite starkly outlined in Demeas' angry words to Chrysis in the *Samia,* as he kicks her out of the oikos: "A fine figure you make! Once you're on the town, you'll very quickly find your true value. Other girls, Chrysis, not at all in your style, run off to dinner parties for a minimum wage, and swallow strong drink until they die; or they starve, if they're not prepared to do this and do it smartly. You'll learn the hard way, like everyone else."[48]

Glykera has a close historical analogue in the person of Neaira, whose remarkable career is told with great rhetorical flourish by Apollodorus in [Demosthenes] 59, "Against Neaira." Like many a heroine in New Comedy, Neaira was abandoned as an infant, but picked up and reared in Corinth as a slave and courtesan/prostitute. With the help of her clients, she managed to buy her own freedom and then moved to Athens where she cohabited with a certain Phrynion. When he mistreated her (and here the historical account is considerably more brutal than the dramatic, even allowing for the larger cultural significance of "shearing" a woman's hair), she left him. In a private arbitration between Phrynion and Stephanos, her new "partner," she was judged to be *kyria tes heautes* ("her own mistress"; 497), and the two men were told to share her company and services. This peculiar judgment and the career of Neaira itself are a strong antidote to the modern tendency to sentimentalize the position of the courtesan and to focus anachronistically on her independent status as "mistress of herself." To be "mistress of herself" meant that a woman did not belong to a household, which was represented by a male *kyrios* in law and litigation. In actuality it left her without protection. The "mistress of herself" was therefore outside the traditional net of protection which household membership afforded a woman. Indeed "mistress of herself" may imply the limited nature of her resources—her own body was in many cases all that she had with which to support herself. Neither the courtesan who was free to operate in the public sphere nor the wife who, except in certain circumstances, was not, is easily cast as feminist "hero" or "victim," but both are part of the Athenian society which Menander depicts, and to which he appealed. On this score, Menander is illuminating but not innovative, and on balance justifies rather than challenges the social status quo.

But what of Polemon's intense and fervently expressed experience of *eros*, matched as well by that of a good number of other young men in Menander's drama? Could this be something new? P. G. McC. Brown presents the guarded thesis that "the notion of marrying for love was not seen as a comic absurdity in the time of Menander." Rather, according to Brown, the argument of a father to his son in the *Dyskolos* would have made sense to a "real-life" Athenian: "I not only want you to marry the girl you're in love with, but I say you ought to" because "a young man's marriage will be secure if he is persuaded to enter on it by eros."[49] The argument is supported by the principle that the arguments or speeches of "good" or "successful" characters can usually be assumed to have struck a sympathetic chord in the Athenian audience. Another "good" character (who expresses his love for the woman he has made pregnant) is Moschion in the *Samia*. At the end of that play Moschion decides not to leave home for a military career because of his obligations to and love for "the girl next door." Eros, he says, is his master.[50]

In considering how significant, how novel or how traditional, such sentiments were in Menander's Athens, two things should be kept in mind. First, the importance of eros, sexual desire and affection, to a successful marriage is an established feature of the Greek literary tradition. The principle is admittedly honored more in the breach than in the observance; but in the *Odyssey* Homer provides a paradigm of marriage to which eros is essential. In one of his more remarkable similes, Homer describes the reunion of Odysseus and Penelope:

> Now from his breast into his eyes the ache
> of longing mounted, and he wept at last,
> his dear wife, clear and faithful, in his arms,
> longed for
> as the sunwarmed earth is longed for by a swimmer
> spent in rough water where his ship went down
> under Poseidon's blows, gale winds and tons of sea.
> Few men can keep alive through a big surf
> to crawl, clotted with brine, on kindly beaches
> in joy, in joy, knowing the abyss behind:
> and so she too rejoiced, her gaze upon her husband,
> her white arms round him pressed as though forever.[51]

In honor of this couple's reunion, Homer continues, Athena herself

> slowed the night
> when night was most profound, and held the Dawn
> under the Ocean of the East.[52]

But recognizing the importance of eros within a marriage (and even in a middle-aged marriage) is not the same thing as approving a marriage made for love alone, as in modern popular sentiment. If indeed Menander or his characters were recommending "marrying for love" in the early third century B.C.E., it would be a notable event in Greek social history—and one meriting more comment perhaps than Brown's disclaimer: "the social history of Athens is far too large a subject to be tackled here."[53] But they are not. On consideration, it appears that love and marriage are connected quite differently in Menander than in our contemporary popular culture. Although Menander's young men do express their desire to marry the women for whom they experience eros, it is also true that these young men happen to "fall in love" with what turn out to be very suitable young women and brides; and eros is by itself by no means a sufficient cause for them, or their parents, to make the marriage. On the other hand, or on the other side of the relationship, eros is not permitted Menander's "brides"; this is an active, unruly force appropriate only to men.[54] Although Menander's characters do occasionally show a concern for the bride's happiness in a suitable marriage and acknowledge the existence of marital affection for that happiness (for example, *Aspis* and *Epitrepontes*), the romantic and erotic asymmetry of gender relations in Menander's world (if not necessarily in Athenian society of the time) is clear.

In sum, Menander's suggestion (through his characters) that eros can and should play a role in marriage is dramatically effective but hardly socially revolutionary. What does, however, seem interesting and distinctive in Menander's romantic plots is the way in which violence is a central feature of the eros that drives the actions of young men, and is restrained or moderated only if the young man knows that the object of his love is a free citizen and eligible bride. The quality or control (quality-control) of eros is determined by status. So Charisios, overcome by drink and eros, raped Pamphile in ignorance of her free status (470 ff.), whereas Moschion, who knew Plangon's identity, admits to shame at having made her pregnant but does not describe his act as a violent one. His slave simply says that his master has "made a mistake against a free girl" (*exemarten eis eleutheran koren;* 646–647), while Moschion himself claims that "thousands" of men have done the same. Although this attitude may seem disingenuous, it is nonetheless clear that Menander's society drew a distinction between seduction and rape, and that violent rape of a free woman was not an insignificant crime. According to the protective brother in the *Dyskolos,* it is a crime truly deserving the death sentence (292). And in the same play, the appropriate expression of eros in accord with the woman's status is made quite explicit in the advice of one young man to another: if she's a hetaira, "carry her off, get drunk, burn the door down," but if she is free, investigate *genos, bios,* and *tropoi* (birth, livelihood, and character; 65–66). And in both the *Dyskolos* and the *Aspis,* the infatuated young suitors protest, somewhat proudly perhaps, that though desperately in love they have exercised self-control and have not acted violently toward the young citizen women whom they hope to marry (*Dyskolos* 301–313; *Aspis* 289–298).[55] The image emerges of a highly sophisticated and also markedly hierarchical attitude toward both love and sexual violence—completely in keeping with the social class and intellectual community to which Menander belonged. This articulation of criteria for sexual behavior, like the portraits of "good courtesans," is best understood as supporting by dramatic amplification the norms of family life, which were and remained eminently traditional—and in this sense Aristotelian.[56]

Menander's Households

Historical change is evident, however, in the dynamics of interaction between Menander's households and the larger public or political world. There is a marked distancing between the society of private households and that of politics and law, with the latter now relegated to the margins of the drama and the former occupying center stage. In contrast to classical drama, such as the *Oresteia* or the Oedipus plays, in which a single (usually royal) household illuminates the problems and issues of the larger polis community, public interest and the polis itself seem remote from Menander's dramatic world.

Furthermore, to the extent that specifically public/polis law or activities do enter into the lives of Menander's characters and their households, it is with largely negative implications for their well-being. Rather than protecting family and household interests or assuming a synonymy between those interests and the public interest, as in the archaic and classical eras, the polis in Menander's dramatic world is a remote presence. Its laws are typically invoked by foolish or unsympathetic characters, while the more sensible members of this community of households solve their problems without public or polis help. A closer look at four of Menander's better-preserved plays, *Dyskolos* (The Grouch), *Samia* (The Samian Woman), *Aspis* (The Shield), and *Epitrepontes* (The Arbitrants), will illustrate this significant change of perspective. (See Figure 6 for Menander's household relationships.)

Dyskolos

The *Dyskolos,* produced in 316 and the only securely dated of Menander's plays, is the story of a distempered "loner" named Knemon who lives in a remote part of Attica, cultivating his rocky farm with only the help of his daughter and an old female servant. Near his farm is a shrine of Pan, and it is from the god himself that we learn about the title character:

> He's a real hermit of a man [*apanthropos tis anthropos sphodra*], who snarls at everyone and hates company—company isn't the

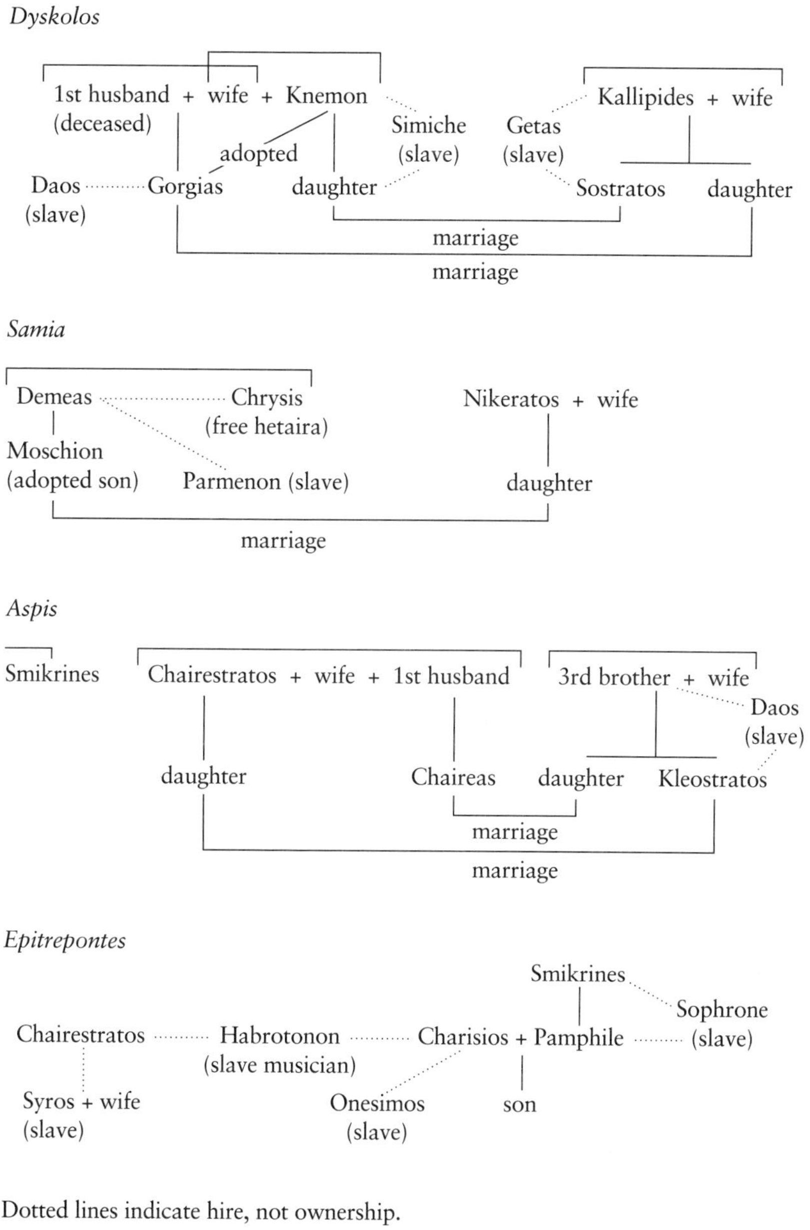

Dyskolos

1st husband + wife + Knemon   Kallipides + wife
(deceased)   Simiche   Getas
        adopted   (slave)   (slave)
Daos ········· Gorgias   daughter ·······   Sostratos   daughter
(slave)
                                        marriage
                                    marriage

Samia

Demeas ····················· Chrysis   Nikeratos + wife
  | (free hetaira)
Moschion
(adopted son)   Parmenon (slave)   daughter
                            marriage

Aspis

Smikrines   Chairestratos + wife + 1st husband   3rd brother + wife
                                                            Daos
                                                            (slave)
        daughter   Chaireas   daughter   Kleostratos
                                    marriage
                                marriage

Epitrepontes

                                    Smikrines
                                        | Sophrone
Chairestratos ········· Habrotonon ········· Charisios + Pamphile ········ (slave)
                  (slave musician) |
Syros + wife   Onesimos   son
(slave)   (slave)

Dotted lines indicate hire, not ownership.

Figure 6. The interrelation of households in Menander

word: he's getting on now, and he's never addressed a civil word to anyone in his life except myself . . . and that's only because he lives beside me, and can't help passing my door.

and about his family:

In spite of being such a hermit, he did get married, to a widow whose former husband had just died, leaving her with a small son. Well, he quarreled with his wife, every day and most of the night too—a miserable life. A baby daughter was born, and that just made things worse. Finally, when things got so bad that there was no hope of change and life was hard and bitter, his wife left him and went back to her son . . . He [the son] owns this small-holding here, next door, there he's now struggling to support his mother, himself and one loyal family slave [oiketes] . . . The old man lives alone with his daughter, and an old slave woman [therapaina]. He's always working, fetching his own wood and doing his own digging—and hating absolutely everyone.[57]

The action of the play begins when Pan puts a spell on a rich young gentleman (Sostratos) out on a hunting trip, causing the young man to fall desperately in love "at first sight" with Knemon's daughter—a young woman who Pan notes is "innocent of evil" (35–36). A friend (Chaireas) offers the advice noted earlier based on the criterion of status: if she is a hetaira, "grab her, carry her off, get drunk, burn the door down"; but if she is marriageable and free, check on "family, finance and character."[58] Sostratos, however, has already taken matters into his own hands—and has sent his slave to speak to Knemon directly. So Knemon's peace and solitude are disturbed at the very opening of the play, and increasingly so as the action proceeds.

As it happens, Sostratos' mother arrives at the shrine of Pan for a picnic-sacrifice. According to her son, she spends her days traipsing around Attica making sacrifices to various and sundry gods and goddesses. Since she and her party have forgotten their cooking pot, a slave is sent on another mission to Knemon's door. Already furious after his first visitor and protesting that his land is becoming a "public highway" (demosia hodos; 118) and a public stoa (175), upon the arrival of the second, Knemon decides that he will have to stay indoors for the day and angrily greets the slave sent to borrow a pot: "Is there any contract [*symbolaion*], you godless wretch [*anosie*], between you and me?" (469). When the slave insists that he is not on public business, "demanding payment of a debt or serving a summons" (469–470), Knemon uncomprehendingly turns him away. A friendly loan is not in his social repertoire. In Knemon's view, strangers and visitors turn his private domain into a public highway, and the only reason he can imagine for their being there is a "contract" which he insists does not exist. For Knemon, all persons and business not within the immediate bounds of his household, indeed anyone who would have the effrontery to knock on his door, must be part of the public world of which he wants no part. The line between public and private is thus drawn in an extreme and antagonistic fashion.

In the course of the drama, however, Knemon's narrow and polarized perception of the private sphere is challenged by the emergence of a private community built upon the household relations of the increasingly intertwined families and distinct both from the political world of the remote city-center (with its summons and stoas) and from Knemon's earlier hermit existence. Further, unlike the public sphere, where strict lines of political privilege based on economic status prevail, the rustic shrine of Pan in this play is the scene of romantic love—at least on the part of Sostratos—leading to two marriages which join wealthy and "poor" households.

But that is jumping ahead to the "happy ending." Returning to the action of the play, we find Sostratos, though intimidated by Knemon's vehemence, even more enamored of the "grouch's" daughter. Her distress over a bucket lost down the well and a jug which still needs to be filled wins his heart (190 ff.). By offering the young woman his help, however, he raises the suspicions of her half-brother Gorgias' slave, and so must confront Gorgias' earnest accusation of improper intentions: "Your idea is to seduce an innocent girl [literally: to persuade a free young woman to go wrong]—a respectable man's daughter, too—or you're watching your chance to do something that deserves the death-sentence, several times over."[59] Presumably, Gorgias is distinguishing seduction of a free girl from rape. The latter is what "deserves the death sentence." Protesting that his only crime is falling in love, and that he is ready to marry her without a dowry and will swear an oath to cherish her forever, he wins Gorgias' goodwill. The two then hatch a plan to put the question to Knemon while the old man is working in his field, which adjoins that of Gorgias. And for the sake of making a better impression, Sostratos even takes up a hoe himself and sets out to do some unaccustomed physical labor.

Unfortunately Sostratos' pain and labor are, for a time, in vain. Although the alliance with Gorgias will eventually pay off, Knemon himself has already decided to stay at home in the face of the "public" invasion of his property (455). The old man soon discovers, however, that being "at home" is no guarantee of safety, for when he attempts to retrieve the lost bucket and now a hoe from the bottom of the well, he falls in himself. And there he remains, to the considerable pleasure of the cook who was so rudely refused a cooking pot, until Gorgias jumps down into the well himself and, playing the part of Atlas (in the words of Sostratos, who watched the whole operation from above), manages to bring him up.

The experience has severely shaken Knemon and inspires him to make the following interesting admission:

> One mistake I did perhaps make, is thinking that I could be completely self-sufficient [*autarkes*], and would never need anyone's assistance. Now that I've seen how sudden and unexpected death can be, I realize I was stupid to take that line. You always need to have—and to have handy—someone to help you. When I saw how people lived, calculating everything for profit, I swear I grew cynical, and I never even imagined that any man would ever do a disinterested kindness to another [literally: would be *eunous* to another].[60]

Then, recognizing the bond of gratitude that now unexpectedly ties him to Gorgias, whom he has till now treated as a complete stranger, with never a kind word or a friendly deed, Knemon adopts (literally "makes"; 731) Gorgias as his son and entrusts the full care of his household and his daughter to him.

But the "grouch" is not yet willing to give up his life of private isolation, or his suspicion of all society outside his doors. He instructs Gorgias to get his daughter a husband, saying: "Even if I make a complete recovery, I won't be able to do that, for I'll never find anyone I approve of. If I live, leave me to live my own life [*zen eath' hos boulomai*]," and then offers this explanation of the advantages of his way of life: "If everyone was like me, there'd be no lawsuits [*dikasteria*] or dragging one another off to jail [*desmoteria*], and no wars: everyone would be satisfied with a moderate competence."[61] It is striking that Knemon uses the democratic slogan "to live as one pleases" to justify living a life separate from those institutions and activities which had typified democratic politics in the classical era.[62] Even though he now admits that some sort of society is essential for both his own and his household's welfare, he still holds to his highly polarized view of the public and private worlds—and prefers the life of isolation, even with its dangers, to that of lawsuits and war. His daughter does need a husband, but now even that is Gorgias' responsibility, and Knemon himself can be left in peace.

But the story does not end there, or even with the double betrothal of Knemon's daughter to Sostratos and Sostratos' sister to Gorgias. In the end, Knemon is convinced to join this family community—indeed, to join the wedding dance. This unlikely conclusion is brought about by the household slaves of Sostratos with the blessing of Knemon's own old slave woman, who heads off to the wedding party with some pointed words of warning for her master: "You can lie there all on your own. You're a real misery. They wanted to take you to the shrine, but you wouldn't go. Something awful [*mega kakon*] will happen to you, you mark my words, something much worse than you're suffering now."[63] That "something awful" comes by way of the two slaves who have previously suffered under his tongue and lash, and now resolve to take some revenge. As they see it, however, their revenge is also a means of getting Knemon to join the human world and the newly created society of households joined by marriage. So says one to the other (in lines discussed earlier in this chapter): "It is positively our duty to make him a better man. For we're related to him, now that the families are connected." Their method of "domestication" or "civilization" is first to carry the injured and sleeping Knemon out of his own house, and then to bang loudly on the door asking to borrow not merely one cooking pot, but tables, rugs, and a big bronze mixing bowl as well. Knemon groans, unable to move because of his injuries. Then, telling him that if he won't join the party he will have to sit there and hear about it, the slaves describe how his wife and daughter arrived amid kisses and embraces, and how the wine was poured and the young girls danced. Knemon is visibly suffering, and now, when invited once again to join the party ("Dance! On your feet. We'll help you"), he finally relents, concluding that it may be better to put up with what is going on inside than to continue to suffer outside (see 957–958). The play ends as the slave Getas makes a last appeal: "You've enjoyed our victory over the old man, now please applaud us, young and old. Any laughter-loving Victory, daughter of a noble line, smile upon us all our days."[64] The audience is sent home on the festive notes of the wedding party, having seen love and marriage triumph together over even the most entrenched "grouch" and most extreme polarization of self and society. Although Knemon doesn't have much to say at the end of the play, his final position—within the wedding party rather than outside it—reveals his final acceptance of the possibility and desirability of a middle ground between the extremes of private isolation and public lawsuits: the community of households joined by common interests and affection and by marriage. Knemon's daughter will marry her infatuated aristocratic suitor, and Knemon's newly adopted son will marry that aristocratic suitor's sister. Two households—one rural, poor, and newly reunited, the other urban, rich, and in need of entertainment—are now bound together in a community beneficial to all.[65] In the *Dyskolos,* the benefits of such a community are for the most part set off against the dangers and vulnerability of Knemon's life of isolation. In the *Aspis, Samia,* and *Epitrepontes,* we shall see that same community of interconnected households and their members—slave and free, male and female—first create and then resolve their social problems without the benefit of, and in fact often in striking opposition to, polis interest and public law.

Aspis

The story of the *Aspis* (The Shield) centers on what is still arguably the most frequent source of family and household conflict and what was in Greek history one of the earliest topics of public law: property and inheritance. When a young man (Kleostratos) is mistakenly thought to have been killed while serving as a mercenary in Lycia, the news has a disruptive effect on the relations of several households back in Athens. Although Kleostratos' father has died sometime earlier, two paternal uncles still survive. The elder of the two, Smikrines, the play's "villain," is, like Knemon in the *Dyskolos,* a solitary sort ("he lives alone"; 121); but rather than shun the world of law and lawcourts, this loner attempts to use the threat of both to get what he wants from his family. The younger brother, Chaerestratos, is, in contrast, a wealthy and sympathetic character who has brought up Kleostratos' sister together with his own daughter and stepson. Kleostratos' "death" while in service (undertaken to raise money for his sister's dowry; 8) results in the sister's becoming an heiress, both to whatever property her father has left Kleostratos and to the booty (gold and slaves) which Kleostratos had won before he "died" and which his slave Daos has dutifully brought home.[66] According to Athenian law, an heiress could be claimed in marriage by her father's nearest male kindred. So the stage is set: the old and greedy uncle claims the young woman over the protests of her other uncle and of the stepcousin who has grown up with her and also happened to fall in love with her (288 ff.). Only a clever plot involving a second false death manages to put all to rights. Staging the sudden illness and death of Chaerestratos, the plotters tempt Smikrines with the prospect of a still richer heiress, Chaerestratos' own daughter. Although very little of the last two acts survives, Smikrines clearly falls into the trap and is no doubt appropriately humiliated.

Smikrines is perhaps the most interesting character for present purposes, given his appeal to Athenian inheritance law contrary to the interests of his own family. But the slave Daos' opening mournful soliloquy on his lost master also contains an interesting comment on the relation of public and private life. "Every day is a sad day for me now," says Daos,

and life's balance sheet is not at all what I hoped it would be when I set out. For I thought you'd come safely back from the war, a hero, and that you'd live the rest of your life in some style, with the title of General [*Strategos*] or Privy Councillor [*Symboulos*]. And your sister, for whose sake you enlisted, would marry a man you approved of, when you'd come home to those who loved you.[67]

What is notable is that the offices of democratic public life—the generalship and service in the council of 500—are represented here more as indicators of status and prestige than as vehicles for action and political power. Coming home a hero and winning such positions will, says the slave, allow Kleostratos to live a comfortable and honored life with his family. The reward of an active military and political life is, from this perspective, a successful and secure private life.

In contrast to Kleostratos, who after returning home alive at the end of the play could expect to live a life of private contentment, Smikrines is without family and friends and is noticeably bitter about that situation. He is introduced by the goddess Chance *(Tyche)* as a man who "takes no account of the claims of relatives or friends and who "wants everything for himself" (117–120). So he, like Knemon, lives alone with only an old housekeeper. On his own account, however, Smikrines blames his brother for mistreatment and lack of respect: "He treats me like a family servant [*oikotribes*] or a bastard [*nothos*]" (175–176). Since, he argues, his own brother considers him a "foreigner," he will reciprocate the treatment *and* claim his niece in marriage according to the letter of the law—or, at least, according to the law as he presents it from his selfish perspective (186–187).

It is immediately apparent that in contrast to the interpretation of early Athenian inheritance law, which views the laws on the *epikleros* as supporting the stability of households by legislating the responsibility of a man's *anchisteia* for his daughter's marriage, Smikrines interprets both the law and the law court as appropriate means for "foreigners" to confront one another and pursue individual self-interest regardless of family relationship. Although some have argued that the villainous Smikrines' appeal to this law constitutes an implicit criticism by Menander of what was in his day an obsolete and potentially cruel law,[68] it is also possible that Menander's audience would have seen Smikrines' position as itself a simplistic misrepresentation of Solonian law. It is at least worth noting that Aristotle speaks of Solon's laws (plural) on heiresses (*Ath.Pol.* 9) and that Plutarch, in his life of Solon, suggests that these laws included provisions against extreme mismatches in age and matches made only for mercenary reasons (*Solon* 20.2). Smikrines' legal position may not be as solid as some have thought. One could say that rather than bringing the force of law and justice to the defense of his wronged property rights, he is using rhetorical distortion (an acknowledged feature of the law court) in order to launch an attack on his own family.

The military metaphor is in fact employed by Smikrines himself in a revealing comment made later in the play, when the old man is under the mistaken impression that the wealthier daughter and the household property are now his. Suspicious that he will be cheated by his own family, he imagines that the women of the household are carrying off property "as if from the enemy" and that they are communicating with the neighbors through the drainpipes (465–467). It is hard to imagine a more hostile family relationship. In the end, of course, the hostility rebounds in the form of an appropriately comic plot against Smikrines himself—who, we can assume, is suitably punished for his unfamilial behavior. By the end of the play, Menander's interconnected households will be free of Smikrines' threat to impose "law and justice" against their larger interest. Indeed, they will in all probability have celebrated the double marriage of Kleostratos with Chaerestratos' daughter and Kleostratos' sister with Chaereas, Chaerestratos' stepson, and further reinforced their family or household community. Once again the community of households triumphs over both individual isolationism and an intrusive public law.

Samia

In the *Samia,* Menander presents the perspective of both public law and tragic drama on family relationships and behavior through the parodic character of Nikeratos, eventually the "father of the bride" but throughout the play a man notably given to interpreting the behavior of his fellow players as either high tragedy or high treason. Nikeratos' use of both the legal and the dramatic language of adultery and murder in his misguided attack on his eventual son-in-law suggests, as in the *Aspis,* that public "law and justice" is not the means to household harmony. Instead, it is the marriage of Nikeratos' daughter with the son of his next-door neighbor, who is also the father of her child, that brings to an end the confusion and hostility between various members of both households and also joins the two families together.

The story again features two households, this time actual neighbors, who by the end of the play are happily connected by marriage. On the one side of the stage is the house *(oikia)* of Demeas, a bachelor of some wealth who has adopted a son (Moschion) and more recently fallen in love with and, on his son's advice, taken in a concubine (Chrysis). On the other side of the stage lives the poorer household of Nikeratos—Nikeratos himself, his wife, and his daughter. Presumably they have slaves, but none are mentioned. The audience receives the necessary background information about these households not from a goddess but from young Moschion himself, who has a confession to make but takes some time getting to the point. He begins by saying, "I have done wrong" *(hemarteka;* 3), but then decides to describe in some detail the family background of his "error." Moschion opens his soliloquy by expressing gratitude for his father's kindness and generosity. He grew up, he says, having everything he wanted and treated "just like every other boy of good family."[69] As a young man he did all the things an elite young man should: he sponsored a dramatic production, raised dogs and horses, completed military service in a dashing way *(lampros),* and had enough money to make his friends a loan. All of this Moschion sums up by saying that his father has made him a "man"—an *anthropos* (17). He does not say, it can be noted, "he made me a citizen"; and it is clear that the reward of Moschion's public citizen service, like that of Kleostratos in the *Aspis* (as imagined by Daos), is the enhancement of social status and reputation, and not necessarily the assumption of further political responsibility. So, in an interesting reversal of traditional or classical public versus private priorities, worthy public service is here cited as evidence of a civilized and successful father-son relationship, not as a goal in itself.

Moschion then turns to the figure of Chrysis, his father's concubine, and although part of his story is lost at this point, he makes it clear that it was because of Chrysis that he got to know "the girl next door." When Chrysis became friendly with Nikeratos' wife, he explains, the two households came to be on quite familiar terms: "She [Chrysis] was often in their house, and they'd visit us, too." One day Moschion happened to find the women engaged in celebrating the festival of Adonis on the rooftop of his house and decided to join them as a spectator *(theates;* 43); and now finally he comes reluctantly and somewhat obliquely to the point: "I hesitate to tell you the rest of the story. Perhaps I am ashamed, where shame is no help, but I'm still ashamed—the girl got pregnant. Now I've told you that, you know what went before, too." Still, Moschion insists, his behavior was civilized under the circumstances: "I didn't deny that I was responsible, but went without being asked to the girl's mother, and promised to marry her daughter as soon as my father came home. I gave my word I would."[70] And now, with the baby born and recognized as his, Moschion unwittingly further complicates things for himself by entrusting the infant to Chrysis, who, in what Moschion considers a lucky coincidence, had become pregnant at about the same time but did not produce a live child.[71] As a result, she was available to care for and nurse the new child, and the matter could be kept under wraps at least until the fathers, Demeas and Nikeratos, returned and could approve the marriage. At that point it seems likely that Moschion would have reclaimed the child as his own, but this is not made completely clear in the play as it survives.

When Demeas and Nikeratos do return, there is at first a happy coincidence of desire, since the two men have themselves planned during their trip abroad the very marriage alliance that Moschion's "error" has already anticipated. Initial arrangements for the wedding are immediately and happily under way when Demeas just happens to overhear an old servant speak affectionately of the infant as Moschion's own son. Since he has been told that the infant's mother is Chrysis, Demeas jumps to the logical conclusion that in his absence Moschion and Chrysis have betrayed him. Judging—because it suits his fatherly prejudices—that Chrysis was the truly guilty party, he throws the woman into the streets, without, however, explaining the source of his anger.[72]

When Chrysis takes refuge in the house next door, the circle of confused characters expands—and Nikeratos enters the fray. Nikeratos has decided that Chrysis is being mistreated, and so urges Moschion to approach Demeas on her behalf. To this move toward family reconciliation Demeas responds: "Someone's organizing a diplomatic approach to me" (454). And finally, when Moschion's solicitation on Chrysis' behalf has driven his father into a fit of rage, Demeas reveals that he knows Moschion to be the child's father. The son acknowledges the fact but, still not comprehending his father's rage, dismisses the act with the comment: "What I did isn't such a terrible crime [*pandeinon*]. I'm sure thousands of men have done it before" (484–486). Demeas' response—"By Zeus, what nerve! In the face of this audience I ask you, who is the baby's mother: Tell Nikeratos, if you don't think it so terrible [*deinon*]"—finally enlightens Nikeratos, and he immediately launches into a tragic denunciation of the "dreadful deed" of incest: "O deed most dread! O Tereus, Oedipus, Thyestes! O all the incestuous loves of legend! You put them all in the shade."[73] Nikeratos urges Demeas to act for himself in a mythic/tragic mode and "assume Amyntor's rage and blind your son" (498–499), and of Moschion he says again in highly dramatic language: "How did you dare [*etolmesas*] to do such a thing?" (498). Continuing in his call for punishment, Nikeratos now turns to legal sanctions: If I were you, he says to Demeas—"if he had shamed my bed"—I would immediately sell that *pallake*[74] and disinherit the son (507–510). The public character of these recommended sanctions is clear from his next comments: "There wouldn't be an empty seat in barber's shop or public garden—the whole world would be there from first light, talking about me and saying, 'Nikeratos is a man, prosecuting for murder, and quite right too.'"[75] When Moschion, now totally confused, asks, "Murder, what murder?" Nikeratos responds that any act of rebellion such as he understands Moschion to have committed against his father is in fact equivalent to murder. In his dramatic manner, Nikeratos has created a comic parody of the conflation of household and polis order, and of the crimes of adultery, treason, and murder, which is so central to fifth-century Athenian tragedy.[76] Only now does Moschion finally realize the full extent of his father's misconception. He immediately sets him straight: "The baby's mother is Nikeratos' daughter. I'm the father."[77]

Nikeratos, however, is still in his highly tragic mode of public outrage—and now the outrage has been committed against him (through his daughter). He continues to act outraged and to spout hyperbolic charges—for example, Moschion is a "*moichos* caught in the act, admitting his guilt" (717–718)[78]—up until the very moment that he formally marries his daughter to Moschion, with the traditional formula "I give you this woman to be your wife, for the procreation of legitimate children." As Nikeratos himself realizes, however, no one takes him seriously (719); for the prevailing view is that private household troubles are not in fact best settled by public murder or adultery laws—or by invoking either such laws as a threat, or tragic drama as a model. It seems only appropriate then that Demeas turns against Nikeratos his own mythic mode of argument with an appeal to the story of Zeus's "golden" seduction of Danaë: "You're surely just as good as Danaë's father. If Zeus honored her, then perhaps your daughter . . ."[79] Believe what you want, Demeas seems to suggest in this clearly comic response to Nikeratos' tragic performance, but don't turn a private household matter into the stuff of public drama or litigation. It's time for these households to get on with the practical business at hand. And so, after one last family crisis created by Moschion's pretense of leaving home for a military career, Demeas can finally say: "Chrysis, send out the women, the water-carrier, and the musician . . . [Moschion], put on your garland, and deck yourself like a bridegroom."[80]

And it is also time for a reminder that all that has preceded has been part of a festival moment: Demeas concludes the play with an appeal to Victory, that she "be favorable to our choruses" (737); the play, like all of Menander's other comedies, is not simple imitation of private life, but a self-conscious dramatic reflection of an interesting renegotiation of the public and private spheres in Menander's Athens. In the fifth-century world of Aeschylus' *Oresteia,* adultery was a public crime meriting death; in the *Samia,* Nikeratos' invocation of tragedy's moral stance is only further evidence of his comic lack of understanding.

Epitrepontes

Such self-conscious reflection back upon the conventions of classical tragedy is also a feature of the *Epitrepontes,* a play which takes its title from the arbitration judgment delivered by the character Smikrines to two slaves, Daos and Syros, in a case with a common mythical pattern. It seems that one of the slaves, Daos, while engaged in shepherding his sheep, had found an abandoned (or "exposed") infant. He brought the child home, together with the trinkets and jewelry which had been left with it. But having second thoughts about the responsibility of childrearing, he gave the infant (but not the jewelry) to the second slave, a charcoal burner named Syros whose wife happened to have just lost a baby.[81] When Syros learns of the existence of "property" which he considers rightfully his—or the child's—he insists that the case go to arbitration, and coming by chance upon Smikrines, the two together ask him to arbitrate. "You've been to the theater, I'm sure," Syros says to Smikrines in making his plea, "and know all the stories."[82] If Daos had taken off with the birth tokens of the heroes of tragedy, suggests Syros, Neleus and Pelias, and others as well, would have gone through life unrecognized.

The self-conscious humor of this "title" scene of *Epitrepontes* speaks also to the larger argument of this chapter. First, there is the clear irony produced by the fact, probably known to the audience through a prologue, that the child in question is Smikrines' own grandson, born to his daughter Pamphile after she was raped at an all-night festival by, as it turns out, her future husband, Charisios. So in his ignorance, the grandfather unwittingly preserves the birth tokens and thereby the future status of his own grandson. Then, as the play progresses, Smikrines spends his energy asserting his legal right to take back his daughter and her dowry from what he considers an unworthy and extravagant husband, that is, from Charisios, who left her and took up with the courtesan and musician Habrotonon when he discovered that Pamphile had given birth to a "five-month" child. Pamphile herself, however, resists her father's will, making in the process the Aristotelian distinction noted earlier between the relation of parent and child and that of master and slave. In the end, of course, husband and wife are reconciled—with the husband acknowledging the "double standard" he has used in judging his wife—and their child is recognized as fully legitimate.[83] To this happy ending, the legalist Smikrines has contributed only the unwitting decision in favor of the "property rights" of his own grandson.

A second and equally significant source of irony in this scene is the way in which slaves speak the language of justice and the law court—or, as Smikrines puts it to the two slaves directly: "Damn you! Traipsing about in working clothes,/Presenting *cases?*" Syros himself, the "aggrieved party," evokes the principle of justice as a community responsibility:

> On all occasions justice should prevail,
> The whole world over. Any man should feel
> Concerned about it—that's a general
> Rule of society.[84]

But the only community to which, as a slave, Syros has a claim is the community of households; and beneath the comic parody of slaves preaching the importance of civic responsibility and justice lies the implication that it is this community—and not that of the official polis courts—that will bring about a resolution of the confusion and conflicts of the play.

Throughout the play, slaves continue to appropriate the language of law and justice. The slave musician Habrotonon, a key player in the production of a "happy ending," upbraids another fellow slave for his timidity in investigating the identity of the exposed child:

> Ah! poor thing! Well, if
> It really is your master's baby, could you see
> It brought up as a slave? You'd merit death for that![85]

Later in the play, as Smikrines is about to assert his legal right to reclaim both his daughter and her dowry,[86] he complains that by resisting this action his old servant Sophrone is acting as his judge *(krinomai pros Sophronen)*. And finally, from the other household involved, Onesimos (slave of Smikrines' son-in-law Charisios) gives Smikrines a lecture on the importance of character rather than law in producing both good behavior and happiness—then urges him to "drop all charges" and go to meet his grandson.

The text of the *Epitrepontes* is considerably damaged, and some elements of both plot and character remain unclear. What does happen, for example, to Habrotonon, and what is her relationship with Charisios' good friend Chairestratos? The play nonetheless illustrates once again Menander's interest in the community of interconnected and interrelated households as a social alternative to both the public world of legal rights and law suits and a private world of extreme isolation, whose inhabitants either show extreme hostility to the public world, like Knemon, or try to employ its rules and methods for their own antifamilial purposes, like the two Smikrines.

Smikrines in the *Epitrepontes,* like Smikrines in the *Aspis,* would impose his legal rights against the interests and desires of the members
of the household community. His ignorance of the past experience of
his own household is only part of the problem. He is simply, says
Chairestratos in a restored line of the very fragmentary first act, a *ki-
nados* (cheat or rogue) who "turns an *oikia* upside down" (165).
Here again the implication is quite clear: the social community created by human relationships within and among households—those
of father and son, husband and wife, master and slave, brother and
brother-in-law—provides an alternative to the classical ideal of an
active and public citizen life. The important role played by household slaves in the "happy endings" of Menander's comedies, as well
as the slaves' appropriation of public language and law for their own
purposes, or rather their household's purposes, speaks clearly to this
changed perspective on the relation of public and private in Athens:
Menander depicts a community not of public citizens with individual
legal rights and responsibilities, but of private households bound together by human needs and familial relationships.

The apolitical character of Menander's comedies is particularly striking to those familiar with the highly political character of earlier
fifth-century drama and the explicit political commentary of Aristophanes' comedies. Menander's comedies contain no references to, or
attacks upon, contemporary politicians, and no proposals, even of a
comic or fantastic sort, for contemporary politics. In contrast, it is
frequently noted, his plots deal with "private" matters and his characters "are concerned with their own rather than the state's affairs,
with money and marriage, not with politics." Further, his detractors
point out that Menander's comedies may not be a particularly accurate record of even this limited social milieu: the size of dowries in
Menander, for example, is historically unreliable. On this line of argument the best appraisal of Menander as a historical source would
be something like "inaccurate, if contemporary, depiction of the private life of an inane elite."

    In contrast to these familiar judgments, I have argued here that
Menander's plays offer a more significant reflection of the historical
experience of Athens in the early decades of Macedonian rule and

are in fact quite "political" in the broader sense of the word. Rather than a simple retreat away from the public and into private life, Menander's plays reveal a new emphasis on the benefits of a community which stands between the public polis and the private individual (and his family). This is a community or society of interrelated and interdependent households, organized hierarchically and including both free and slave, and providing a sense of community and order which neither the polis nor a life of private isolation can offer. It is not so much a new community (neighborhoods and interrelated households were certainly a long-term part of Athenian social life) as a newly emphasized one—in contrast with the strictly political community of the assembly or law courts. The contrasting, and also in some ways similar, figures of Knemon in the *Dyskolos* and Smikrines in the *Aspis* illustrate the point clearly. Both men are unsympathetic characters who live alone and at odds with almost everyone and especially their immediate family. Both are isolated, but in contrasting ways. Dyskolos lives a life of extreme isolation or "privacy" and sees all social interaction as a dangerous "public" intrusion on that privacy. Smikrines, on the other hand, tries to use the force of public law to win his own private, and quite selfish, gain against the interests of the larger community of his brothers' households. Both men fail in their efforts, while the community of households emerges triumphant in both plays, for in both the *Dyskolos* and the *Aspis* the happy ending celebrates not one but two marriages. Similarly, in the *Samia* and the *Epitrepontes* Nikeratos and another Smikrines put themselves at odds with the community of households when they oppose the new marriages of those plays—Nikeratos more comically than Smikrines—with the threat of public law and legal right. And again the community of households emerges happily triumphant: in the one, a marriage is celebrated; in the other, a marriage is restored.

Marriage is indeed the key to the resolution of Menander's plots— as it is also, for better or worse, in earlier Athenian drama. What is different in Menander is the way in which Menander's marriages are arranged by and for the households involved, against the obstruction produced by both public interference and private isolation. The polis is neither the protector of household interests, as in the archaic era, nor the metaphorical household itself, as in the classical era. In

Menander, the polis as the locus of political and judicial decision-making (Aristotle's polis) is moved to the margins while his community of interconnected households holds center stage. But insofar as we understand the polis (*pace* Aristotle) as rooted in a broader sort of participation than the strictly political, we can see Menander's comedies as creating a polis community as well, as his characters and interrelated households carry on their activities of commerce, religion, arbitration, and marriage celebrations. In this larger respect, Menander could indeed be said to be quite political.

The roles played by slaves in Menander's plays present perhaps his most interesting challenge to the classical conception of the polis community, and underline an important difference between Menander's dramatic world and the elite family-community of Plato's *Republic* or the community of active male citizens of Aristotle's *Politics*. When slaves act to support the common welfare of the household and speak the language of public law in doing so, while free male citizens attempt to use that same public law to undermine that same common welfare, it is clear that the latter have lost their privileged social position and that the lines of public and private interest and responsibility have been substantially redrawn.

Thus, Menander's plays with their assertion of the centrality of the household society or community present a significant challenge to the traditional view of the "primacy of politics" in Greek history. "The primacy of politics," of course, can mean a variety of things, depending on what is taken to constitute "politics" (or "nonpolitics"). For example, as was argued earlier, while politics can indeed be said to have "primacy" in both Plato's and Aristotle's construction of the ideal state, there is a significant difference in the ways the two philosophers construct the political realm. For Plato, the polis is ideally a single organic household, in contrast both to the isolated Cyclops on his mountaintop (*Laws* 3) and to the stasis-ridden or "sick" *poleis* depicted in the *Republic*. For Aristotle, on the other hand, the polis is essentially a collection of active male citizens, those who have the privilege of participating in judicial and deliberative decision-making, and "politics" has accordingly a quite narrow meaning. Menander, however, parts company from both Plato and Aristotle, depicting a community of households, a civil society which stands against both the isolated hermit and the crowded law courts.

So Menander, living in an age in which the traditional institutions of Athenian government were often a facade for unencumbered Macedonian military rule, seems to have taken the significant and perhaps even "modern" step of asserting the "primacy of the social."[87] And so his comedies, for all their appearance of triviality, have a historical significance beyond the size of Athenian dowries or the social habits of an inane elite.

CONCLUSION

From Homer to Menander, from the household of Odysseus to that of Knemon, the family is a part of Greek history. As constituted through the household, the family retains its identity, but the part it plays is hardly insignificant or unchanging. The private sphere is not a secluded "women's quarters" but the source and focus of relationships that were essential to the well-being of the community as a whole throughout Greek history. The engagement of the long-separated "private and public spheres" enlarges the historical stage and increases our appreciation of the historical drama.

Since the Enlightenment, the history of the private family has traditionally been presented as a moral history, as is evident in the persistent focus on the issue of the "status" or "position" of Greek women.[1] As J. P. Mahaffy put it, the "social position of women" is the "test point" for an evaluation of the moral progress of Greek or any society, and it is a test which according to Mahaffy (and more recent critics) the Greeks, most notably in Athens, conspicuously failed. From Henry Maine's criticism of a social order which entails the "seclusion and degradation of an entire sex" to Louis Henry Morgan's puzzlement that the Greeks failed to "develop and utilize the mental, moral and conservative forces of the female intellect," nineteenth-century writers insisted not only that the Greek family was privatized by the rise of the Greek state, but that the other side of male political participation in the public sphere was female "seclusion and degradation" in the private sphere.

The rhetorical character of Maine's and Morgan's sweeping judgments is obvious, as is the fact that the women whose treatment sparks their indignation were primarily the free mothers, wives, and daughters of Athenian citizens—the ancient counterparts of their own mothers, wives, and daughters—not slave, foreign, or lower-class women. Nonetheless, the question of "women's status" has been passed down to the twentieth century with much of the same moral and ideological charge as it had in earlier centuries, from A. W. Gomme's explicit claim, now in defense of the Greeks, that "Athenian society was, in the main, of the normal European type," to Sarah Pomeroy's influential discussion of the diverse sources for understanding women's "status," emphasizing the profound effects of male bias in Greek literature and of male control over women's lives.[2] Women's status in this discussion has remained essentially connected to the value they are judged to have had in men's eyes: subjective status is seen as prior to objective status (legal rights, economic authority, family privilege)—that is, the exclusion of women from the male public world is generally seen as deriving from the low esteem in which women are held by the men who inhabit that public world. Thus, women's status is the ideological construction of men, and the discussion remains centered on the question: "Did Greek men value, respect, and love Greek women or not?" Affirmative and negative answers are heard today as in the past, recently with an increasing insistence on the inaccessibility of women's own views, desires, and experiences, generally assumed not to coincide with men's.

Perhaps, however, these are neither the most useful questions to ask nor the most secure assumptions from which to begin. That women's status in the eyes of men should dominate discussions of women's history seems to be as much a consequence of the "privatization" of family history as is the traditional focus of family history on the "minutiae of quotidian details of reality." As Marilyn Katz has further pointed out, the discussion of "women in antiquity" has tended to be either highly ideological or highly antiquarian; it is only rarely historical.[3] If, however, the family—its interests, structures, and relationships—can be seen as an important participant in the historical development of Greek society, so also will women enter the historical realm. And they will enter not solely as objects of male gaze but as participants in social institutions.

It is time—indeed, past time—to rethink the traditional categories of analysis and their use in the interpretation of past societies. The argument of this book has been therefore in an essential way revisionist. It has attempted to disrupt the nineteenth-century paradigm, first by opening it up to critical scrutiny and then by reengaging the history of the "private family" with the "public polis" through focused discussion of polis-oikos or state-household interaction from Homer to Menander. Noticeably missing is any discussion of "Did the Greeks love their children?" or "Did Greek men love their wives?"—or "Why did they hate them?" The question of the "status of women" has not itself motivated or delineated the chapters of this book, although each chapter contains important conclusions about the institutions that shaped women's lives and structured their social experience. My theme throughout has been the interaction of the family and the state, oikos and polis, in Greek history; my focus has been the reasons for and the nature of public, communal interest in private, familial behavior, and on the institutions of both polis and oikos that tell the story of that engagement.

Family history in the late twentieth century is on several significant counts a different enterprise from family history in the late nineteenth or even mid-twentieth century. Gone is the nineteenth-century confidence in evolutionary progress toward the "civilized" bourgeois family. "Family" now is a word which needs to be defined and often expanded, as well as given historical and cultural context. Gone (or going) also is the more recent twentieth-century enthusiasm for reified separate spheres as an interpretive tool for understanding the subordination of women in a patriarchal society. What remains, I suggest, is an appreciation that in the diverse domain of historical experience the family is still constituted of or created by relationships which are essentially those basic relationships identified by Aristotle. Yet, like households, families come in many forms; they are products of fission, fusion, mutation, and adaptation. The family, then, is fully historical; it is not an idealized type or a separate sphere, but very often the focus of social identity and the mediator between public and private experience. The family is not the passive

relic of political development, but the active fashioner of relationships and identities from which and with which its members engage
the larger world. From the perspective of the late twentieth century,
the family is a remarkably creative and resilient bundle of essential
human relationships whose history is vitally connected with that of
the larger society of which it is a part. The Greek family is a participant in *l'histoire mobile.*[4]

In discussing the family in Greek history I have employed neither
strictly qualitative nor quantitative analysis, but rather have tried to
illuminate the interaction of the Greek family and its essential relationships with the history and institutions of the public world, the
polis. In doing so I have relied extensively on the evidence of law and
social norms, particularly in regard to the inheritance of property
and the protection of marriage, as known from legal statutes as well
as legal and dramatic rhetoric. This approach and this evidence fit
particularly well specific topics at the heart of the book: property
ownership and sexual behavior are not only key points of public-
private intersection but also persistent topics in surviving Greek law
and literature. From that perspective, the book may be said to discuss the topic of the Greek family history on "its own terms."
Nonetheless, it is also necessarily written in twentieth-century terms
typified by a keen interest in the diversity and complexity of social
forms and participation, and a strong suspicion of linear historical
theories (as well as linear families) and of idealized historical images.
The interest of history, including family history, lies in complexity.

NOTES

Introduction

1. Cf. the comments of Suzanne Dixon in *The Roman Family* (Baltimore 1992) p. 1. Her final point is applicable to the study of the Greek family as well: "The variety [of English uses] does not usually cause difficulty because the situation makes the particular meaning clear, but discussion of 'the Roman family' requires a common reference point. It is my belief that some scholarly differences about the nature of the family come down to this failure to define the central topic."

2. In "The *Oikos* in Athenian Law," *CQ* 39 (1989) 10–21, Douglas MacDowell distinguishes between what he considers the "original" and legal meaning of *oikos,* which is "property," and the later colloquial use of *oikos* as "family," i.e., "line of descent from father to son through successive generations" (p. 15). In this book I argue, in contrast, that *oikos* referred inclusively to both persons and property, and not at all to a "line of descent." Although Aristotle defined the oikos as a "natural association for everyday purposes" (*Politics* 1252b12–14), MacDowell specifically rejects this definition.

3. For the meaning of *genos,* see the convenient summary of S. D. Lambert, *The Phratries of Attica* (Ann Arbor 1993) 59–74. For an extended discussion see F. Bourriot, *Recherches sur la nature du genos* (Lille 1976); and D. Roussel, *Tribu et cité* (Paris 1976).

4. I use these terms metaphorically—and would also argue that "women's quarters" were more an ideological construction than a physical reality in Greek houses, where the simplicity of the architecture argues for rooms with multiple uses; see M. H. Jameson, "Private Space and the Greek City," in *the Greek City from Homer to Alexander,* ed. Oswyn Murray and S. Price (Oxford 1990) 171–195.

5. See Dixon, *The Roman Family,* p. 17.

1. The Nineteenth-Century Paradigm of Greek Family History

1. J. J. Bachofen, "My Life in Retrospect," in *Myth, Religion, and Mother Right,* trans. R. Mannheim (Princeton 1967) (hereafter cited as *Mother Right*) p. 17. On nineteenth-century social evolutionary thought see J. W. Burrow, *Evolution and Society* (Cambridge 1966); G. W. Stocking, *Victorian Anthropology* (New York 1987); A. Kuper, *The Invention of Primitive Society* (London 1988).

2. See Jennifer T. Roberts, *Athens on Trial: the Antidemocratic Tradition in Western Thought* (Princeton 1994).

3. See M. I. Finley, "Anthropology and the Classics," in *The Use and Abuse of History* (London 1975); S. C. Humphreys, *Anthropology and the Greeks* (London 1978).

4. R. Fagles, "The Serpent and the Eagle," in *The Oresteia* (New York 1966) pp. 16 and 21; Sue Blundell, *Women in Ancient Greece* (Cambridge, Mass., 1994) pp. 75 and 129; Claudine Leduc, "Marriage in Ancient Greece," in *A History of Women in the West,* vol. 1, ed. Pauline Schmitt-Pantel, trans. Arthur Goldhammer (Cambridge, Mass., 1992) p. 239.

5. E.g., Josine Blok, "Sexual Asymmetry: A Historiographical Essay," in *Sexual Asymmetry,* ed. J. Blok and P. Mason (Amsterdam 1987) pp. 1–57; Beate Wagner-Hasel, "Das Privat wird politisch," in *Weiblichkeit in geschichtlicher Perspektive,* ed. A. J. Becher and J. Rusen (Frankfurt 1988); idem, "Frauenleben in orientalischer Abgeschlossenheit?" *Der Altsprachliche Unterricht* 2 (1989) 18–29; Marilyn Katz, "Ideology and 'the Status of Women' in Ancient Greece," *History and Theory* 31 (1992) 70–97.

6. Cf. Richard Saller, "*Patria Potestas* and the Stereotype of the Roman Family," *Continuity and Change* 1 (1986) 7–22.

7. For one standard definition of patriarchy ("male-dominated institutions") see Gerda Lerner, *The Creation of Patriarchy* (Oxford 1986) p. 239. In her commentary on Xenophon's *Oeconomicus,* Sarah Pomeroy defines patriarchy as an economic system, in addition to a social one, "in which the male who heads the *oikos* appropriates the labour of his wife, children, and slaves"; *Xenophon, Oeconomicus: A Social and Historical Commentary* (Oxford 1994) p. 58. The connection between patriarchy in this sense and misogyny is clear in Pomeroy's earlier comment, "most Greek thought tended to reduce the value of a wife to the primary function of sexual reproduction. Athenian marriage indeed was based on such a misogynistic concept" (p. 35).

8. For the bilateral character of inheritance in Athens see Roger Just, *Women in Athenian Law and Life* (London 1989) chap. 5. On the issue of seclusion see David Cohen, "Seclusion, Separation, and the Status of

Women in Classical Athens," *Greece and Rome* 36 (1989) 3–15. For women at the theater see now A. J. Podlecki, "Could Women Attend the Theater in Ancient Athens? A Collection of Testimonia," *Ancient World* 21 (1990) 27–43; and Jeffrey Henderson, "Women and the Dramatic Festivals of Athens," *TAPA* 121 (1991) 133–147. Despite his arguments against the exclusion of women from the theater, however, Henderson still considers the "notional audience" of Athenian drama as male.

9. Quotations in the text are from Bachofen, *Mother Right*; Friedrich Engels, *The Origin of the Family, Private Property, and the State,* trans. West Barrett (London 1986); Lewis H. Morgan, *Ancient Society,* ed. Leslie A. White (Cambridge, Mass., 1964); D.-N. Fustel de Coulanges, *The Ancient City,* trans. W. Small (1873; reprint New York 1929); and Henry Maine, *Ancient Law* (New York 1965). Although Bachofen is traditionally thought of as the "discoverer" of prehistoric Greek matriarchy, he did not himself use either the word "matriarchy" or "patriarchy." As Stella Georgoudi notes, however, Bachofen's use of the terms "mother-law" and "gynecocracy" implied "the superiority of women over men in the family as well as in society" ("Creating a Myth of Matriarchy," in Schmitt-Pantel, *History of Women in the West* pp. 450–451) and so allows the common English usage.

10. For comments on other contributors to the debate, including J. Lubbock and J. M. McLennan, see Kuper, *The Invention of Primitive Society,* chap. 3. Thomas Trautman's *Lewis Henry Morgan and the Invention of Kinship* (Berkeley 1987) focuses on Bachofen, Fustel, and Maine, along with McLennan, as "Kinship's Other Inventors" in chap. 8.

11. Bachofen, *Mother Right* pp. 75, 76.

12. On Bachofen's place in the nineteenth-century debate on woman's place, see Blok, "Sexual Asymmetry." For examples of the "credo" of the nineteenth-century "scientific history" see Fritz Stern, *Varieties of History* (New York 1972), including essays by Fustel de Coulanges, "The Ethos of a Scientific Historian," and J. B. Bury, "The Science of History."

13. See Bachofen, *Mother Right* pp. 69–84, for the expression of these ideas.

14. Ibid., pp. 92–95, 110. Engels objected to the term "hetairism" on the ground that it is taken from the Greek for "prostitute" or "courtesan" and so implies the existence of the distinction wife/prostitute, clearly inappropriate in a proposed state of indiscriminate sexual coupling; *Origin of the Family* p. 40. Objection sustained.

15. Bachofen, *Mother Right* p. 86.

16. On nineteenth-century use of these ideas see Amanda Vickery, "Golden Age to Separate Spheres? A Review of the Categories and Chronology of English Women's History," *Historical Journal* 36 (1993) 383–414.

Note how different this is from the "myth of matriarchy" described by J. Bamberger, "The Myth of Matriarchy: Why Men Rule in Primitive Society," in *Women, Culture, and Society* (Stanford 1974), in which women are guilty of misrule and abuse of religion and so are punished with loss of power. See further Georgoudi, "Creating a Myth of Matriarchy."

17. Bachofen, *Mother Right* p. 109.

18. Ibid., p. 110.

19. Ibid., p. 111.

20. Fustel avers that he "would rather be mistaken in the manner of Livy than that of Niebuhr" (quoted in Arnaldo Momigliano, "Fustel de Coulanges, *The Ancient City,*" in *The Family, Women, and Death,* ed. S. C. Humphreys [London 1983] p. 137). Cf. Bachofen's caustic reference to German scholars as "philistines" and "hyperboreans" (*Mother Right* p. 13). For a thorough account of Bachofen's aversion to German scholarship in the person of Mommsen, see L. Gossman, *Orpheus Philologus: Bachofen versus Mommsen on the Study of Antiquity* (Philadelphia 1983).

21. Fustel de Coulanges, *The Ancient City* pp. 11–12.

22. Ibid., p. 25.

23. Ibid.

24. Ibid., p. 33. Fustel's reliance on Servius here is typical of his method—and of his disregard for the Germanic style of source criticism.

25. Ibid., p. 38. Oddly enough, Fustel justifies this claim by reference to "the idea that generation was due entirely to the male": "The belief of primitive ages, as we find it in the Vedas, and as we find vestiges of it in all Greek and Roman law, was that the reproductive power resided exclusively in the father" (p. 39). Even Aristotle, however, did not go that far, and the Hippocratic corpus indisputably recognizes the female contribution to reproduction; see G. E. R. Lloyd, *Science, Folklore and Ideology* (Cambridge 1983).

26. Fustel de Coulanges, *The Ancient City* pp. 42, 47. The incorporation of the wife into the husband's family, *"filiae loco,"* is also a central feature of Claudine Leduc's presentation of what she calls "daughter-in-law marriage"; "Marriage in Ancient Greece" pp. 235–294.

27. Fustel de Coulanges, *The Ancient City* pp. 51, 49.

28. We are routinely informed that the Greeks (and especially the Athenians) did not marry for love, but only "for the production of legitimate children" (see Roberts' statement of this view as historical fact in *Athens on Trial* p. 277). Yet that Greeks and Athenians did often hope for pleasure and affection, as well as children, within marriage is quite evident, for example, from a close look at marriage rituals and celebrations; see R. Sinos and J. Oakley, *The Athenian Wedding* (Madison 1993). See also Plutarch's essay "Advice on Marriage" (with my discussion in "Plutarch's 'Advice on

Marriage': Traditional Wisdom through a Philosophic Lens," *ANRW* II.33.5 [1992] 4709–23) for a view of marriage focusing on the relationship, sexual and intellectual, between husband and wife.

29. Fustel de Coulanges, *The Ancient City* pp. 57, 59.

30. See Suzanne Dixon, *The Roman Family* (Baltimore 1992) chap. 1. Cf. S. C. Humphreys, "Kinship in Greek Society," in *Anthropology and the Greeks* pp. 193–202.

31. Fustel de Coulanges, *The Ancient City* p. 74.

32. Ibid., p. 77.

33. Ibid., book 4, "The Revolutions."

34. See ibid., chap. 10, sec. 2: "An Examination of Certain Opinions That Have Been Put Forth to Explain the Roman Gens."

35. Ibid., p. 109.

36. Ibid., p. 106. The notion of "fictive kinship" which so annoyed Fustel still causes problems in current work on the Greek family, where there is sometimes a slippage between the notions of fictive kin and actual kin. For example, Robert Littman considers fictive kinship a type of kinship, which it certainly may be, but then refers to the phratry, a fictive kin group recruited patrilineally, as a "descent group," which it is not; *Kinship and Politics in Athens, 600–400 B.C.* (New York 1990) p. 18.

37. Fustel de Coulanges, *The Ancient City* p. 255.

38. Peter Rose, for example, uses the term frequently without clarification in *Sons of the Gods, Children of Earth: Ideology and Literary Form in Ancient Greece* (Ithaca 1992), so confusing, and to an extent undermining, the description of historical class structure on which he bases his literary interpretation. He refers to "great houses" as both *oikoi* and clans (e.g., p. 196 and following discussion) and equates the patronymic suffix –*idai* with oikos identity (p. 204).

39. See George Feaver's discussion of the American reception of Maine's *Ancient Law* and the interest of Oliver Wendell Holmes and Henry Adams; *From Status to Contract: A Biography of Sir Henry Maine* (London 1969) pp. 128–148.

40. Maine, *Ancient Law* pp. 72, 76.

41. Ibid., pp. 76, 78.

42. Ibid., p. 78.

43. The Cleisthenic reforms in Athens in the late sixth century, by which ten new tribes constituted of local demes (districts or villages) replaced the four old Ionian "tribes," is usually taken as the standard historical example of this transition.

44. So Feaver (*From Status to Contract* p. xvii) summarizes the theory which provides his biography with its title.

45. Maine, *Ancient Law* pp. 86, 98. See Feaver, *From Status to Contract* pp. 48–49.

46. Maine, *Ancient Law* p. 87. Recent scholarship has moved away from the extreme legalistic view of paternal power in Rome toward a more realistic appraisal of family relations; see Richard Saller, "*Patria Potestas* and the Stereotype of the Roman Family," *Continuity and Change* 1 (1986) 7–22.

47. Henry Maine, "The Early History of the Settled Property of Married Women," in *Lectures on the Early History of Institutions* (1875; reprint London 1966) p. 340.

48. Ibid.

49. See Carl Resek, *Lewis Henry Morgan, an American Scholar* (Chicago 1960).

50. See Feaver, *From Status to Contract* pp. 159–170.

51. Morgan, *Ancient Society* p. 60.

52. It is remarkable how often this completely unsupported notion of "clan exogamy" crops up in discussions of the Greek family. See, for example, Ronald Willetts' reconstruction of the marriage system of Gortyn in *The Law Code of Gortyn* (Berlin 1967), which I discuss in Chapter 3.

53. Morgan, *Ancient Society* p. 192.

54. Ibid., pp. 192, 196.

55. This epithet appears in *Origin of the Family* p. 137. Engels apparently relied on Marx's notes on *Ancient Society* (collected in *The Ethnological Notebooks of Karl Marx,* ed. Lawrence Krader [Assen, Netherlands, 1972]) when writing—in the space of some three months—his own treatise. For the story of its composition, as well as critical response and appraisal, see Barrett's introduction to the Penguin translation (London 1986).

56. Engels, *Origin of the Family* p. 95.

57. Engels echoes Morgan in insisting, without any evidence, on the exogamous character of the *gentes*—i.e., marriage was possible only to someone from a different (matrilineal) gens. In historical times, marriage to close kin on both the paternal and maternal sides was in fact quite common.

58. Engels, *Origin of the Family* p. 116.

59. Ibid., p. 129.

60. A desire to make Athens speak to issues in contemporary society is evident in two recent books on classical Athens: J. Ober, *Mass and Elite in Democratic Athens* (Princeton 1989); and David Cohen, *Law, Sexuality, and Society: The Enforcement of Morals in Classical Athens* (New York 1991).

61. Cf., for example, Sylvana Tomaselli, "The Enlightenment Debate on Women," *History Workshop Journal,* 1985, pp. 101–124; and Joan Landes, *Women and the Public Sphere in the Age of the French Revolution* (Ithaca 1988).

62. Engels, *Origin of the Family* p. 152. For an American historian's interesting analysis of the effect this paradigm has had on the writing of women's history, see Linda K. Kerber, "Separate Spheres, Female Worlds, Women's Place: The Rhetoric of Women's History," *Journal of American History* 75 (1988) 9–39.

63. Engels, *Origin of the Family* pp. 96, 105, 99.

64. See Stern, "Introduction," in *Varieties of History.*

65. John Stuart Mill, *Dissertations and Discussions* 2: 521, quoted by M. L. Clarke, *George Grote: A Biography* (London 1962) p. 121.

66. See Clarke, *George Grote,* for a brief account of the intellectual and political achievements of this energetic man. On the *History* see also Roberts, *Athens on Trial* chap. 10.

67. On Mitford's *History of Greece* in its historical and intellectual context, see again Roberts, *Athens on Trial* chap. 10.

68. So wrote A. P. Stanley in *Quarterly Review* 86 (1850) 394 (quoted by Clarke, *George Grote* p. 123).

69. See "Grecian Legends and Early History," in *The Minor Works of George Grote,* ed. A. Bain (1883; reprint New York 1974).

70. Bachofen, *Mother Right* p. 73; George Grote, *History of Greece* (1888; reprint New York 1971) 2: 1. See Grote's quotation of Niebuhr, 2: 3.

71. Grote, *History of Greece* 2: 25, 27–28.

72. The proper classification of the Alcmeonidae is a persistent problem. It is clear, however, that this was not a "lineage" strictly speaking, since one could be an Alcmeonid from either the maternal or the paternal side (e.g., Pericles, son of Agariste). Possibly it was a group to which an Athenian might claim (or be accused of) some connection—through a mother, father, sister, or great-aunt if necessary—if the political benefit seemed great and the risk manageable. For the idea that Athenian kinship was an inherently flexible set of relationships, fashioned variously in the interests of those to whom it was useful, see David Cohen, *Law, Violence, and Community in Classical Athens* (Cambridge 1995) pp. 163–180.

73. Grote, *History of Greece* 2: 428.

74. Ibid., 5: 24.

75. Ibid., p. 25.

76. The nineteenth-century elevation of Aspasia is colorfully illustrated in Alma-Tadema's painting of Pericles, Socrates, Alcibiades, Phaedias, *and* Aspasia, standing together on the scaffolding, examining the Parthenon frieze. For further discussion of the figure of Aspasia, see Madeleine Henry, *Prisoner of History: Aspasia of Miletus and Her Biographical Tradition* (Oxford 1995).

77. W. B. Stanford and R. B. McDowell, *Mahaffy, a Biography of an Anglo-Irishman* (London 1971) p. 11.

78. James Mahaffy, *Social Life in Greece from Homer to Menander* (London 1874) preface.

79. Ibid., pp. 111, 234.

80. Ibid., pp. 257, 208, 174.

81. Ibid., pp. 199, 201.

82. For a useful compilation of evidence for women's public activities, with sensible use of comparative evidence, see Cohen, "Seclusion, Separation, and Status of Women" and *Law, Sexuality, and Society* chap. 6. One of the clearest pieces of evidence for an "outside the home" role for Athenian women comes from Aristotle, who noted (or complained) that in a democracy, "who could prevent the women of the lower classes from going out when they want to?" (*Politics* 4.15). The implication is that in a democracy, where citizenship extends to the lower classes, it is not possible to keep the citizen women under close supervision, since they necessarily go out to work and do business for their households. Cf. Ober's presentation of Aspasia as the one woman capable of membership in the "educated elite" of classical Athens; *Mass and Elite in Democratic Athens* pp. 89–90.

83. Paul Rahe, "The Primacy of Politics," *American History Review* 89 (1984).

84. See, e.g., ibid.; and Ober, *Mass and Elite in Democratic Athens,* for whom by definition women (with slaves and metics) were unable to have public and political status in Athens (p. 249). In critique of this view see also Beate Wagner-Hasel, "Das Privat wird politisch," on Jürgen Habermas' *Structural Transformation of the Public Sphere,* trans. Thomas Burger (Cambridge, Mass., 1989) pp. 28–29, as illustrative of the difference between modern European conceptions of public and private and the Greek institutions of polis and oikos.

85. See chap. 1, "La famille dans la cité," for a clear statement of Glotz's Fustelian position; *La solidarité de la famille* (1904; reprint New York 1973). Note, e.g., his use of the phrase "le démembrement du *genos*" (p. 15). In the same chapter Glotz refers to the views of Grote, Morgan, and Maine.

86. Note also George Thomson's comment in introducing his translation of the *Oresteia:* "The clearest account of the organization of tribal society and its significance for the early history of Greece and Rome is still L. H. Morgan's *Ancient Society,* where the misconceptions of Niebuhr, Grote and Mommsen are corrected"; *The Oresteia of Aeschylus* (Cambridge 1938) p. 7.

87. Peter Rose's Marxist analysis of the *Oresteia (Sons of the Gods, Children of Earth* pp. 185–265) presents a variation on this theme, arguing

that the trilogy dramatizes the conflict between the elite, clan-based aristocracy (the "great houses" or "*oikoi*") and the emerging democracy.

88. M. I. Finley, *The World of Odysseus,* 2d ed. (New York 1965) p. 111.

89. Ibid., pp. 77–78.

90. W. K. Lacey, *The Family in Classical Greece* (London 1968) p. 9.

91. See, e.g., ibid., p. 20: "In these [Athens and Megara] and other mainland communities the process of emancipating the individual from his family units was very slow indeed"; p. 29: "A possible—and perhaps more likely—date [for the legal definition of the *anchisteia*], however, is the time when the liberation of the individual *oikoi* from their *genos* made a definition of the limits of the kinship-group highly desirable—that is, in Solon's day, in the early sixth century"; and p. 52: a reference to "state law," which "liberated the family *oikos* from its *genos* and even the individual from his *oikos.*"

92. Ibid., p. 51.

93. Ibid., pp. 15, 24.

94. Ibid., p. 176.

95. See Dixon, *The Roman Family,* with bibliography citing such scholars as Richard Saller, Keith Bradley, Elizabeth Rawson, Susan Treggiari, and Jane Gardner.

96. Sarah Pomeroy, *Goddesses, Whores, Wives, and Slaves* (New York 1975) pp. 30–31. The seclusion of women in later classical Greece is assumed, as is lack of sexual attraction between husbands and wives.

97. Ibid., p. 80. On the evidence which does notice women in the theater, see Podlecki, "Could Women Attend the Theater in Ancient Athens?"; and Henderson, "Women and the Dramatic Festivals of Athens."

98. For a sober appraisal of the realities, rather than the myths, of Spartan family life see S. Hodkinson, "Land Tenure and Inheritance in Classical Sparta," *CQ* (1986) 378–406; J. Redfield, "The Women of Sparta," *CJ* 73 (1977–78) 146–161; P. Cartledge, "Spartan Wives: Liberation or Licence?" *CQ* 73 (1981) 84–109; and further in Chapter 3 of this volume.

99. E. Fantham, H. Foley, N. Kampen, S. Pomeroy, and H. A. Shapiro, eds., *Women in the Classical World* (Oxford 1994), pp. 5 and 7.

100. Sue Blundell, *Women in Ancient Greece* (Cambridge, Mass., 1995) pp. 114, 119, and, e.g., 63, 66, 114, 116, 119.

101. Ibid., p. 101. Cf. Nancy Demand, *Birth, Death, and Motherhood in Classical Greece* (Baltimore 1994); and my review in *AJP* 119 (1996) 323–325.

102. See Katz, "Ideology and 'the Status of Women'"; Wagner-Hasel, "Das Privat wird politisch"; Blok, "Sexual Asymmetry"; Pauline Schmitt-

Pantel, "Women and Ancient History Today," in *History of Women in the West,* with bibliography.

103. Mahaffy, *Social Life in Greece* p. vii.

104. The phrase is Barzun's and is quoted by Stern in the "Introduction" to *Varieties of History* p. 27.

105. Adam Kuper uses this term to describe the relation of the early anthropologists to their "primitive" subjects: "primitive society proved to be their own society (as they understood it) seen in a distorting mirror"; *The Invention of Primitive Society* p. 5.

106. Virginia Woolf, "On Not Knowing Greek," in *Collected Essays* (London 1966) 1: 1. The significance of the title may be misunderstood. Virginia Woolf knew Greek; it was their world (and their laughter) that she found so distant.

107. E.g., Lawrence Angel, "Geometric Athenians," *Hesperia,* suppl. 2 (Athens 1939) 236–246.

2. The Family in Homer and Hesiod

1. The epigraph is from T. A. Sinclair's translation of the *Politics* (Harmondsworth 1962).

2. *Iliad* 15.497–499, trans. Richmond Lattimore.

3. In using the term "Homeric society" I am not thereby assuming that this is a strictly historical society. Rather, the world depicted in Homer's poems is a poetic society that reflects only imperfectly and partially the social structures and values of the world or worlds in which the poems were created and transmitted from one generation to the next. There is of course a long and complex ongoing discussion of this issue, about which I make no final judgment here. Among the competing candidates for "Homer's world," however, I favor the later dates, the ninth or eighth centuries, over Finley's tenth-century "World of Odysseus." For a recent contribution to the debate and a strong argument for a later date, see Ian Morris, "The Use and Abuse of Homer," *Classical Antiquity* 5 (1986) 81–138.

4. Whether the *kleros* was inalienable in early Greece is another much-debated issue, and one with some relevance here, given that a belief in the inalienability of land is usually connected with a belief in a larger clan or extended family to which the land belongs and which oversees its maintenance within that family. There is, however, no clear evidence that inalienability of land was typical in early Greece. For discussion of this issue, with bibliography and with particular reference to Athens, see B. Manville, *The Origins of Citizenship in Ancient Athens* (Princeton 1990) chap. 5. Manville notes that

proponents of original inalienability are all "indebted, in one way or another, to the view of Fustel de Coulanges" (p. 96 n. 8).

5. For this and other terminological points I have used the now indis-
pensable Ibycus program.

6. *Iliad* 1.18 and passim; 1.113; *Odyssey* 1.355; 2.136. Note also the
use of adverbial forms such as *oikoi* and *oikade*.

7. *Odyssey* 6.181; 1.248 and 251; *Iliad* 24.240.

8. For a different view see Douglas MacDowell, "The *Oikos* in Athenian Law," *CQ* 39 (1989) 10–21. MacDowell maintains that *oikos* has two
distinct senses, "property" and "family," and that when it means "family,"
it refers to a patrilineally based group (p. 15). I can see no clear basis for
this claim.

9. Cf. M. I. Finley, *The World of Odysseus*, 2d ed. (New York 1965)
chap. 4. More recently, Claudine Leduc ("Marriage in Ancient Greece," in
A History of Women, vol. 1, ed. Pauline Schmitt-Pantel, trans. Arthur Goldhammer [Cambridge, Mass., 1992]), returns to the position that Homeric
society was organized in "segmented lineages, each located in a discrete
household" and that "between the eighth and the fourth century B.C., Hellenic societies . . . abandoned unilineal households and moved from discrete
to overlapping or interconnected households" (pp. 238–239). These two hy-
potheses are not, however, convincingly demonstrated by historical argument.

10. Oswyn Murray, *Early Greece* (London 1980) pp. 41, 42.

11. Robert Littman, *Kinship and Politics in Athens, 600–400 B.C.* (New
York 1990). For example, in discussing the Alcmeonidai he says: "so powerful was the clan that at least in the seventh and sixth centuries the head of
the clan ipso facto was a major political leader" (p. 4). This construct is also
quite prominent in some recent work in literary criticism emphasizing the
connection between literature and society. See, for example, Peter Rose,
*Children of Gods, Sons of the Earth: Ideology and Literary Form in Ancient
Greece* (Ithaca 1992), where the *genos* as corporate clan plays an important
role. For example, the "Atreidai" and "Priamidai" are both termed "clans"
(pp. 201 and 205). In general, Rose equates "great houses," or *oikoi*, with
clans, or *genew*.

12. *Dictionary of the Social Classes*, ed. H. Reading (London 1977).

13. See Walter Donlon, "The Social Groups of Dark Age Greece," *CP* 80
(1985) 302; and (as quoted by Donlon) R. Fox, *Kinship and Marriage: An
Anthropological Perspective* (Baltimore 1967) p. 167.

14. The use of *genos* to refer to a "fictive kin group," such as the Eumolpidai or the Eteoboutadai, looking to a common ancestor and responsible for
the maintenance of a specific cult/sanctuary, is a specialized use of the general

term which has caused considerable confusion in discussions of Athenian kinship structures. In his organic description of the origin of the polis in *Politics* 1 (part of which was quoted at the opening of this chapter), Aristotle implies that members of villages were often related to one another in a way which was apparently imagined by contemporary Greeks as typical of the members of a *genos* of this sort: the village "comes into being through the processes of nature in the fullest sense, as offshoots of a household are set up by sons and grandsons. The members of such a village are therefore called by some 'homogalactic' [from the same milk]" (*Politics* 1252b). The same term is used in a fragment of Philochorus, who speaks of "*homogalaktes* whom we call *gennetai*" (frag. 35 Jacoby). The common Greek extension of the language of kinship to nonkin and political relationships should not, however, be allowed to obscure the fact that Eteoboutadai and Eumolpidai were not true clans. They can legitimately be called corporate groups, but not corporate kin groups. See further F. Bourriot, *Recherches sur la nature de genos* (Lille 1976); D. Roussel, *Tribu et cité* (Paris 1976); and S. D. Lambert, *The Phratries of Attica* (Ann Arbor 1993) pp. 59–78.

15. I refer here first to a statement by Ian Morris: "The old orthodoxy that Dark Age societies were 'tribal' and evolved into the more political systems in Archaic times has now been challenged, and a new consensus is emerging. This view holds that kinship groups larger than the family were relatively unimportant in structuring life in the Dark Age, and that the *phylai* and *genē* of classical Greece were late and 'artificial' developments"; "The Gortyn Code and Greek Kinship," *GRBS* 31 (1990) 233. It is precisely the terms *phylai* and *genē* which ancient historians have been accustomed to translate as "tribe" and "clan." The problem is the lack of English alternatives. Perhaps, as with *polis*, transliteration is the best solution. The second quotation is from Donlon, "Social Groups of Dark Age Greece" p. 304.

16. Murray, *Early Greece* p. 42.

17. Passages cited in text (in sequence): *Iliad* 6.209; *Odyssey* 24.508; *Iliad* 4.57; 5.896; 13.354; 6.180; 21.186; 2.852.

18. Recall Murray's linking of "hereditary descent," *genos*, and "family" (*Early Greece* p. 41). See also Peter Rose, *Sons of the Gods, Children of Earth: Ideology and Literary Form in Ancient Greece* (Ithaca 1992); and Leslie Kurke, *The Traffic in Praise* (Ithaca 1991), for examples of historically based literary criticism which assume a patrilineal clan-based structure for early Greek society.

19. Murray, *Early Greece* p. 64. I join Murray (and also Kurt Raaflaub, "Homer to Solon: The Rise of the Polis," in *The Ancient Greek City-State* [Copenhagen 1993]) in holding that as seen in the Homeric epic "the polis already existed in all essential aspects." At what point the emerging polis

can be termed a "state" is another question. But at least by the time of organized colonization in the later eighth and seventh centuries, revealing the existence of governmental authority (to force people to emigrate) and decision making, there would seem to be "states" in archaic Greece. The development of codified law is another indication of the existence of a state, if not again a state in its full modern sense. On this question see Ian Morris, "The Early Polis as City and State," in *City and Country in the Ancient World,* ed. J. Rich and A. Wallace-Hadrill (London 1991). Morris offers the "innocent" definition of a state as "a complex, permanently hierarchical social and political organisation, with formal office of government" and asserts that "most historians agree that Homer's Ithaca does not merit the title 'state'" (pp. 40–41).

20. On Penelope's role in the successful return of Odysseus, see Jack Winkler, "Penelope's Cunning and Homer's," in *The Constraints of Desire* (New York 1990) pp. 129–161. On Penelope see also Sheila Murnaghan, *Disguise and Recognition in the Odyssey* (Princeton 1987); Marilyn Katz, *Penelope's Renown: Meaning and Indeterminacy in the Odyssey* (Princeton 1992); Nancy Felson-Rubin, *Regarding Penelope: From Character to Poetics* (Princeton 1994).

21. *Iliad* 6.237–240 (282–285), trans. Robert Fagles. Here and in later references, I give the line numbers of the Greek text, followed by the line numbers of Fagles' text in parentheses.

22. *Odyssey* 8.577–586 (Alcinoos to Odysseus), trans. Robert Fitzgerald (modified).

23. See *LSJ* s.v. ἔτης, giving a Homeric meaning of "clansman, kinsman and dependent on a great house" but simply "citizen" in later Greek. Cf. G. S. Kirk, *The Iliad: A Commentary* (Cambridge 1990), who suggests that *etai* here might be more distant male relatives, but elsewhere could refer to "fellow-citizens." The point to be gained from this uncertainty is that both friends and fellow citizens could be imagined as extensions of the oikos—as "family."

24. For Homer's account of Meleager see *Iliad* 9.566–567.

25. Cf. Thomas Gallant, *Risk and Survival in Ancient Greece* (Stanford 1991) p. 23 on the proper identification of these households as "joint," not "extended."

26. M. I. Finley, "Marriage, Sale, and Gift in the Homeric World," *Revue internationale des droits de l'antiquité* 2 (1955) 167–194 (= *Economy and Society* pp. 233–245) p. 243.

27. Nestor to Telemachus: *Odyssey* 3.195, trans. Fitzgerald.

28. Theoklymenos to Telemachos: *Odyssey* 15.272, trans. Fitzgerald (modified). *Emphylos* is translated "cousin" by Fitzgerald, but it seems rather to refer to someone who is an "insider" in the community. (Cf. Plato,

Laws 871a.) The term is rooted in the word *phyle,* which is generally translated "tribe." But the *phyle* in the later Greek polis was essentially a political (not "tribal") division. As far as I can see, there is no suggestion of kinship here. *Kasignetoi* are "kinsmen" in Fitzgerald's translation. Cf. *LSJ,* which also suggests that a wider group than siblings may be denoted. However, "brother" usually seems the most straightforward meaning. As is well known and often noted, the common Indo-European root for "brother" was taken over by the fictive kin relationship of the Greek phratry. On the implications of this for our understanding of the phratry, see Lambert, *The Phratries of Attica,* with full bibliography.

29. Eupeithes to the brothers and fathers of the dead suitors: *Odyssey* 24.484, trans. Fitzgerald.

30. Ajax to Achilles: *Iliad* 9.632–636 (771–777), trans. Fagles.

31. On the conceptual overlap between "friend" and "kin" see Donlon, "Social Groups of Dark Age Greece" p. 300: "Blood relatives, in-laws, dependents, retainers, and friends are all called *philoi.* A similar kind of relationship is reflected in the words *etes* and *hetairos* in Homer. *Etes,* usually glossed as 'kinsman,' 'relation,' and *hetairos,* 'companion,' are both derived from the proto-Indo-European stem **swe-,* 'one's own,' 'belonging.'" Despite his clear recognition of and emphasis on the inappropriateness of the nineteenth-century theories of tribes and clans for a historical understanding of early Greece, and despite his very clear explanation of why the "functional kin group" beyond the oikos was bilateral, ego-centered, "structurally shapeless," with "no corporate functions," Donlon still wants to give some credit to the idea that the pre-Homeric oikos might have been something like an extended "clan village" (p. 299). On this issue see also S. C. Humphreys, "Kinship in Greek Society," *ASNP* 4 (1974) 357–358.

32. This point is hardly new; it was made by H. J. Treston in his 1923 study of compensation in early Greek society (*POINE: A Study in Ancient Greek Blood-Vengeance* [New York 1923] pp. 76–77) even though the work as a whole is based on a tribal and clan model. Murray (*Early Greece* p. 42) comments that "curiously it is only killing within the family which involves a wider group of relatives or supporters." He cites *Iliad* 2.661, the story of Tlepolemos, who killed his father's uncle and fled from the "rest of the sons and grandsons of Herakles"; and *Odyssey* 15.272, the passage quoted in the text.

33. W. K. Lacey, *The Family in Classical Greece* (Ithaca 1968) p. 54.

34. *Iliad* 18.497–508 (580–592), trans. Fagles (modified). Although Fagles translates "over the blood-price of a kinsman just murdered," the text simply says "of a man" (*andros;* 499).

35. There is an extensive literature on this scene and its significance for the development of Greek legal procedures. See esp. H. J. Wolff, "The Ori-

gin of Judicial Litigation among the Greeks," *Traditio* 4 (1946) 31–87. Cf. the interesting comments of W. R. Connor on the role of the *histor* in this passage as a Homeric model for Herodotus' *historie*; "The *Histor* in History," in *Nomodeiktes: Greek Studies in Honor of Martin Ostwald* (Ann Arbor 1993) pp. 3–16.

36. Helene Foley, "The Conception of Women in Greek Drama," in *Reflections of Women in Antiquity,* ed. Foley (London 1981) p. 151.

37. *Odyssey* 9.106–115, trans. Fitzgerald. Literally, lines 7 and 8 of this passage read: "they have no *agorai boulephoroi* nor *themistes*"—no assemblies for making plans and no traditional legal rules. "Tribal" is a loaded term.

38. In the passage of the *Politics* with which this chapter began, Aristotle cites the Cyclopes as an example of a society organized on (and limited to) the village level.

39. On the meaning of *kouridios/e* see P. Chantraine, *Dictionnaire etymologique de la langue grecque* (Paris 1968). For *kouridie alochos,* see *Iliad* 1.114 (Clytemnestra) and 19.297 (Briseis' hoped-for status). For a *kouridios posis* see *Iliad* 5.514.

40. Finley, "Marriage, Sale, and Gift," showed that the language of marriage was not at all that of sale—and indeed that there was no language of sale in the Homeric poems on which any such equation of marriage with sale could be based.

41. Morris, "The Use and Abuse of Homer." Another strong critique came from A. Snodgrass some years earlier ("An Historical Homeric Society?" *JHS* 94 [1974] 114–125). A clear motive behind Finley's argument on Homeric marriage was his project of establishing a historical identity for Homer's society in the tenth and ninth centuries. Such a historical society required a coherent marriage system appropriate to its circumstances, as Finley reconstructed them. Snodgrass, however, argued (with help from cross-cultural analysis) that two incompatible marriage systems, bridewealth and dowry, were operating in the society of the poems and that therefore that society could not be historical. However, even granting Snodgrass his particular point, it does not seem that his conclusion necessarily follows, since in fact "historical" societies often have conflicting or competing social customs.

42. Morris, "The Use and Abuse of Homer" pp. 113–114 with n. 181. The anthropological analysis on which Morris relies is that of Jack Goody, as outlined in "Bridewealth and Dowry in Africa and Eurasia," in *Bridewealth and Dowry,* ed. Goody and S. J. Tambiah (Cambridge 1973), and also in *Production and Reproduction* (Cambridge 1976). Morris holds to a late (eighth-century) date for "Homeric society."

43. Morris, "The Use and Abuse of Homer" pp. 110–111, 115.

44. Finley, "Marriage, Sale, and Gift" p. 245.

45. Lacey, *The Family in Classical Greece* pp. 41, 42, 43.

46. See Cynthia B. Patterson, "Marriage and the Married Woman in Athenian Law," in *Women's History and Ancient History,* ed. S. B. Pomeroy (Chapel Hill 1991).

47. *Iliad* 18.491–497 (573–579), trans. Fagles.

48. Postulating what effects Penelope's remarriage might have is made especially difficult by the complicated picture drawn by the poet of Penelope's position and options. J.-P. Vernant seems to believe that whoever married Penelope would inherit the "kingship" of Ithaca ("Marriage," in *Myth and Society in Ancient Greece* [The Highlands, N.J., 1980]); others see the two as unattached (e.g., Lacey, *The Family in Classical Greece,* whose attempt to disentangle the complexity of Penelope's position is admirable). But there is no doubt that her marriage was a matter of public interest.

49. *Odyssey* 18.281–283. See also Athena's earlier warning to Telemachos about what he might stand to lose if Penelope should remarry: "You know what heart there is in a woman's breast. She wishes to increase the house of the man she weds" (15.20–21).

50. *Odyssey* 4.76; 23.228 (Penelope's slaves).

51. *Odyssey* 7.67–74.

52. This is evident from the genealogy Homer provides for both Alcinoos and Arete (7.55–66). Bachofen typically took Arete's authority as a vestige of the earlier matriarchal order, an idea that still seems to have some appeal.

53. *Odyssey* 7.68. Nausicaa's instructions to Odysseus, that he should throw his arms around Arete's knees (6.310) when he enters the palace, can be compared with Themistocles' supplication of the wife of the king of the Molossians (Thucydides 1.136) and with some Cylonian partisans' supplication of the wives of the Athenian archons (Plutarch, *Solon* 12). Matriarchal relics?

54. Lewis H. Morgan, *Ancient Society,* ed. Leslie A. White (Cambridge, Mass., 1964) p. 399.

55. Thomas D. Seymour, *Life in the Homeric Age* (New York 1907) p. 128. The contrast is most pointedly with later classical Athens, for Seymour has commented on the previous page that his "survey of the most prominent women and goddesses of the Homeric poems shows that the Greek women of the poet's time were far from being kept in semi-Oriental seclusion" (p. 127). The author of another early twentieth-century "Homeric handbook" (Henry Browne, S.J., *Handbook of Homeric Studies* [London 1908]) remarks: "There is no sort of sign or hint of gross or perverted

passion," but "if a single exception to this rule can be detected in the *Odyssey,* it is in the doings of certain of the Olympians who were Asiatic importations, and represent a more unbridled lustfulness than the Homeric people claimed for themselves or even for their own native divinities" (pp. 212–213). On the ideology of the "orient" in regard to the status of women, see now Beate Wager-Hasel, "Frauenleben in orientalischer Abgeschlossenheit?" *Der Altsprachliche Unterricht* 2 (1989) 18–29.

56. Sarah B. Pomeroy, *Goddesses, Whores, Wives, and Slaves* (New York 1976) pp. 30–31.

57. On the problems in the way the traditional debate has been framed, see now Marilyn Katz, "Ideology and 'the Status of Women' in Ancient Greece," *History and Theory* 31 (1992) 70–97; cf. Katz's earlier essay (published under the surname Arthur), "Early Greece: The Origins of the Western Attitude toward Women," in *Women in the Ancient World,* ed. John Peradotto and J. P. Sullivan (Albany 1984), in which she takes issue both with those who argue that the status of Homeric women was higher and with those who argue it was lower than in later classical Greece.

58. Hesiod, *Works and Days* 373–374, trans. Richmond Lattimore.

59. *Works and Days* 57, *Theogony* 602—both referring to Pandora.

60. *Theogony* 586, 588, 604, trans Lattimore.

61. *Works and Days* 11–26. Though now somewhat dated in its analysis (particularly of Greek sexuality and gender relations), Alvin Gouldner's chapter "The Greek Contest System," in *Enter Plato* (New York 1965), makes important observations about the effect of "strife" on all facets of Greek life, public and private.

62. *Works and Days* 519–524, trans. Lattimore. This kind of leisure apparently seems to Hesiod totally appropriate for a young daughter.

63. *Works and Days* 371–372, trans. Lattimore.

64. *Works and Days* 376–380, trans. Lattimore (modified). "One single son" translates *monogenes pais.* Grammatically, this could also refer to a single daughter. Lattimore translates *oikos* as "house" and *megaroisin* in line 377 (where the wealth will pile up) as "household." For clarity I have changed this to "storerooms."

65. I refer to the work of Jack Goody and specifically to his distinction between "homogeneous" and "diverging" inheritance systems, the latter being typical of societies practicing plow agriculture; see *Production and Reproduction* (Cambridge 1976), a collection of earlier papers.

66. Marilyn Arthur Katz has suggested that Hekate, "the only child of her mother [Asteria]," who receives special honors from Zeus himself in the *Theogony* (404 ff.), might be considered a Hesiodic *epikleros;* "Cultural

Strategies in Hesiod's Theogony," *Arethusa* 15 (1982) 69. Like Arete in the *Odyssey,* however, Hekate's special status is not specifically explained in those terms.

67. So Katz in 1978 ("Early Greece: Origin of the Western Attitude toward Women" p. 22) stated that "there was some family property which was obliged to be returned to the clan in default of male heirs" and refers to these lines.

68. So Arnaldo Momigliano summarized Fustel de Coulanges' image of early Greek society; see his further comments on that image in "Fustel de Coulanges, *The Ancient City,*" in *The Family, Women, and Death,* ed. S. C. Humphreys, 2d ed. (Ann Arbor 1993) pp. 131–136.

69. *Works and Days* 733–734, trans. Lattimore.

70. See S. C. Humphreys, "Family Tombs and Tomb-cults in Classical Athens: Tradition or Traditionalism?" *JHS* 100 (1980) 96–126 (= *The Family, Women, and Death* chap. 5), for a thorough review of the archaeological evidence—and also a thorough debunking of some conventional ideas on this topic.

71. *Works and Days* 180–201, trans. Lattimore.

72. *Works and Days* 321–322, trans. Lattimore. "Out of season" or "untimely" would be a more literal translation of *parakairia.*

73. See, e.g., Bjorn Qviller, "The Dynamics of the Homeric Society," *Symbolae Osloenses* 56 (1981) 109–155.

74. See Murray, *Early Greece* pp. 57–68. Although the assembly in the Achaean camp described in *Iliad* 2 is traditionally seen as reflecting the institutions of the early polis, it should at least be noted that this was not a single polis but an army recruited from a broad array of Greek communities.

75. On these issues see Morris, "The Early Polis as City and State."

76. See Raaflaub, "Homer to Solon," with bibliography.

3. Early Greek Law and the Family

1. Richmond Lattimore, trans., *Greek Lyrics* (Chicago 1960) pp. 42–43. The title is Lattimore's.

2. Aristotle, *Politics* 1274b4. Note that the lawgiver is an outsider in each of these cases, so making the Athenian choice of "one of their own" as lawgiver (Solon) more remarkable.

3. On the historical significance of these stories, even when clearly apocryphal, see A. Szegedy-Maszak, "Legends of Greek Lawgivers," *GRBS* 19 (1978) 199–209.

4. *Inscriptiones Creticae,* ed. M. Guarducci (Berlin 1935–1950) col. IV.72. In the following discussion I use the edition and translation of Ronald Willetts, *The Law Code of Gortyn* (Berlin 1967). On the character of early Cretan law see M. Gagarin, *Early Greek Law* (Berkeley 1986) and also (on the Gortyn Code) "The Organization of the Gortyn Law Code," *GRBS* 23 (1982) 129–146.

5. Study of this inscription and of the society that produced it has been dominated by the work of Ronald Willetts, whose *Law Code of Gortyn* contains a complete text and translation with historical introduction and commentary; see also his recently revised *Civilization of Ancient Crete,* 2d ed. (Amsterdam 1991). Willetts views Gortynian society (of the code) as in the process of evolution from a primitive tribal order, based on family groups larger than the oikos, to the historical polis order rooted in the individual oikos (*Law Code of Gortyn* p. 18). He makes extensive use of the nineteenth-century paradigm of family history, with particular reference to the work of L. H. Morgan and his followers (p. 19 and passim).

6. See Eberhard Ruschenbusch's collection of Solonian law, ΣΟΛΟΝΟΣ NOMOI (Wiesbaden 1966); and, on the issues of the historical status and survival of those laws, A. Andrewes, "The Survival of Solon's Axones," in *Phoros: Tribute to Benjamin D. Merritt* (Locust Valley, N.Y., 1974); and N. Robertson, "Solon's Axones and Kyrbeis and the Sixth Century Background," *Historia* 35 (1986) 147–176. Cf. also Ian Morris on the difficulty of comparing the evidence of the Athenian courts with the Gortyn Code; "The Gortyn Code and Greek Kinship," *GRBS* 31 (1990) 236.

7. Xenophon begins his *Politeia of the Lacedaimonians* with the comment that Lycurgus "adopted opposite institutions to the majority with outstandingly successful results"; at its conclusion, however, he admits that all is not well in Sparta, but attributes this to the failure of contemporary Spartans to maintain the Lycurgan law unchanged (14). On the textual and historical problems raised by this chapter see Douglas MacDowell, *Spartan Law* (Edinburgh 1986) pp. 8–14. Quotations are taken from *The Polity of the Spartans,* trans. J. M. Moore, in *Aristotle and Xenophon on Democracy and Oligarchy* (Berkeley 1975).

8. Plutarch, *Lycurgus* 8.3–6; 16.1.

9. *Lycurgus* 16.1–2, trans. Dryden-Clough (modified). Plutarch says that the decision was taken by the "oldest of the *phyletoi,*" a term essentially equivalent to "the elders of the city." In Sparta, as in other Greek *poleis,* the *phyle* was a division of the citizen population for purposes of administration and military organization. On "tribal" organization throughout the Greek world, see N. Jones, *Public Organization in Ancient Greece* (Philadelphia 1987). Cf.

Walter Donlon, "The Social Groups of Dark Age Greece," *CP* 80 (1985) 293–308, for a strong argument against the traditional view of the *phyle* as originally a primitive clan-based group.

10. Stephen Hodkinson, "Land Tenure and Inheritance in Classical Sparta," *CQ* 36 (1986) 378–406. Hodkinson develops his argument further, and with broader consequences for the full scope of Spartan history, in "Inheritance, Marriage, and Demography: Perspectives upon the Success and Decline of Classical Sparta," in *Classical Sparta: Techniques behind Her Success,* ed. A. Powell (London 1989). Similar conclusions about Spartan family life are reached by Claude Mossé, "Women in the Spartan Revolutions of the Third Century B.C.," in *Women's History and Ancient History,* ed. S. B. Pomeroy (Chapel Hill 1991).

11. Hodkinson, "Land Tenure and Inheritance" pp. 392 and 404. In terminology and analysis Hodkinson relies, like many classical historians, on the anthropological work of Jack Goody (e.g., *Production and Reproduction* [Cambridge 1973]; with S. J. Tambiah, *Bridewealth and Dowry* [Cambridge 1973]).

12. Hodkinson, "Land Tenure and Inheritance" pp. 383 ff. Although Hodkinson does not press the argument, and indeed adds it as something of an afterthought (p. 394), Plato's silence on any such Spartan system of indivisibility and inalienability of *kleros* while setting up just such a system in the *Laws* (in the presence of a Spartan) is strong evidence that there was none.

13. *Politeia of the Lacedaimonians* 1.8. Xenophon's further comment, that Lycurgus "approved many such arrangements, for the women wish to run two households [*oikoi*], and the men to get more brothers for their children—brothers who will share in their power and *genos,* but not in the property" (1.9), may not be reliable in regard to the lawgiver's motivation, but reveals once again the basic household structure underlying the peculiar Lycrugan rules and communal structures. As Hodkinson notes, the "practices of wife-sharing, uterine half-sibling marriage and polyandry," all of which have been thought to contribute to the antifamily character of Spartan society, in fact "make sense on the supposition that land was transmitted hereditarily by means of partible inheritance"; "Land Tenure and Inheritance" p. 393.

14. Hodkinson, "Land Tenure and Inheritance" pp. 405–406.

15. See also Paul Cartledge, "Spartan Wives: Liberation or Licence?" *CQ* 31 (1981) 84–105, for an analysis and critique of the ancient and modern traditions about the status of Spartan women. Cartledge emphasizes that even though Spartan women received some form of physical and perhaps intellectual education and could inherit and own their own property, their role in the state was primarily that of childbearer, and their position in

the marital system was largely passive. From this perspective, perhaps the widows and the heiresses, who Aristotle implies sat unmarried upon their property, were the only Spartan women "liberated" to any significant extent. But these were an indication of the failure of the Spartan order, not of its advanced gender equality.

16. Cf. Mossé, "Women in the Spartan Revolutions" pp. 138–153, who also dismisses Plutarch's account of Spartan marriage as unhistorical, preferring that of Xenophon.

17. The argument went like this: When asked by a stranger what punishment was suffered by adulterers *(moichoi)* in Sparta, Geradas replied that there were none. When the stranger persisted, asking, "What if there were?" Geradas answered that the offender would have to present the plaintiff with a bull having a neck so long that it could stretch from the top of Taygetos to drink from the Eurotos river below. The stranger protested that it was impossible to find such a bull, and Gerasas "concluded" (Q.E.D.) that it was likewise impossible to find a *moichos* in Sparta (*Lycurgus* 15).

18. See also Mossé, "Women in the Spartan Revolutions"; cf. MacDowell, *Spartan Law*, who seems to believe that although adultery (or "seduction") was clearly recognized as an offense in the "early period," later on Spartan women had (or took) more sexual freedom.

19. *Law Code of Gortyn* col. IV.41–43. This is the model for Hodkinson's "universal female inheritance" in which daughters inherit one-half the amount of their brothers—as opposed to "residual female inheritance" in which daughters only inherit in the absence of sons, generally assumed to be the rule in Athens. The institution of the dowry in Athens, however, complicates this contrast.

20. As indicated above, I use Willetts' translation of the code. His is still the standard translation and also the standard interpretation. Though thorough and learned, it should be used with a clear recognition of the evolutionary paradigm that stands behind it. For a critique of Willetts' anthropological argument on "cross-cousin" marriage, an essential feature of Morgan's evolutionary analysis, see Ian Morris, "The Gortyn Code and Greek Kinship," *GRBS* 31 (1990) 233–254.

21. Willetts translates this as "serf." In his recent revision of *The Civilization of Ancient Crete* (1991) Willetts defends his use of this term against the criticism of Pierre Vidal-Naquet (p. 183).

22. *Law Code of Gortyn* col. II.2–15.

23. The code employs a complex system of age categories, including *anoros* and *anebos,* apparently indicating someone below the age of puberty, and *apodromos* and *dromeus* for "minor" and full adult status. See Willetts for a discussion of all these terms.

24. For Willetts' arguments, see *Law Code of Gortyn* pp. 23–27, with Morris' criticism ("The Gortyn Code and Greek Kinship").

25. Jones, *Public Organization in Ancient Greece*, regards the requirement that the Gortynian heiress marry within her father's *pyla* as evidence that "the fifth century Gortynian phylai were in some substantial sense genuine personal associations" (p. 225). He does not explain further.

26. The passage in question refers somewhat obscurely to the time "when the Aithalian *startos*, those with Kyllos, formed the *kosmos* [*ekosmion*]." Aristotle, *Politics* 1272a, notes that the Cretan *kosmoi* were chosen on the basis of *genos*, which Willetts takes to support his position in the following paragraph from the Gortyn Code: "The clan is apparently referred to as *startos* and we have seen that Aristotle stated that the *kosmoi* were drawn from 'certain clans.' This apparatus of clans, phratries (groups of clans) and tribes (groups of phratries) was organically related, as ancient authorities testify, and, together with such other important institutions as the Men's House, they have been investigated in many other societies by anthropologists" (*Law Code of Gortyn* p. 11). Willetts also notes (p. 65) the connection between *startos* and *stratos* (army). A word with military connotations, however, seems an unlikely candidate for a patrilineal descent group. Cf. Jones, *Public Organization of Greece* pp. 225–226.

27. Willetts, *Law Code of Gortyn* col. IV.23–46.

28. Ibid., col. V.9–28. The final clause is a difficult and much-debated passage which reads as follows: αἰ δέ κ' οἰ επιβαλλοντες, τὰς Ϝοικίας οἴτινες κ' ἰοντι ὀ κλᾶρος, τούτους ἔκεν τὰ κρέματα. Willetts uses "composing" to translate what is elsewhere simply the verb "to be"; thus his translation implies that the dependents of the household, who are themselves household property and so part of the *klaros*, are here given the final claim to the household property, or *kremata*. There are other possible interpretations, for which see Willetts' commentary. Simply by moving the comma from before to after *tas woikias*, Guarducci eliminated the *woikeus*' claim.

29. Willetts, *Law Code of Gortyn* p. 18. I can find no justification offered here or elsewhere for this interpretation—other than an a priori assumption of an archaic tribal/clan order characterized by Morgan's "classificatory" kinship (see pp. 18–19).

30. On Willetts' interpretation of *kadestas* (which an ancient lexicographer defined as *syngeneis*, or "relatives") as a classificatory term denoting "cross-cousin relationship and classifying one set of relative of one exogamous group" (*Law Code of Gortyn* p. 19), see Morris, "Kinship in the Gortyn Code." It is indeed a complex structure.

31. See Willetts, *Law Code of Gortyn*, esp. pp. 18–27. I do not mean to imply that it is impossible to detect historical change or revision within the

code. Given the length both of the code and of Cretan legal traditions, it would be surprising if such changes or revisions could not be found. Rather, my point is that the code cannot be forced into the evolutionary model of change without significant distortion.

32. The best-known evolutionary reading of the *Oresteia* is probably George Thomson's *Aeschylus and Athens,* 2d ed. (London 1946); see also idem, *The Oresteia of Aeschylus* (Cambridge 1938).

33. See Brook Manville, *The Origins of Citizenship in Ancient Athens* (Princeton 1990), for a recent assessment and bibliography.

34. Aristotle, *Ath.Pol.* 5; Plutarch, *Solon* 15.

35. *Ath.Pol.* 12.4, trans. J. M. Moore.

36. On the importance of Solon's reforms for the concept of Athenian citizenship see Manville, *Origins of Citizenship in Ancient Athens* chap. 5.

37. See, e.g., Josiah Ober's summary of Solon's place in Athenian history in *Mass and Elite in Democratic Athens: Rhetoric, Ideology, and the Power of the People* (Princeton 1989).

38. *Solon* 21, trans. Dryden-Clough.

39. Demosthenes 46.14, Loeb trans. A. T. Murray. Perhaps "woman" should rather be "wife" here; the divided loyalty of the wife was a topos in ancient Greek society. This law is quoted as if it is a genuine law of Solon, and the last series of extenuating circumstances are perhaps distinctive enough to make that assumption a plausible one. Adopted sons could not bequeath property, but could only pass it on to a natural heir or leave the estate intestate.

40. See, e.g., Manville, *Origins of Citizenship in Ancient Athens* pp. 128–129: "The new state of affairs can be illuminated by observing the motives behind the creation of testamentary laws in other tribal societies. Elsewhere in time and place, regulations of inheritance typically evolve to protect the property farmed by individual families against the claims of a holding lineage or authority. As a general rule, wills and other institutions created by laws of succession transform the individual cultivator's rights of residence and labor on a plot to a privilege of ownership."

41. On the artificial character of the historical genos see further F. Bourriot, *Recherches sur la nature du genos* (Lille 1976); for a useful summary of current discussion on the genos see S. D. Lambert, *The Phratries of Attica* (Ann Arbor 1993).

42. Herodotus 5.92. Aubrey de Selincourt translates "one clan—the Bacchiadai, who intermarried only amongst themselves—were in power there." *Genos* is not in the text.

43. See Cynthia B. Patterson, *Pericles' Citizenship Law* (New York 1981) app. 2.

44. Failure to clarify use of the term "clan" in reference to both the Eupatridai and *genē* such as the Eumolpidai is a problem common to recent

books as different as Robert Littman, *Kinship and Politics in Athens, 600–400 B.C.* (New York 1990); and Peter Rose, *Sons of the Gods, Children of Earth: Ideology and Literary Form in Ancient Greece* (Ithaca 1992).

45. For the reconstruction of the *anchisteia* through citations in the orators see Roger Just, *Women in Athenian Law and Life* (London 1989) pp. 85–89.

46. Athenian court speeches on matters of inheritance, however, reveal that the formal definition of the *anchisteia* was not necessarily well known to all Athenians and that it was possible for a speaker to present, within limits, his own view on who should be considered "nearest." For this point and a discussion of the way in which "family" was a rhetorically variable word, see David Cohen, *Law, Violence, and Community in Classical Athens* (Cambridge 1995) chap. 8.

47. On the character and political importance of the Athenian phratry as the overseer of legitimacy and citizenship, see now Lambert, *The Phratries of Attica*; also C. Hedrick, "The Athenian Phratry" (Ph.D. diss., University of Pennsylvania 1984), and Patterson, *Pericles' Citizenship Law.*

48. *IG* I.115; Russell Meiggs and David Lewis, *Greek Historical Inscriptions to the End of the Fifth Century* (Oxford 1969) 86; for discussion see R. Stroud, *Drakon's Law on Homicide* (Berkeley 1968); M. Gagarin, *Drakon and Early Athenian Homicide Law* (New Haven 1981).

49. Note, e.g., the role played by the phratry and phratry members in Isaeus 3, "On the Estate of Pyrrhus."

50. Cf. Lambert, *The Phratries of Attica.*

51. For a detailed discussion of the meaning of the word *nothos* and the status it denotes see Cynthia B. Patterson, "Those Athenian Bastards," *Classical Antiquity* 9 (1990) 40–73.

52. The problem is that the quotation of law is embedded in a joke. The clever Athenian and mortal Pisthetairos explains to the less than clever *nothos* and immortal Heracles that he has no vested interest in the cause or property of his father Zeus, since the law of Solon established that "a *nothos* has no right of inheritance [*anchisteia*] if there are *gnesioi*. If there are no *gnesioi*, the property falls to the next of kin"; *Birds* 1661–66.

53. Demosthenes 23.53–55; cf. Plutarch, *Solon* 23.

54. David Cohen asserts that democratic Athens was distinguished by the principle of noninterference in private life—by the principle that everyone should be allowed to "live as he chooses"; *Law, Sexuality, and Society: The Enforcement of Morals in Classical Athens* (New York 1991) p. 229; cf. *Law, Violence, and Community* p. 42. This claim seems to overlook the significant ways in which private sexual behavior could have consequences for the public position of a household and so drew public attention and regulation.

55. See Menander, frags. 333 and 334, including one husband saying to another about his heiress wife: "Mine's a real Lamia [monster, vampire] . . . she's a perfect plague." Cf. Aristotle, *Nicomachean Ethics* (1161a1–4) on the heiress as an "oligarchic" ruler.

56. J. J. Bachofen, *Myth, Religion, and Mother Right,* trans. R. Manheim (Princeton 1967) p. 86.

57. See R. Sinos and J. Oakley, *The Athenian Wedding* (Madison 1993); also R. Rehm, *Marriage to Death: The Conflation of Wedding and Funeral Rituals in Greek Tragedy* (Princeton 1994).

58. So W. K. Lacey speaks of the "disaster" of having only female children (*The Family in Classical Greece* [London 1968] p. 24). As Plato's account suggests, however, the real misfortune for a father was not to have provided his daughters with appropriate husbands before his death (*Laws* 8.924).

59. See Goody, *Production and Reproduction* pp. 86–98 with app. 2, "The Probability of Family Distributions." Goody's calculations are based on a pre-industrial model of population, with high mortality and an average of six children born per household. On this model, 17 percent of households would be childless.

60. Willetts asserts that *epiballon* means "clansman" except in this section dealing with the heiress, where it means "to whom it falls to marry" or "groom elect"; *Law Code of Gortyn* p. 23. The distinction seems to be based on the fact that in the regulations for the marriage of the heiress the *epiballontes* come from the restricted circle of brothers and sons of brothers of the deceased, which is not the case in its earlier usage for those who claim an estate after the children of a man's brothers and sisters. Raphael Sealey simply translates the term as "heir," which of course has its own problems, since the woman, not her husband, is technically the heir; *Women and the Law in Classical Greece* (Chapel Hill 1990) pp. 63–69. I suspect that the term is not so specific as Willetts supposes, and simply denotes what it means literally: "the one to whom something falls," here specifically limited to brothers and sons of brothers. In the summary in the text, therefore, I simply use the transliteration *epiballon.*

61. Cf. Sealey, *Women and the Law* pp. 63–69.

62. *Law Code of Gortyn* col. VIII.20–33. Sealey provides a useful summary of these rules (*Women and the Law* p. 65).

63. *Law Code of Gortyn* col. V.9–22.

64. One might ask why this would not also have been seen as a problem in the case of an intestate estate, in which not only did sisters and sisters' children inherit but also the property could apparently end up in the hands of the *woikeus* of the estate. Also in this case division of the property *(kre-*

mata) is envisioned as a possible solution in the presence of several *epibal-lontes*. Perhaps, however, *kremata* do not necessarily include the full *kleros* upon which the oikos rested.

65. See *Law Code of Gortyn* col. IV.31–37.

66. David Schaps, *The Economic Rights of Women in Ancient Greece* (Edinburgh 1976) p. 44.

67. Douglas MacDowell, "The *Oikos* in Athenian Law," CQ 39 (1989) 10–21, does argue that *oikos* as "family" referred to "descendants through the male line" and cites Demosthenes 43.48 to establish the point: "Makartatos. Who was his father? Theopompos . . . Who was Theopompos' father? Kharidemos. Who was Kharidemos' father? Stratios. Who was Stratios' father? Bouselos. This, men of the jury, is the *oikos* of Stratios, one of the sons of Bouselos. And those men, whose names I have given you are descendants [*ekgonoi*] of Stratios." The quotation, as cited, is misleading. The speaker is opposing the claim of Makartatos to what he is calling the estate of Hagnias, another of the sons of Bouselos, with the claim of his own client. He then immediately goes on to do the same thing for that client as he did for Makartatos, leading back to what he calls a "second *oikos*," the *oikos* of Hagnias and the estate in question. Somewhat earlier (in another passage MacDowell cites) the speaker says that "out of the one *oikos* of Bouselos, five *oikos* came into being" (43.19). Thus it seems clear that *oikos* is not lineage but household. Demosthenes simply uses a line of descent to get back to the *oikos* around which he wants to argue his client's case.

68. Schaps, *Economic Rights of Women* p. 44.

69. *Law Code of Gortyn* col. XI.42–45.

70. Isaeus, frag. 25 Thalheim. Modern discussions of this law have generally followed the view that the law required the relative to marry the heiress, and required her divorce if she was already married. This seems to me an unnecessary conclusion from the evidence available and unduly influenced by the rhetorical language of the orators, who could move easily from "the law allows" to "the law requires" (e.g., Lysias 1). The prime passage is Isaeus 3.64, where the speaker claims that "many men who were already married have had their own wives taken away from them"—i.e., through remarriage to the *anchisteus*. This seems to have been the case, however, only if the woman put in a claim to the full paternal estate (or *kleros*); if she did not make such a claim she apparently could opt to remain married (see, e.g., Isaeus 10.19). Also if she had already borne children, the *anchisteus* may have had no claim, but this view is based on some lines in Terence's *Micio* which are relevant but not necessarily authoritative. In any case, the Athenian laws on the *epikleros* should, on my view, be read more as delegating re-

sponsiblity to a group than as legislating marriage for a particular member. Here the Gortyn Code, with its series of alternative marriage possibilities, provides a useful comparison.

71. For the sources of Athenian law on the *epikleros* see A. H. R. Harrison, *The Law of Athens,* vol. 1 (Oxford 1968) pp. 132–138; and Schaps, *Economic Rights of Women* pp. 25–42, with bibliography. Of the earlier discussion, see esp. L. Gernet, "Sur l'épiclerat," *REG* 31 (1921) 337–379.

72. Plutarch, *Solon* 20, trans. Scott-Kilvert (modified).

73. Schaps, *Economic Rights of Women* p. 32.

74. Some well-known Athenians were named from the maternal side, e.g., Cleisthenes the "founder" of Athenian democracy. Thucydides the historian's father was named Olorus, presumably the name of his maternal grandmother's non-Athenian father. And so forth.

75. Note the scattering of members of the Alcmeonid family in various demes and tribes. This was a family in a quite loose and definitely bilateral sense; two of its most famous members, Pericles and Alcibiades, were connected to the historical Alcmeon through their mothers. See J. K. Davies, *Athenian Propertied Families* (Oxford 1971) s.v. Alkmeon.

76. On the property rights of Athenian women, see Foxhall, "Household, Gender and Property," which appears back to back with MacDowell's quite different appraisal of the oikos and Athenian law of property. Despite a growing recognition that Athenian women did use and manage property, even if without the full rights of alienation assumed in the modern use of the word "own," it is still asserted baldly that women in Athens had no property rights. See Sarah Pomeroy's *Xenophon, Oeconomicus: A Social and Historical Commentary* (Oxford 1994) p. 256 (reviewed by Virginia Hunter, *CP* 91 [1996] 184–189).

77. See Hodkinson, "Land Tenure and Inheritance" p. 395, for a discussion of this passage; also, in general on Spartan marriage practices, "Inheritance, Marriage, and Demography." The term *patrouchos,* as MacDowell has emphasized in his discussion of Spartan inheritance law, is found only in Herodotus. Although it seems to be related to the Gortynian *patroiokos* and is probably Doric, we do not in fact know what term the Spartans used; *Spartan Law* p. 96.

78. For discussion of Sparta's demographic history, see T. J. Figueira, "Population Patterns in Late Archaic and Classical Sparta," *TAPA* 116 (1986) 165–213; and Hodkinson, "Inheritance, Marriage, and Demography," with bibliography. Hodkinson has developed his interpretation of Spartan society, its contradictions and social tensions, further in "Spartan Society in the Fourth Century: Crisis and Continuity," in *Le IV siecle av. J.-C.: Approches historiographiques,* ed. P. Carlier (Nancy 1996).

79. On this question see G. Morrow, *Plato's Cretan City* (Princeton 1960).

80. Plato's philosophical and pedagogical preambles are a distinctive feature of his lawgiving (see *Laws* 4 for his explanation of his purposes).

81. Although *Politics* 1252b (quoted at the opening of Chapter 2) is the better-known statement, Plato said essentially the same thing in book 3 of *Laws*.

4. Marriage and Adultery in Democratic Athens

1. Solon, frag. 4 West, translated by Richmond Lattimore, *Greek Lyrics* (Chicago 1960) p. 21.

2. I have argued for the centrality of marriage in Athenian democratic ideology and for the importance of legitimacy for citizen participation in a number of articles—"Those Athenian Bastards," *CA* 9 (1990) 40–73; "Marriage and the Married Women in Athenian Law," in *Women's History and Ancient History*, ed. S. B. Pomeroy (Chapel Hill 1991); "The Case against Neaira and the Ideology of the Athenian Family," in *Athenian Identity and Civic Ideology*, ed. A. Scafuro and A. Boegehold (Baltimore 1994)—as well as in *Pericles' Citizenship Law of 451/0 B.C.* (New York 1981).

3. Thucydides 2.37, trans. Rex Warner. Perhaps sexual pleasures which violated marriage were not exactly what Pericles had in mind in this passage of his eulogy of Athens. Indeed, it may reveal more about twentieth-century America than fifth-century B.C.E. Athens that Pericles' words are often taken to refer implicitly to sexual behavior and enjoyment. See, for example, David Cohen, *Law, Sexuality, and Society: The Enforcement of Morals in Classical Athens* (New York 1991), p. 90.

4. Aristotle, *Politics* 1253b. For the view of marriage as essentially de facto, see J.-P. Vernant, "Marriage," in *Myth and Society in Ancient Greece* (Atlantic Highlands, N.J., 1986); and esp. R. Sealey, "On Lawful Concubinage in Athens," *CA* 3 (1984) 111–133.

5. Literally: "[the woman] whom father or brother or grandfather entrusts [*engyese*], from this woman are born legitimate children [*paidas gnesious*]"; Demosthenes 44.49.

6. For this often-used language see Menander, *Dyskolos* 842.

7. Although some still persist in the view that since Pericles' law does not mention marriage and legitimacy, they were not a necessary ingredient of legitimate citizenship, the position is not a convincing one. First, the law is not a definition of citizenship; and second, there is abundant testimony, particularly from the courts, that Athens did not separate private and public legitimacy. Both required married parents.

8. Aristotle, *Ath.Pol.* 26.4. For the meaning of *astos/e* and the implications of the Athenian (and here Periclean) use of the term, see C. B. Patterson, "*Hai Attikai:* The Other Athenians," *Helios* 13 (1986) 46–67.

9. Aristophanes, *Birds* 1661–66, trans. William Arrowsmith (modified).

10. D. M. MacDowell, *The Law in Classical Athens* (Ithaca 1978) p. 89: "The law that a citizen could not marry an alien was part of the same enactment as the law that a child of a citizen and an alien was not to be a citizen." There is no evidence, however, for the existence of this "other provision of Pericles' law" (p. 67).

11. On the question of bastards and citizenship see Patterson, "Those Athenian Bastards." Part of the problem is that modern discussion has focused on the illegitimate Athenian as the child of two unmarried Athenian parents, whereas the Athenian discussion focused on the *nothos,* who was typically the child of parents of different status (i.e., free and slave, or Athenian and foreign). The difference is critical.

12. On the argument, see Patterson, "The Case against Neaira."

13. Various dates have been suggested for the passage of these laws, which seem to belong together; given that they seem to assume the development of the Athenian court system, an early fourth-century date seems reasonable. See D. Whitehead, "Women and Naturalisation in Fourth Century Athens: The Case of Archippe," *CQ* 36 (1986) 109–114; and C. Carey, "Apollodorus' Mother: The Wives of Enfranchised Aliens in Athens," *CQ* 41 (1991) 84–89, on the status of Apollodorus' mother, Archippe. MacDowell assumes that such prohibition (or invalidization) of marriages to foreigners was a part of the Periclean law, but he considers it possible that the imposition of penalties began only in the fourth century; *The Law in Classical Athens* p. 87.

14. See, e.g., the speaker's argument against the existence of such proof in Isaeus 3.

15. Aeschylus, *Eumenides* 217–222, trans. Richmond Lattimore. Cf. Aristotle, *Politics* 1252a24–33, for whom marriage is also both a natural and a political relationship.

16. C. Sourvinou-Inwood disputes this view of Antigone's familial and polis responsibility, arguing instead that Antigone is a "bad woman" who enters the public realm and usurps properly male roles in defying Creon's order and giving her brother a public burial; "Assumptions and the Creation of Meaning: A Reading of Sophocles' *Antigone,*" *JHS* 108 (1988) 118–136. Helene Foley, using some interesting comparative evidence from the Mani of southern Greece, argues that it is only because she is the last surviving member of her family that Antigone, as a woman, enters the public arena and undertakes the burial of her brother, a physical action nor-

mally left to the male members of the family; "Antigone as Moral Agent," in *Tragedy and the Tragic,* ed. M. Silk (Oxford 1996). However, Antigone connects her burial of Polyneices with her similar care of the bodies of her parents, Oedipus (who apparently died in Thebes in this version of the story) and Jocasta, as well as that of Eteocles (900–902). The issue in the case of the burial of Polyneices is Antigone's refusal to obey Creon's public decree, not a rejection of traditional gender roles.

17. On this topic see also Sheila Murnaghan, "Antigone 904–920 and the Institution of Marriage," *AJP* 107 (1986) 192–207. Murnaghan initially discusses marriage as a patriarchal institution of the male polis but ends by stressing its personal, male and female, character. She concludes: "the splitting up of the personal and the political . . . is untenable and . . . there can be no adequate justification for Antigone's loss of a full life containing not only close and properly honored family ties but the experiences of marriage and motherhood as well" (p. 207).

18. Sophocles, *Antigone,* trans. Wyckoff. For the history of the interpretation of these lines, see Murnaghan, "Antigone 904–920"; and Foley, "Antigone as a Moral Agent."

19. *Pace* Murnaghan ("Antigone 904–920" p. 206 n. 31), Creon's words do not "echo the language of the Athenian marriage ceremony." They echo the language of the *engye*. In this play, both Creon and Antigone present an "impersonal conception of marriage" (Murnaghan p. 206).

20. On this theme see R. Rehm, *Marriage to Death* (Princeton 1994).

21. So Lin Foxhall characterizes David Cohen's stirring up the discussion on *moicheia* in her "Response to Eva Cantarella," in *Symposion 1990: Papers on Greek and Hellenistic Legal History,* ed. M. Gagarin (Vienna 1991).

22. Cohen, *Law, Sexuality, and Society.* See my review in *AHR,* June 1993, pp. 845–846.

23. Cohen, *Law, Sexuality, and Society* pp. 102, 124.

24. For this view of adultery in ancient Mediterranean society, see also David Cohen, "The Augustan Law on Adultery: The Social and Cultural Context," in *The Family in Italy from Antiquity to the Present,* ed. J. Kertzer and R. Saller (New Haven 1991).

25. Cohen, *Law, Sexuality, and Society* p. 220. See also his similar comments in *Law, Violence, and Community in Classical Athens* (Cambridge 1995).

26. The supposed *moicheia* of Epaenetos with Neaira's unmarried daughter ([Demosthenes] 59.65) is a crucial piece of evidence which Cohen reinterprets to support his position; *Law, Sexuality, and Society* pp. 108–109 with n. 32.

27. See S. Treggiari, *Roman Marriage* (Oxford 1991) pp. 262–264.

28. Kenneth Dover, *Greek Popular Morality in the Time of Plato and Aristotle* (Oxford 1974) p. 209.

29. The law is interpolated into Demosthenes' text, but since the terms are repeated by Demosthenes himself in his argument, they are probably genuine. The translation is that of the Loeb text with brackets added to indicate where the Greek text has been expanded. That the preposition *epi* refers to sexual intercourse is generally taken for granted. Cf. a similar use of *epi* in the Gortyn Code (col. VII.3); Ronald Willetts, ed., *The Law Code of Gortyn* (Berlin 1967).

30. Cohen, *Law, Sexuality, and Society* p. 105; see also E. Harris, "Did the Athenians Regard Seduction as a Worse Crime than Rape?" *CQ* 40 (1990) 370–377; Susan Cole, "Greek Sanctions against Sexual Assault," *CP* 79 (1984) 97–113; and, most recently, C. Carey, "Rape and Adultery in Athenian Law," *CQ* 45 (1995) 407–417. Cf. Plato's similar phrasing in *Laws* 874c for a law specifically dealing with rape (sexual assault).

31. Plato, *Laws* 9.866d–869e. These comments are in part a response to Susan Treggiari's comments on a paper I gave at the 1993 APA meetings in Washington, D.C., as part of a panel on "Legislation and Morality."

32. So Susan Treggiari, personal communication; see previous note.

33. Lysias 1, "On the Murder of Eratosthenes."

34. See, e.g., Lysias 1.4, 15, 33, and 36.

35. Lysias 1.29–31, trans. W. R. M. Lamb.

36. Lysias 1.27. Cf. the similar broad claim made by a character in Menander, *Dyskolos* 290.

37. See Cohen, *Law, Sexuality, and Society* pp. 98–132, on the various laws appealed to by Lysias.

38. So Sarah Pomeroy wrote in 1976: "whether adultery came about through rape or seduction, the male was considered the legally guilty or active party, the woman passive" (*Goddesses, Whores, Wives, and Slaves* [New York 1975] p. 86). Susan Cole noted in 1984: "the issue of sexual assault of women raises special problems, because in certain circumstances sexual assault could have been treated as adultery"; "Greek Sanctions against Sexual Assault" p. 97. And in 1990 Lin Foxhall explained that because "rape, seduction and *moikheia* [she does not define the last term] were all equally and essentially offenses against men's authority over the household," they were "sometimes not easily distinguished"; "Response to Eva Cantarella" pp. 299–300. Lysias seems to have won the day. The distinction that Lysias does explicitly draw between what we would call rape and adultery, making the latter a worse crime because it corrupts both mind and body, is also generally repeated as culturally authoritative. The question is, of course, "worse" from whose or from what perspective?

39. Literally "to the one who took him" *(toi helonti)*, usually translated as "who caught him in the act" but which can also mean the one who convicted him. In an unpublished paper, "The *Graphe Moikheias*," Adele Scafuro argues that the later meaning is more consistent with Athenian usage (personal communication).

40. The phrase "without a knife" has, not surprisingly, provoked considerable comment; that it refers to castration is one possible view. As I learned recently during a discussion of this question, in animal husbandry the castrating of an animal is often termed "using the knife."

41. I quote here the interpolated law, which Apollodorus paraphrases and expands upon in his argument. The substance of the interpolated law, however, seems completely in accord with the paraphrase—and is certainly more concise. The fact that in Apollodorus' catalogue of legal actions concerning *moicheia* there is none for the prosecution of the specific act of *moicheia* itself is a key point in Cohen's argument that Athenian law regulated the aggrieved husband's use of self-help against the adulterer but let the act itself alone. In general, Cohen argues, "there were no sexual offences in Athenian law"; *Law, Sexuality, and Society* p. 123. The *Ath.Pol.*, however, includes the *graphe moicheias* as the last in a long list of legal actions that were brought before the *thesmothetai* (57). Cohen argues that this should be understood as a reference to Apollodorus' action employed against the husband who holds another man as a *moichos*. The argument, however, is tendentious. The fact that Aristotle "only mentions one *graphe* concerning adultery" is inadequate support for the conclusion that "there is no reason to suppose that this [i.e., Apollodorus' *graphe*] was not the one he had in mind" (p. 123).

42. Hipponax, frag. 30 West.

43. On the character of Hipponax's poetry, see Ralph Rosen, *Old Comedy and the Iambographic Tradition* (Atlanta 1988). Although the concept here is not necessarily our own modern notion of what is obscene, there was in archaic and classical Greek vocabulary a category of words frequently used in invective (and in Aristophanic comedy) but not in polite society.

44. Pierre Chantraine, *Dictionnaire étymologique de la langue grecque* (Paris 1968) s.v. *moichos*.

45. J. N. Adams, *The Latin Sexual Vocabulary* (Baltimore 1982) p. 142.

46. Xenophanes, frag. 10 Diehl.

47. On Aristophanes' language see Jeffrey Henderson, *The Maculate Muse* (New Haven 1975). Henderson, however, does not include *moichos* in his catalogue. It is also significant that Hesiod does not use the term *moichos* in his condemnation (in the moral language of epic) of the man who "goes up into the bed of his brother, to lie in secret love with his brother's

wife, doing acts that are against nature"; *Works and Days* 328–329, trans. Richmond Lattimore.

48. Kenneth Dover, *Greek Homosexuality* (Cambridge, Mass., 1978) pp. 105–106 in reference to *Clouds* 1083. Do the quotes around radish imply that Dover does not take the term literally? The point is left unclear. On this punishment and related matters, see Virginia Hunter, *Policing Athens: Social Control in the Attic Lawsuits, 420–320 B.C.* (Princeton 1994) chap. 6.

49. Cohen, *Law, Sexuality, and Society* p. 116 n. 56.

50. Aristophanes, *Lysistrata* 124. Cf. Douglas Parker, *Lysistrata* (New York 1964) p. 11, who rejects the literal translation in favor of "total abstinence from sex."

51. Willetts, *Law Code of Gortyn* col. II.21.

52. Lysias 13.66.

53. Cf. Cohen's comments on the connection of adultery and thievery (*Law, Sexuality, and Society* p. 113 n. 45). Cohen cites a seventeenth-century English "Exposition of the Ten Commandments" which explains that "the adulterer is a thief, by intruding his child into another man's possession," and also Dr. Johnson, who commented that "the thief merely makes off with the sheep, but the adulterer gets the sheep and farm as well." The adulterer (and his child) gets the farm, it can be added, because he has also got the wife, and it is this further sexual thievery that escalates the crime of adultery beyond ordinary theft. Also, in ancient law in general, nighttime crime, of which adultery is a quintessential example, is considered especially dangerous and threatening to social order.

54. If this is not apparent now it should become so in the next chapter, where the specific legal cases of *moicheia* are discussed in detail.

55. Willetts, *Law Code of Gortyn* col. II.21. The clause seems to imply that the woman is a daughter, sister, or wife. Note once again the emphasis on the entry into another man's house.

56. Cohen, *Law, Sexuality, and Society* p. 102.

57. Ibid., p. 109; cf. p. 106.

58. Ibid., p. 109. Cohen then continues: "to put it more cynically, [the violation] of the husband's claim to exclusive sexual access to his wife."

59. Beate Wagner-Hasel, "Frauenleben in orientalischer Abgeschlossenheit? Zur Geschichte und Nutzanwendung eines Topos," *Der Altsprachliche Unterricht* 2 (1989) 8–29. One thinks of Mozart's "Abduction from the Seraglio."

60. Paul Rahe, "The Primacy of Politics," *AHR* 89 (1984) 270, quoted above in Chapter 1.

61. On the shape and definition of domestic space in the Greek house, see M. H. Jameson, "Private Space and the Greek City," in *The Greek City from Homer to Alexander,* ed. O. Murray and S. Price (Oxford 1990). On p. 193 Jameson notes that "it is inescapable that by the fourth century B.C. most Greek houses used portable terracotta braziers or had makeshift fires wherever it was convenient"; this physical reality, however, does not lessen the conceptual importance of the hearth for the Greek oikos: "The archaeological evidence, just because it does not provide confirmation of the physical reality of round hearth and door gods, enables us to appreciate the ideological power of the symbolic figures that defined the classical Greek conception of domestic space" (p. 195). The same can be said of the *gynaikeion.*

62. Cohen, *Law, Sexuality, and Society* p. 149. See also his "Seclusion and Separation," *Greece and Rome* 36 (1990) 3–15.

63. See A. R. W. Harrison, *The Law of Athens,* vol. 1 (Oxford 1968).

64. See Lin Foxhall, "Household, Gender and Property in Classical Athens," *CQ* 89 (1989) 22–44, for an excellent critique of the view that Athenian women did not "own" property. On women's use and management of property, see also Virginia Hunter, "Women's Authority in Classical Athens: The Example of Kleoboule and Her Son (Dem. 27–29)," *EMC/CV* 8 (1989) 39–48.

65. An example of the anachronism present in the law is that it was not at all typical in the classical era for a [slave] concubine to have been kept within the household "for the purpose of producing legitimate children." On the identity of the *pallake* see my comments in Gagarin, *Symposion 1990* pp. 281–287.

66. See Cohen, *Law, Sexuality, and Society* chap. 7.

67. One of the best examples is Demosthenes' mother (see Hunter, "Women's Authority"), and there are others. Although traditionally the orators have been considered a source for the more extreme view of female seclusion, when read carefully they speak to women's active involvement in maintaining the public and economic status of their households.

68. Sue Blundell, *Women in Ancient Greece* (Cambridge, Mass., 1994) p. 128. Blundell comes to this conclusion after carefully noting, among other things, that women did own property, might be literate, and could participate in outdoor exercise and games (pp. 114, 132–133).

69. This is, in summary, Cohen's provocative thesis in *Law, Sexuality, and Society* pp. 122–124.

70. This is a difficult claim to prove or disprove, given the nature of our knowledge of Athenian law. Moreover, as in his insistence on a narrow meaning for *moicheia,* the argument here seems tendentious.

71. [Demosthenes] 59.87, quoted earlier in text. See also Aeschines 1.183.

72. Cohen, *Law, Sexuality, and Society* pp. 123–124.

73. For the punishment of citizen crime in classical Athens, see now Hunter, *Policing Athens*, esp. pp. 174–184 on the evidence on the use of torture against citizens and free men in extreme situations of treason or endangered state security. Normally, torture was inflicted only upon slaves. Cf. Page duBois, *Torture and Truth* (New York 1991).

74. On the nature of female citizenship in Athens, see Patterson, "*Hai Attikai.*"

75. Cohen minimizes this part of her punishment with the comment "such women could, and did, remarry" (*Law, Sexuality, and Society* p. 124). Euripides' *Electra* 920 ff., however, does not adequately support this statement, nor does the marriage of Neaira's daughter, since she was not a convicted *moicheumene*. Cohen has no real evidence for this claim, and it seems unlikely that such a woman would easily find a new household. No historical examples exist.

76. Plato, *Laws* 774a–c, trans. Saunders (modified).

77. *Laws* 840e, trans. Saunders. The cover story of the August 1994 *Time* magazine, however, on the biological roots of infidelity, suggests that Plato was wrong about the birds, or at least about some of them.

78. *Laws* 784e, trans. Saunders. Plato does not explain further his view of what moderate adultery might be.

79. *Laws* 838c, trans. Saunders.

80. Lattimore, *Greek Lyrics*. This is the continuation of the poem with which this chapter opened.

5. Adultery Onstage and in Court

1. In introducing his analysis of adultery in the nineteenth-century European novel, Tony Tanner looks back to the Greek tradition with the comment: "Western literature as we know it starts with an act of transgression, a violation of boundaries that leads to instability, asymmetry, disorder, and an interfamilial and intertribal clash that threatens the very existence of civilization (as then known) itself"; *Adultery in the Novel* (Baltimore 1988) p. 24. He refers to the abduction of Helen; in this chapter, however, I concentrate on the less ambiguous adultery of Clytemnestra.

2. Cf. ibid., pp. 368–377.

3. The same story can of course be retold to different audiences with different purposes. See, e.g. (in addition to Athenian drama), William Morris' nineteenth-century "Defence of Guenevere," with the comments of Virginia Hale and Catherine Barnes Stevenson, "Morris' Medieval Queen: A Paradox Resolved," *Victorian Poetry* 30 (1992) 171–178.

4. It is also possible, of course, to consider the *Iliad* as motivated by an act of rape or abduction, especially when Helen's state of mind is not the focus of attention. There is an interesting similarity here with the strategy of Lysias' "On the Murder of Eratosthenes" (see discussion in text).

5. *Odyssey* 8.268–270, trans. Robert Fitzgerald.

6. By taking the story of Agamemnon, Clytemnestra, and Aegisthus as a paradigm of adultery, I am not suggesting that it presents a standard or typical case, but rather that in larger-than-life fashion it illuminates the moral structure of adultery in its distinctive Athenian context. Adultery is here a crime of corruption and gender reversal committed over time within the household itself. Standing in notable contrast is the construction of adultery in the nineteenth-century novels studied by Tanner *(Adultery in the Novel)* or in Hawthorne's *Scarlet Letter,* where the emphasis is on a single moment of passion. The fact that it would be possible to tell the story of the *Oresteia* in a way which downplayed adultery and emphasized the simple act of murder (perhaps taking Aegisthus as husband rather than lover—note the potential ambiguity of *Odyssey* 1.35) seems only to reinforce the significance of the Aeschylean (and Athenian) emphasis on the central theme of adultery in this trilogy. Cf. the comments of Simon Goldhill, *The Oresteia* (Cambridge 1992) pp. 37–45, on the centrality of the theme of adultery as a threat to public order in Aeschylus' *Oresteia.*

7. From this perspective, one could modify—and I think improve—David Cohen's argument that Athenian public interest lay essentially in the violence produced by adultery; *Law, Sexuality, and Society: The Enforcement of Morals in Classical Athens* (New York 1991). The inherent violence of adultery against the household and its relationships is as central to its "public danger" as is its potential for provoking private revenge or feuding.

8. Aeschylus, *Agamemnon* 35–39, trans. Robert Fagles (38–43).

9. *Agamemnon* 1405, 208, 1525, trans. Fagles (1430, 209, 1553).

10. *Agamemnon* 1231–32, trans. Fagles (1241).

11. See *Libation Bearers* 120, where Electra asks whether she should look for a *dikastes* or a *dikephoros* to bring justice to her house.

12. Aeschylus, *Libation Bearers* 989–990, trans. Fagles (981–982 modified). "The one who shames" is a literal translation of *aischunter* at 990, which Fagles translates as "adulterer."

13. *Libation Bearers* 991–996, trans. Fagles (983–989).

14. *Libation Bearers* 132–138, trans. Fagles (139–143).

15. Cf. Tanner's distinction between "family" and "lineage"; *Adultery in the Novel* p. 368. He seems to imply, however, that the importance of adultery in the modern novel presupposes the development of the modern family, and quotes Philippe Ariès on the earlier importance of lineage: "only the

line was capable of exciting the forces of feeling and imagination. That is why so many romances of chivalry treat of it" (*Centuries of Childhood* p. 355, as quoted by Tanner). It is unfortunate that Tanner has relied so heavily on Ariès' interpretation of the premodern family. A Homeric hero fought not for his genos but for his oikos. The household was the true emotional center of the early Greek family.

16. *Libation Bearers* 262–263, trans. Fagles (267–268 modified). Aeschylus uses *domos, domata,* and *oikos* interchangeably for house and household; all three words are unmistakably concrete in their reference and are rooted in the sense of family as household.

17. Tantalus served his son Pelops to the gods, and Pelops' son Atreus served his brother Thyestes' children to their father in return for Thyestes' adultery with Atreus' wife. And then there is also Helen.

18. Cf. Hesiod, *Works and Days* 328–329, quoted in the previous chapter.

19. Aeschylus, *Eumenides* 739–740, after Fagles (754–755). *Gyne* means both "woman" and "wife"; here "wife" seems the better translation.

20. Aeschylus, *Eumenides* 858–866, trans. Lattimore.

21. *Eumenides* 984–986, trans. Fagles (993–995).

22. A common reading of the *Oresteia* is that the play reflects the struggle between matriarchy and patriarchy, whether prehistorical (Bachofen et al.) or ideological (see esp. Froma Zeitlin, "The Dynamics of Misogyny," in *Women in the Ancient World,* ed. J. Peradotto and J. P. Sullivan [Albany 1984] pp. 159–191). On this view, Clytemnestra represents female interests and powers distinct from those of the male and is defeated by the arguments of patriarchal authority—and henceforth women will be subjected to patriarchal marriage and excluded from patrilineal inheritance. Despite the force and appeal of such an interpretation, it does not do full justice to the complexity of the dramatic representation of adultery or to the trilogy's conclusion, in which Athena's female persuasion brings the still-powerful Furies into the circle of Athenian public religion as the guardians of marriage and the oikos. It is at least possible to view this as an improvement for all concerned. And despite the frequency with which the idea is repeated (e.g., by Zeitlin), inheritance in classical Athens was not strictly patrilineal.

23. The authorship of the reforms was attributed by Aristotle (*Ath.Pol.* 25) to a certain Ephialtes, about whom not much is known apart from the interesting story that he was a victim of assassination. That much, however, may be an indication of the depth of the feelings aroused by the reforms.

24. On the workings of these institutions (and also the demographic implication ot the numbers), see esp. M. Hansen, *The Athenian Democracy: The Age of Demosthenes* (Oxford 1991).

25. See Thucydides 1.102–111.

26. Thucydides 1.107, trans. Rex Warner. The truth of this claim cannot be established, but that it was believed at all—if only by Thucydides himself—is nonetheless significant.

27. Sophocles, *Electra* 1505–07, trans. Grene (modified).

28. Sophocles, *Electra* 1508–10, trans. Grene.

29. Sophocles, *Electra* 33–34, trans. Grene.

30. These quotations come from lines 96 ff. as translated by Grene. The translation of these highly charged lines is notably difficult.

31. Euripides, *Electra* 60–63, trans. Emily Vermeule.

32. Euripides, *Electra* 207–212, trans. Vermeule. Notice the contrast between Electra in exile in the mountains and her mother in bed at home. But home should be the place for a young daughter (cf. Hesiod, *Works and Days* 518 ff.) until she is sent out to form an oikos of her own.

33. Euripides, *Electra* 610–611, trans. Vermeule.

34. Euripides, *Electra* 962, 982, trans. Vermeule.

35. Euripides, *Electra* 949–951, trans. Vermeule (modified).

36. Euripides, *Electra* 1027–28, trans. Vermeule.

37. Euripides, *Electra* 1069–73, trans. Vermeule. The last line is literally "indicts herself as a bad woman" *(diagraph' hos ousan kaken)*.

38. E.g., lines 600, 645, 683, 926.

39. Cf. Plato's linking of these two "unholy" crimes against the family in his adultery law in book 8 of the *Laws*.

40. Again, cf. *Laws* 8.836 ff.

41. The implication seems to be that this is unfair to younger women and an infraction of the rules of "gift transactions" in such affairs.

42. Aristophanes, *Thesmophoriazousae* 481–89, trans. Fitts.

43. Thucydides 2.41, trans. Warner.

44. For discussion and illustration of Athenian grave reliefs, see Christoph Clairmont, *Gravestone and Epigraph: Greek Memorials from the Archaic and Classical Periods* (Mainz 1970); for a general overview of the development of Athenian drama, see *The Cambridge History of Classical Literature,* vol. 1 (Cambridge 1982).

45. See, e.g., Josiah Ober, *Mass and Elite in Democratic Athens: Rhetoric, Ideology, and the Power of the People* (Princeton 1989).

46. Cf. the argument of David Cohen, discussed in the previous chapter. It seems to me, however, that the act of adultery was always understood in relation to the household it corrupted. So perhaps it is not really possible to talk about what the Athenian attitude was to the simple sexual act of adultery per se.

47. On this topic, in relation to *moicheia* and other disputes, see A. Scafuro, *The Forensic Stage: Settling Disputes in Graeco-Roman New Comedy* (Cambridge forthcoming).

48. This is [Demosthenes] 59, "Against Neaira." For a discussion of the argument of this speech, especially as it relates to the marriage and legitimacy, see Cynthia B. Patterson, "The Case against Neaira and the Ideology of the Athenian Family," in *Athenian Identity and Civic Ideology,* ed. A. Scafuro and A. Boegehold (Baltimore 1994).

49. The speech "Against Alcibiades" was collected in antiquity among the speeches of Andocides but was clearly not written by the young Andocides in 417.

50. For these charges see also Plutarch, *Alcibiades.*

51. The reference is to the tradition that Aegisthus was born from the adulterous and incestuous relationship of Thyestes and Atreus' wife.

52. When the issue of adultery emerged in the 1992 U.S. presidential campaign, the American press generally rejected its relevance and insisted on the separation of private and public morality. Ross Perot, on the other hand, was quoted as saying that, for his part, he would have no adulterers (or homosexuals) in his cabinet.

53. This does seem a severe penalty for stealing clothes. Perhaps there is something more involved. Note, however, the frequency of the death penalty in Plato's legislation in the *Laws,* as for example in the case of theft of public property at 941e, which seems to be taken as a kind of treason. Still, the penalty for "clothes stealing" deserves more attention—just how were clothes stolen from a person in ancient Athens? (Charles Kahn has suggested in conversation that it was "at the gym.")

54. Cf. the argument of Lysias 1. Although Lysias might claim that the proper or possible punishment for *moicheia* was death, it seems that in general the Athenians handled the situation with less extreme, but frequently quite humiliating, penalties. It may also be useful to remember Jack Winkler's suggestion that "the texts we study are, for the most part, rather like men's coffeehouse talk. Their legislative intent contains a fair amount of bluff, of saving face; they regularly lay down laws which are belied by the jokes those same men will later tell"; "Laying Down the Law: The Oversight of Men's Sexual Behavior in Classical Athens," in *The Constraints of Desire* (New York 1990) p. 70.

55. The speech is basic to K. J. Dover's *Greek Homosexuality* (New York 1978) and to the numerous discussions that have followed the publication of that book. See David Halperin, *One Hundred Years of Homosexuality and Other Essays on Greek Love* (New York 1989); also Winkler,

"Laying Down the Law." For a different view, see Cohen, *Law, Sexuality, and Society* chap. 7.

56. Notice that Aeschines cites (using the term loosely, as is appropriate for Athenian rhetoric) the same law on the treatment of the woman caught with a *moichos* as cited by Apollodoros in [Demosthenes] "Against Neaira"; see "Against Timarchos" 183.

57. Winkler, "Laying Down the Law" p. 57.

58. For the procedure of *eisangeleia*, by which prominent Athenians, generals, or politicians could be put on trial for such crimes as attempted tyranny or subversion of the democracy, see M. H. Hansen, *Eisangelia: The Sovereignty of the People's Court in Athens in the Fourth Century B.C. and the Impeachment of Generals and Politicians* (Odense 1975). It is extremely interesting to find adultery among the "subversive activities" covered by the procedure, but unfortunately the case is very obscure and the speeches fragmentary.

59. For the case, see Lycurgus, "Against Lycophron" (fragments); and Hypereides, "In Defense of Lycophron," both in *Minor Attic Orators*, Loeb Classical Library.

60. Lycurgus, "Against Lycophron" 11 and 12. Quoted fragments are from Suidas s.v. *mochtheria,* Harpocration s.v. *andrapodistes,* and Stobaeus, *Florilegium* lxviii.35, respectively.

61. He seems to have argued that it was inappropriate because he was not at that time a public official, general, or politician. See Hansen, *Eisangelia* pp. 106–107.

62. Hypereides, "In Defense of Lycophron" 12.

63. [Hypereides], "Second Oration in Defense of Lycophron," frag. 1.

64. The date has been deduced from the known activities and Olympic victory of Dioxippos, the wrestler and brother of the woman with whom Lycophron is accused of *moicheia.*

65. I assume that he was a bachelor since, in the surviving fragments, he never mentions a wife, which could have been rhetorically advantageous. He does mention his relatives (*oikeioi:* 3) who relayed the news of the *eisangelia* to him when he was abroad, but generally he does not emphasize his family relations.

66. There is a suggestion in Hypereides' speech that other relatives had some interest in establishing that the woman's child was not her husband's. Once again, the concern would seem to be not lineage purity but the material interest of living members of the family in family property. Although the prosecution by Lycurgus seems openly political in character, it may be worth noting that Lycophron is Lycurgus' father's name. Is there some family conflict entangled here with the public?

67. On the avoidance of the use of proper names for "proper" women in Athenian society, see D. Schaps, "The Woman Least Mentioned: Etiquette and Women's Names," *CQ* 27 (1977) 323–330.

68. Lysias 1.16–17, trans. W. R. M. Lamb.

69. Lysias 1.32–33, trans. Lamb (modified).

70. Plutarch, *Solon* 23, trans. Scott-Kilvert. The 1981 Penguin edition has "illegal" for "legal" in the first line of this passage, but I imagine that this is a misprint rather than a mistranslation.

71. The term is that of E. Keuls, *The Reign of the Phallus* (New York 1986).

72. However, the quite similar language of Plato's law on assault (*Laws* 9.874c) suggests that Lysias' misreading may be more extreme than is usually recognized. For critical appraisal of Lysias' rhetoric see Susan Cole, "Greek Sanctions against Sexual Assault," *AJP* 79 (1984) 97–113; E. Harris, "Did the Athenians Consider Seduction a Worse Crime than Rape?" *CQ* 40 (1990) 370–377; and Cohen, *Law, Sexuality, and Society* pp. 98–132.

73. See Cole, "Greek Sanctions"; Harris, "Did the Athenians Consider?"; and Robin Osborne, "Law in Action in Classical Athens," *JHS* 105 (1985) 40–58, on the significance of the availability of multiple options for prosecution of the same action in Athenian law. S. C. Todd, *The Shape of Athenian Law* (Oxford 1993) chap. 7, describes those options.

74. Xenophon, *Hiero* 3.3. The phrase "by accident" seems to be generally taken to refer to rape rather than to a single case of seduction. In either case, however, it is a significant qualification to the conventional view that such a woman would be considered "damaged goods." It may also suggest a different attitude toward female infidelity from that of nineteenth-century Europe, where a single act of infidelity might brand a woman as an adulteress; see Tanner, *Adultery in the Novel*.

75. He is quite vague about the period involved: *chronou metazu diagenomenou* (15).

76. The fact that drama was not similarly constrained may suggest that at least in this respect literary evidence is more representative of reality than legal evidence. Cf. Susan Cole's comment on the comparative historical value of law and literature: "For our understanding of Greek legal sanctions against rape, we must rely upon two types of sources: legal evidence from inscriptions recording laws or from speeches presented in court; and literary accounts (historical or legendary anecdotes and works of fiction). Evidence of the first kind is, of course, more reliable"; "Greek Sanctions" p. 99. The speeches of the Athenian orators, however, should not really be considered legal data, but rather rhetorical legal argument.

77. Aeschylus, *Libation Bearers* 989–990; Sophocles, *Electra* 1505–08.

78. [Demosthenes] 59.85; Aeschines 1.183.

79. Earlier in the *Politics* (1300a) Aristotle speaks of "superintendents of women" *(gynaikonomoi)* as typical of an aristocracy but impossible in a democracy, since "who could prevent the wives of the poor from going out when they want to?" and antithetic to an oligarchy ("the wives of oligarchs are rich and pampered"). It is clear that he has in mind officials who overlook the public display and behavior of women, not private matters of reproduction.

80. Analogously, Aristotle defines citizenship as precisely those [male] activities which take place in the public realm—being a juryman and member of the assembly—leaving unambiguously aside other kinds of participation more connected to the household, such as Plato's weddings and birthday parties (see *Laws* 6 on the punishment of adulterers).

81. *Rhetoric* 1372a23, 1416a24, 1401b24.

82. E.g., *Nicomachean Ethics* 1107a12, 1132a2.

83. The law may have allowed some ambiguity in the interpretation of this term, and in general, as David Cohen has recently argued, kinship definition was open to rhetorical construction for practical purposes of the litigant; *Law, Violence and Community in Classical Athens* (Cambridge 1994) chap. 8.

84. So citizenship is expressed as inheritance rights, "having a share"; naturalization is "adopting" a citizen; and foreign parentage is "bastardy." On the importance of this theme for understanding the citizenship of Athenian women see C. B. Patterson, "*Hai Attikai:* The Other Athenians," *Helios* 13 (1986) 46–67.

85. Thucydides 2, esp. chaps. 42–44.

86. E.g., *Wasps, Acharnians,* and of course *Lysistrata.* On the relation of private to public, oikos to polis, in the *Lysistrata* see Helene Foley, "The 'Female Intruder' Reconsidered: Women in Aristophanes' *Lysistrata* and *Ecclesiazusae,*" *CP* 77 (1982) 1–20. On this theme in general see also Barry Strauss, *Fathers and Sons: Ideology and Society in the Era of the Peloponnesian War* (Princeton 1993).

87. See W. R. Connor, *The New Politicians of Fifth Century Athens* (Princeton 1971), pp. 96 ff.

88. For a general treatment of this theme see Helene Foley, "Women in Athenian Drama," in *Reflections of Women in Antiquity,* ed. Foley (New York 1981).

89. Simon Goldhill, *Reading Greek Tragedy* (Cambridge 1986) p. 105.

90. Ibid., p. 106.

6. Public and Private in Early Hellenistic Athens

1. Paul Rahe, "The Primacy of Politics in Classical Greece," *AHR* 89 (1984) 265–293, presents a recent clear statement of this perspective; but most influential is perhaps still Hannah Arendt's discussion of the polis in *The Human Condition* (Chicago 1958), part II, "The Public and Private Realm."

2. See Glenn Morrow, *Plato's Cretan City: A Historical Interpretation of the Laws* (Princeton 1960), on the Athenian character of Plato's *Laws*.

3. Plato, *Republic* 464, trans. G. M. A. Grube, rev. C. D. C. Reeve. One of the best examples of Plato's cultural revision is his portrait of Socrates as the hero of philosophic tragedy; see R. Patterson, "The Platonic Art of Comedy and Tragedy," *Philosophy and Literature* 6 (1982) 76–93 and "Philosophos Agonistes: Imagery and Moral Psychology in the *Republic*," *Journal of the History of Philosophy*, forthcoming.

4. Arendt, *The Human Condition* p. 30.

5. In this same section Plato uses the single person or body as a metaphor for a polis with unity of purpose and feeling. The point is that analogously to the ideal polis, or family, or polis-family, which are all composed of separate parts, the body will feel as one even if the pain or pleasure is suffered by one of its parts alone (462d). The single body is an appropriate image of the polis by virtue of its organic unity of parts, not its "idiotic" isolation.

6. Arendt, *The Human Condition* p. 27.

7. Aristotle, *Politics* 1259a37, trans. T. A. Sinclair (Harmondsworth 1962). The suggestion that the rule of men over women is essentially a matter of the permanent control of the external signs of authority is remarkable, especially coming from one who elsewhere insists on the intellectual and physical inferiority (weakness) of women. Since, however, Aristotle attributes to women the ability to deliberate, giving them some "political" recognition in the household may be less surprising.

8. Aristotle actually uses the word *politeia* in two ways in the *Politics*: as the general term for political constitution or order, and as the name for the polis in which the demos rules in the common interest (see, e.g., 2.1279a32). But given the unlikelihood in Aristotle's view of such a disinterested demos, the specific constitution called *politeia* is relatively insignificant in his analysis.

9. And insofar as Plato's *Republic* takes to a philosophical extreme the Athenian ideology of the essential connection between oikos and polis, the point is also a criticism of classical Athenian democracy and its conception of citizenship. That Aristotle was not sympathetic to the organic model of

the polis (which presented citizenship, for example, as a "sharing in the polis") is clear from *Politics* 3.

10. *Politics* 12336b, trans. Sinclair.

11. Cf. Sinclair's comments in the introduction to the Penguin translation. Aristotle's "definition" of citizenship is usually taken as authoritative—if for no other reason than that it is so clear and succinct. I fail to see, however, why this should be taken as more representative of Greek conceptions of citizenship than the Athenian term *metechein tes poleos*. If we call what Pericles proposed in 451 B.C.E. a citizenship law, then *metechein tes poleos* is accordingly what we should consider the Athenian expression of citizenship. For a discussion of the context and character of that law see C. B. Patterson, *Pericles' Citizensip Law of 451/0 B.C.* (New York 1981).

12. Josiah Ober, "Aristotle's Political Sociology: Class, Status, and Order in the *Politics*," in *Essays on the Foundations of Aristotelian Political Science*, ed. C. Lord and D. O'Connor (Berkeley 1991) p. 134.

13. Peter Green, *From Alexander to Actium* (Berkeley 1990) p. 74.

14. A. W. Gomme and F. H. Sandbach, *Menander: A Commentary* (Oxford 1973) p. 24.

15. See Ober, "Aristotle's Political Sociology."

16. Benjamin Meritt, "Greek Inscriptions," *Hesperia* 21 (1952) 355.

17. Diodorus Siculus 18.18.

18. Aristotle, *Ath.Pol.* 29.5; cf. Thucydides 8.66.

19. Despite J. K. Davies' use of the term "alternatives" in his often-cited article "Athenian Citizenship: The Descent Group and Its Alternatives," *CJ* 73 (1977–78) 162–175, the proposed restrictions of Athenian citizenship he discusses (wealth and military service) assume the existence of the birth criterion. I.e., Athenians were not thinking of opening up their citizen doors to a rich Corinthian or a well-trained Spartan, but of limiting citizenship to a narrower group of Athenians.

20. See *Ath.Pol.* 29 and Thucydides 8.66–88 for accounts of this oligarchic coup; both sources, however, present difficulties, for which see the commentary of P. J. Rhodes, *Commentary on the Athenaion Politeia* (Oxford 1981). Given that the free male citizen population may have been in the range of 20,000–25,000 at the time, this is a significant oligarchic restriction of citizen rights.

21. See *Ath.Pol.* 40; Aeschines 3.195. The orator Lysias was apparently one of those who enjoyed a brief moment of citizenship for his services to the democracy before the enfranchisement was declared illegal; [Plutarch], *Lives of the Ten Orators* 835.

22. Plutarch, *Phocion* 34; also Diodorus 18.66–67. In Plutarch's narrative one of the "best citizens" stood up to protest the presence of slaves and foreigners—but apparently not that of women.

23. For the scattered sources on Demetrius' career see William S. Ferguson, *Hellenistic Athens* (London 1911); Green, *From Alexander to Actium;* and Christian Habicht, *Athens from Alexander to Antony* (Cambridge, Mass., 1997).

24. Understanding the social legislation of Demetrius in this way may help to solve one of the traditional puzzles of his career: i.e., the contrast between the rigor of his sumptuary code and his own private lifestyle, one of elegant and luxurious private dinner parties, beautiful courtesans, and notorious boy lovers.

25. J. K. Davies, "Cultural, Social and Economic Features of the Hellenistic World," in *The Cambridge Ancient History,* 2d ed. (Cambridge 1988), vol. 7, p. 306.

26. J. P. Mahaffy, *Greek Life and Thought from the Death of Alexander to the Roman Conquest* (London 1896) p. 125.

27. Green, *From Alexander to Actium* pp. 66 and 74. Cf. the similar sentiments expressed by Green's predecessor in the field of Hellenistic history, W. W. Tarn, *Hellenistic Civilization,* 3d ed. (London 1952) p. 273.

28. F. E. Peters, *The Harvest of Hellenism: A History of the Near East from Alexander the Great to the Triumph of Christianity* (New York 1970) p. 118.

29. See, e.g., Gomme and Sandbach, *Menander: A Commentary* pp. 28–35; T. B. L. Webster, *An Introduction to Menander* (Manchester 1974) chaps. 3 and 4; Elaine Fantham, "Sex, Status, and Survival in Hellenistic Athens: A Study of Women in New Comedy," *Phoenix* 29 (1975) 44–74; Madeleine Henry, *Menander's Courtesans and the Greek Comic Tradition* (Frankfurt 1985); David Konstan, "Between Courtesan and Wife: Menander's *Perikeiromene,*" *Phoenix* 41 (1987) 122–139; P. G. McC. Brown, "Love and Marriage in Greek New Comedy," *CQ* 43 (1993) 281–287.

30. This is implied in some discussions which focus on the plays in isolation from society and politics; the implication, however, is often countered by a direct forswearing of any historical thesis or argument—as, for example, by Henry (*Menander's Courtesans* p. 3: "This essay will strive to keep from the tempting byways of social history") and Brown ("Love and Marriage" p. 192: "The social history of Athens is far too large a subject to be tackled here").

31. Ferguson, *Hellenistic Athens* p. 91. In implicit approval of this view, *The Cambridge History of Hellenistic Literature* does not include Menander, whereas we do find him discussed under the category "Greek drama" in the *Oxford History of Greece and the Hellenistic World.* Cf. Albert Heinrichs' remarks on Menander's Hellenistic identity in his reponse to the papers of Thomas Gelzer and Peter Parsons in *Images and Etiologies: Self-Definition in the Hellenistic World* (Berkeley 1993) pp. 180–187.

32. Ferguson, *Hellenistic Athens* pp. 92 and 93.

33. This seems to be the main line of argument in Netta Zagagi, *The Comedy of Menander: Convention, Variation and Originality* (London 1994). For example, she writes of the *Samia:* "All the characters are ordinary; their aspirations are conventional, and the entire plot takes place in the context of the familiar and the ordinary" (p. 113).

34. On comic costume and the conventions of New Comedy in general, see Eric Handley, "Comedy," in *The Cambridge History of Classical Literature,* ed. P. Easterling and B. M. W. Knox (Cambridge 1985), with bibliography on pp. 774 and 782. On the costumes and masks of New Comedy see also L. Bernabo Brea, *Menandro e il teatro greco nelle terracotte liparesi* (Genoa 1981).

35. On this point, Niall Slater suggests that "Menander never represents an impossibility (such as flight on a dung beetle), only improbabilities," and further, with respect to "realism and art" in general, that "fiction is history with the boring bits left out" (personal correspondence). One person's "boring bit," however, could well be another's fascinating gem.

36. I do not intend to imply that households did not have such connections or that smaller communities than the polis (e.g., neighborhoods) were not important before this time. Certainly they were. Cf. the role played by the neighborhood in Virginia Hunter's analysis of Athenian "self-regulation" (*Policing Athens: Social Control in the Attic Lawsuits, 420–320 B.C.* [Princeton 1994]) and the importance of private arbitration as an alternative to public litigation as discussed by Adele Scafuro in *The Forensic Stage: Settling Disputes in Graeco-Roman New Comedy* (Cambridge forthcoming). Rather, the point is that the emphasis of Menander's dramas on the household community, over and against the political world of agora and law court, was something new.

37. The possibility that this comic usage is ironic can be countered by the fact that the common term for household slave was *oiketes;* Xenophon, *Oikonomikos* passim.

38. The female slave is notably of little interest to Aristotle, who speaks of the slave (the "living tool") with little attention to gender.

39. Henry, *Menander's Courtesans.*

40. See David Konstan, "Premarital Sex, Illegitimacy, and Male Anxiety in Menander and Athens," in *Athenian Identity and Civic Ideology,* ed. A. Scafuro and A. Boegehold (Baltimore 1993), who argues that the fault here is not being either the victim or the agent of rape, but rather being the parent of an illegitimate child.

41. Although Moschion's act is often said to be rape, not seduction, his own account (for what it is worth) of what happened does not include the element of violence: "I joined them as a spectator. In any case, the noise

they were making would be keeping me awake, for they were taking their tray 'gardens' up to the roof, and dancing and making a real night of it, all over the place. I hesitate to tell you the rest of the story. Perhaps I'm ashamed, where shame is no help, but I'm still ashamed. The girl got pregnant. Now I've told you that, you know what went before, too" (lines 41–50, trans. Norma Miller, *Menander: Plays and Fragments* [Harmondsworth 1987]). It is relevant here that Moschion and Glycera seem to have had the opportunity to get to know each other; i.e., Moschion knew what Glycera's status was at the time. Moschion later includes time as one reason why he does not want to give Glycera up. Moschion later professes his love for the girl he seduced or raped, but when did he "fall in love"?

42. See Sophocles, *Ajax* 1304; Euripides, *Hippolytos* 1452–53.

43. *Pace* E. Keuls, *The Reign of the Phallus* (New York 1986) p. 404.

44. Cf. David Konstan, *Roman Comedy* (Ithaca 1983). Thanks to Niall Slater for suggesting an interpretation along these lines.

45. Konstan, "Between Courtesan and Wife."

46. See Miller, *Menander* p. 259 n. 1.

47. Konstan, "Between Courtesan and Wife" p. 134. Although Konstan uses the term *pallake* throughout as equivalent to "mistress," Glykera is not in fact ever called a *pallake.* Nor do I think she was a *pallake,* since, as I have argued elsewhere, the term (which is somewhat archaic) had an essentially servile connotation; see "Response to Claude Mossé," in *Symposion 1990: Papers on Greek and Hellenistic Legal History,* ed. M. Gagarin (Vienna 1991) pp. 281–287.

48. Menander, *Perikeiromene* 390–398, trans. Miller (modified). I have replaced Miller's "a pound or two" with "a minimum wage" for an American audience—even though ten drachmas (the figure in the text) was somewhat more than the standard daily wage in Athens.

49. Brown, "Love and Marriage"; Brown quotes lines 786–790 on this point on p. 189.

50. See Moschion's monologue at *Samia* 623 ff.

51. Homer, *Odyssey* 23.231–240, trans. Robert Fitzgerald. Jack Winkler calls attention to the importance of these lines: "The simile begins as a picture of his feelings and ends as a picture of hers . . . We go into the simile on his side and come out (we do not know how) on hers. At this moment they embrace and feel the same feelings, think the same thoughts, as if they were the same person: for a moment we cannot tell which is which. It is not easy to say in the cultural language of that highly stratified society that men and women are in any sense equal. But the author of the *Odyssey* has succeeded in doing so"; "Penelope's Cunning and Homer," in *The Constraints of Desire: The Anthropology of Sex and Gender in Ancient Greece* (New York

1990) p. 161. Even before Winkler, however, Helene Foley ("'Reverse Similes' and Sex Roles in the Odyssey," in *Women in Antiquity: The Arethusa Papers,* ed. J. Perodotto and J. P. Sullivan [Albany 1984] pp. 59–73) analyzed this and other similes in which Odysseus is compared to a woman or Penelope to a man (e.g., "your fame goes up into the wide heaven, as of some king"; 19.108) as revealing a positive image of "interdependent" gender roles and of a "mature marriage with well-defined spheres of power and a dynamic tension between two like-minded members of their sex" (p. 73).

52. *Odyssey* 23.242–244, trans. Fitzgerald.

53. Brown, "Love and Marriage" p. 192.

54. Cf. ibid., pp. 194–196, on eros in Menander.

55. The case of the *Epitrepontes* presents an obvious problem for this moral system. Did Chairestratos rape Pamphile (the violence is clear in the slave Habrotonon's description) thinking she was a slave or a noncitizen? If so, why did he think so? Pamphile was attending a nocturnal festival, which citizen women did in fact do. Did eros perhaps cloud his discrimination?

56. Cf. Robert Sutton's discussion of the significance of the changing representation of male-female relations on fifth-century Athenian pottery; "Pornography and Persuasian on Attic Pottery," in *Pornography and Representation,* ed. A. Richlin (New York 1992).

57. Menander, *Dyskolos* 5–12, 13–34, trans. Miller.

58. *Dyskolos* 57–66, trans. Miller.

59. *Dyskolos* 289–293, trans. Miller.

60. *Dyskolos* 713–721, trans. Miller.

61. *Dyskolos* 735, 745, trans. Miller.

62. These are just the sorts of public activities that Plato imagines his communal family society would eliminate (*Republic* 464d).

63. *Dyskolos* 875–878, trans. Miller.

64. *Dyskolos* 965–969, trans. Miller.

65. In "Menander's *Dyskolos* and Demetrios of Phaleron's Dilemma," *Greece and Rome* 31 (1984) 170–180, David Wiles suggests that "*Dyskolos* can be seen as a debate, a search for a mean between two extremes. If one extreme is urban decadence, the other is a kind of conservative austerity, exemplified in the play by Knemon and in real life by such men as Phokion and Krates" (p. 175). Wiles's other suggestions of contemporary relevance in the play—e.g., "Demetrios, like Knemon, was finally forced to join the dance, abandoning moderation in order to impress the populace with material symbols of status" (p. 178)—are less convincing.

66. Such devotion in a slave seems rather unlikely. Whatever its explanation, Daos' loyalty contributes further to the construction of an image, how-

ever mythical, of the household as a firmly connected interest group consisting of both free and slave members.

67. Menander, *Aspis* 1–10, trans. Miller (modified).

68. So D. M. MacDowell, "Love versus the Law: An Essay on Menander's *Aspis*," *Greece and Rome* 29 (1982) 42–52, who was answered by P. G. McC. Brown, "Menander's Dramatic Technique and the Law of Athens," *CQ* 33 (1983) 412–420.

69. Menander, *Samia* 10; the text is uncertain, but the sense is clear.

70. *Samia* 36–38, 47–50, 50–53, trans. Miller.

71. The text is incomplete here, but that this is what happened seems quite clear from later events.

72. Chrysis assumes that Demeas is angry because she has reared rather than exposed the infant. Indeed, Demeas was annoyed with the prospect of rearing a *nothos* in his house (see his conversation with Moschion on this question and Moschion's appeal to the principle of natural equality; 139–140) but had apparently become reconciled to the idea. Sexual betrayal by both his son and his concubine, however, is another matter altogether.

73. *Samia* 488–489, 495–497, trans. Miller (modified).

74. This is the only time Chrysis is referred to as a *pallake*, a term which I have argued elsewhere had clear servile connotations ("Response to Mossé"). Throughout the play she has been called a hetaira, a female companion who might be either free or slave.

75. *Samia* 510–513, trans. Miller.

76. On the thematic connections between Menander and Euripidean tragedy, see A. Katsouris, *Tragic Patterns in Menander* (Athens 1975); and Zagagi, *The Comedy of Menander*. The similarities, for example, between the family relationships in *Samia* and Euripides' *Hippolytos* are quite striking; Moschion's protest that virtue, not the circumstances of birth, determines "legitimacy" (140–143) seems a comic echo of Theseus' reevaluation of Hippolytos at the end of that play. Cf. Katsouris, pp. 31 ff.; and Zagagi, chap. 2.

77. *Samia* 528, trans. Miller.

78. The charge of course is comic exaggeration, since neither Moschion nor the circumstances of his "error" fit the specifications of the crime of *moicheia* (see Chapter 3). It is a clever comic exaggeration, however, which includes a reference to one of the odder elements of the Athenian self-help law: admission of guilt on the part of a *kakourgos* "caught in the act" allows the man who arrested him to kill him on the spot. See David Cohen, *Law, Sexuality, and Society: The Enforcement of Morals in Classical Athens* (New York 1991) pp. 98–132. The importation of this venerable rule into

the domestic confusion of the play's private households would undoubtedly have seemed absurdly comic.

79. *Samia* 597–598, trans. Miller.

80. The text of the line is uncertain; Miller has here filled out the sense of 729–732.

81. It is notable that in this common story pattern (cf. the case of Oedipus or Cyrus), it is the lower-class woman who suffers a miscarriage or infant death. Perhaps there is a bit of reality here.

82. Menander, *Epitrepontes* 326, trans. Miller.

83. According to Konstan ("Premarital Sex, Illegitimacy, and Male Anxiety"), when Charisios says to himself, "You have stumbled just the same yourself" (915), he refers not to the sexual experience of either raped or rapist, but to the misfortune of producing an illegitimate child. It really is not possible, however, to make the male and female experience "just the same" in this case, and perhaps Charisios' words should not be taken so literally.

84. *Epitrepontes* 228–230 and 233–236, trans. W. G. Arnott, *Menander,* vol. 1 (Loeb Classical Library 1979).

85. *Epitrepontes* 468–470, trans. Arnott.

86. For this paternal right, see A. H. R. Harrison, *The Law of Athens,* vol. 1 (Oxford 1968) pp. 30–32. It is possible, however, that this was not so much a formal "right" of the father as an informal matter of paternal responsibility and authority; see V. Rosivach, "Aphairesis and Apoleipsis: A Study of the Sources," *RIDA* 31 (1984) 193–230.

87. Cf. Arendt on the realm of the "social" (which she sees emerging only in the modern world), *The Human Condition* pp. 38–49.

Conclusion

1. For the Enlightenment origins of this tradition of moralizing the history of women, see Sylvia Tomaselli, "The Enlightenment Debate on Women," *History Workshop Journal* 20 (1985) 101–124; and Marilyn Katz, "Ideology and the 'Status of Women' in Ancient Greece," *History and Theory* 31 (1992) 70–97. In focusing on the nineteenth-century development of this tradition, I do not intend to imply any lack of appreciation for the earlier roots of the discussion.

2. A. W. Gomme, "The Position of Women in Athens in the Fifth and Fourth Centuries B.C.," in *Essays in Greek History and Literature* (Oxford 1937) p. 99 n. 2; Sarah B. Pomeroy, *Goddesses, Whores, Wives, and Slaves* (New York 1975).

3. See Katz, "Ideology and the 'Status of Women'" p. 78.

4. In her opening chapter of *The Roman Family* (Baltimore 1992), Suzanne Dixon raises the question of the degree to which family history "belongs to *l'histoire immobile,* an expression . . . that stresses the continuity of social institutions as determined by factors such as geography" (p. 17). Recognizing continuity in social or family institutions, however, does not preclude the existence of real historical engagement by those institutions with the larger public and political world.

INDEX

Adams, J. N., 122
adoption, 18, 43, 76, 88, 93, 99–100, 197, 199
adultery: in Athens, 4, 107–179, 190, 193, 215; in courts, 157–174; in drama, 138–157, 193, 215; in Sparta, 77–78
Aegisthus, 140–154, 159–161, 173
Aeschines, "Against Timarchos," 161–163
Aeschylus: *Agamemnon*, 140, 142–144, 156, 201; *Eumenides*, 112; *Oresteia*, 7, 36, 55, 84, 140–149, 153, 157, 178, 206, 219; *The Libation Bearers*, 142
Agoratos, 123, 161
Alcaeus, "Storm in the State," 70–71
Alcibiades, 33, 78, 159–161, 201
Alcmeonidae, 30–31, 237n72
Alexander of Macedon, 165, 186, 195
alochos, 45–46, 56–57
Apollodorus, 111–112, 120–122, 125, 132, 167, 174, 202
anchisteia (*tou genous*), 31, 38, 53–54, 58, 82–83, 87–90, 92, 97–100, 103, 105–106, 112–113, 177, 196, 214. *See also* kindred
Arendt, Hannah, 181–182
Aristophanes, 135, 140, 186, 194; *Birds*, 90, 110; *Clouds*, 155–156; *Knights*, 177; *Lysistrata*, 122, 124; *Thesmophoriazousae*, 154–156, 166
Aristotle, 75–76, 83–85, 97, 108, 180–181, 188, 190–191, 198, 228; on

adultery, 4, 118–121, 123–124, 174–176; *Athenaion Politeia*, 84–85, 97, 118, 120, 214; *Ethics (Eudemian)*, 124, 175; *Ethics (Nichomachean)*, 175–176; on *moicheia* and *moichos*, 174–176; on *oikos*, 44, 68, 182–185; *Politics*, 44, 55, 89, 101–102, 106, 129, 174–175, 182–184, 186, 189, 196–197, 200, 224; *Rhetoric*, 171, 175
Aspasia, 29, 31–32, 34
Athens: adultery in, 107–179, 193; democratic reforms in, 146–147, 158, 188; family law and law codes in, 3, 12, 59, 71–73, 83–91, 92, 108, 157–174; heiresses in, 91–106; Hellenistic, public and private spheres in, 180–225; inheritance in, 8, 82–83, 85–106; marriage in, 107–137, 177–179; patriarchy in, 7–8; theater/drama in, 8, 40, 84, 138–157, 177–179, 185–225; women in, 7, 20–21, 27, 32–34, 39–42, 61, 82, 125–129
atimia, 121, 131, 137, 153, 173–174

Bachofen, J. J., 8–13, 18, 22–23, 25, 29–30, 84, 91, 233nn9,12
bastard (*nothos*), 89–90, 110, 197, 199, 214
Blok, Josine, 42
Blundell, Sue, 41–42, 129
Brown, P. G. McC., 203–204